COMPARATIVE STUDIES OF SOCIAL AND POLITICAL ELITES

COMPARATIVE SOCIAL RESEARCH

Series Editor: Fredrik Engelstad

COMPARATIVE SOCIAL RESEARCH VOLUME 23

COMPARATIVE STUDIES OF SOCIAL AND POLITICAL ELITES

EDITED BY

FREDRIK ENGELSTAD
Institute for Social Research, Oslo, Norway

TRYGVE GULBRANDSEN
Institute for Social Research, Oslo, Norway

ELSEVIER
JAI

Amsterdam – Boston – Heidelberg – London – New York – Oxford
Paris – San Diego – San Francisco – Singapore – Sydney – Tokyo

JAI Press is an imprint of Elsevier

( )

JAI Press is an imprint of Elsevier
The Boulevard, Langford Lane, Kidlington, Oxford OX5 1GB, UK
Radarweg 29, PO Box 211, 1000 AE Amsterdam, The Netherlands
525 B Street, Suite 1900, San Diego, CA 92101-4495, USA

First edition 2007

British Library Cataloguing in Publication Data
A catalogue record for this book is available from the British Library

ISBN-13: 978-0-7623-1379-2
ISBN-10: 0-7623-1379-X
ISSN: 0195-6310

For information on all JAI Press publications
visit our website at books.elsevier.com

Printed and bound in The Netherlands

07 08 09 10 11 10 9 8 7 6 5 4 3 2 1

Working together to grow
libraries in developing countries

www.elsevier.com | www.bookaid.org | www.sabre.org

ELSEVIER   BOOK AID International   Sabre Foundation

CONTENTS

EDITORIAL BOARD

LIST OF CONTRIBUTORS

Peter Munk Christiansen   Department of Political Science, University of Southern Denmark, Denmark

Verona Christmas-Best   Department of Developmental Psychology, University of Jena, Germany

Maurizio Cotta   Centre for the Study of Political Change, University of Siena, Italy

Jean-Pascal Daloz   Centre National de la Recherche Scientifique, Institut d'Etudes Politiques de Bordeaux, France and Department of Political Science, University of Oslo, Norway

Fredrik Engelstad   Institute for Social Research, Oslo, Norway and Department of Sociology and Human Geography, University of Oslo, Norway

Trygve Gulbrandsen   Institute for Social Research, Oslo, Norway and Department of Sociology and Human Geography, University of Oslo, Norway

John Higley   Department of Government and Sociology, University of Texas at Austin, USA

Ursula Hoffmann-Lange   Department of Political Science, University of Bamberg, Germany

Anne Krogstad

Department of Sociology and Human Geography, University of Oslo, Norway and Institute for Social Research, Oslo, Norway

Birgitta Niklasson

Department of Political Science, University of Gothenburg, Sweden and Department of Communication, University at Albany, State University of New York, USA

Ilkka Ruostetsaari

Department of Political Science and International Relations, University of Tampere, Finland

Anton Steen

Department of Political Science, University of Oslo, Norway

Aagoth Storvik

Institute for Social Research, Oslo, Norway

Lise Togeby

Department of Political Science, University of Aarhus, Denmark

INTRODUCTION: SOCIAL AND POLITICAL ELITES IN MODERN DEMOCRACIES

Fredrik Engelstad

How can the existence of elites be compatible with democratic governance? Any democratic society is inevitably confronted by this basic question. All societies are constituted by a certain degree of division of labor that in turn presupposes some form of leadership and asymmetrical distribution of power. Modern democratic societies in particular are built on complex institutions and specialized organizations held together by large formalized hierarchies, whether they are civil service organizations, economic enterprises, or legal bodies. Thereby a paradox is created: societies with equality between citizens as their basic value simultaneously presuppose leadership on a large scale, entailing great power differences between leaders and the majority of citizens.

The early theory of elites, elaborated by Vilfredo Pareto in the early 1900s, had this as its point of departure. Democratic ideals cannot possibly be realized in practice, was his main thesis. Only a small group is able to govern society whereas the majority will always be in a subordinate position. The same idea is widely known in the social sciences through Michels' iron law of oligarchy. Inspired by Machiavelli, Pareto's theory was formed in opposition to the emerging labor movement and the idea that class struggle would entail the liberation of the working class, and thereby of society as a

Comparative Studies of Social and Political Elites
Comparative Social Research, Volume 23, 1–9
Copyright © 2007 by Elsevier Ltd.
ISSN: 0195-6310/doi:10.1016/S0195-6310(06)23001-1

whole. Pareto emphasized the endemic struggle over power. In his view the most important of these are the struggles between rising and falling elite groups, which he termed the circulation of elites. History is not the history of class struggle as maintained by Marx, but the struggle between elites over social domination. Thereby, history is not the history of the emergence of democracy either, because the dream of democratic governance is an illusion, *pace* Pareto.

The attractiveness of the theories of elites in this version faded during the second half of the twentieth century. Democracy, albeit in imperfect versions, has become the dominant mode of governance in most of the world. At the same time, class conflict became a predominant theme in political thinking in large parts of the twentieth century. In their original form, however, these ideas have gradually withered away. The idea that class struggle might lead to the working class taking over power in society, or establishing itself as the hegemonic power in society, has lost support throughout the modern world. Organized conflict of interest between social classes has by no means disappeared, but there is no broad movement that exposes it as a transcendent force as the basis for a new type of society.

When it is acknowledged that social conflicts are fought out within the framework of democratic institutions, theories of social elites increase their importance. Recent elite studies interpret elites within the framework of democracy, not in conflict with them. The conception of how elites are constituted has also changed. Elites are conceived primarily as coalitions of incumbents of top positions in the various social sectors, such as politics, media, civil service, and business. To the extent that people in these top positions form socially integrated groups we may talk about a political elite, a media elite, a civil service elite, or a business elite. Together, these sector elites as a whole may constitute a more or less well-integrated elite on the societal level. The degree of cohesion and dominance of such a central power elite depends on historical circumstances.

This view points in the opposite direction to that of Pareto. Contemporary elite theories assume that elites and democracy are not incompatible. A large set of historical comparative studies have thematized the establishment of democracy by elite groups (Burton & Higley, 1987; Dogan & Higley, 1998) during the last three decades. The replacement of autocratic forms of government by democracy requires that various elite groups see it in their interest to relinquish immediate power and elaborate elite compromises. Thus, to be preserved in the long run, democracy depends simultaneously on well-functioning elite networks and popular support.

As a consequence, studies of modern elites are simultaneously studies of social and political tensions – tensions between democratic ideals and top–down decision making, between various sector elites as well as between elites and citizens.

The contemporary approach to elite formations stands in contrast to several well-established paradigms in sociological theory on social governance and the top levels in society. Primarily, it stands in contrast to the conception of C. Wright Mills (1956) where it is taken for granted that a small and strongly integrated societal power elite is able to run a large country more or less autonomously, without active support from other strata or large social groups. More generally, there is a significant contrast to theories with a strong structuralist leaning, as found for example in the work of Bourdieu. In structuralist thinking there is a tendency to split systemic conceptions of societal functioning, which is described as basically autonomous processes, from descriptions of the highest circles in society the main feature of which is that they culturally distinguish themselves from the other social groups. At the same time, elite theory stands in contrast to idealistic liberal theories that tend to disregard the power embodied in institutions, or assume that power concentration may be abolished by the introduction of market mechanisms.

EMPIRICAL STUDY OF SOCIAL ELITES IN THE TWENTY-FIRST CENTURY

The fruitful development of the theory of elites within the framework of democratic societies, naturally presupposes ample empirical work, allowing broad descriptions of elite structure. Unfortunately, representative data on modern social elites are still relatively scarce. The most ambitious attempt to cover elite formation in Europe is restricted to the political sphere, a large longitudinal data set on parliamentary elites, covering members of parliament in 12 European countries over a period of 150 years (Best & Cotta, 2000). On a more ad hoc basis data sets covering broader sections of European national elites have been collected in Germany, the Nordic countries, and Eastern Europe. These data sets are utilized in several of the articles in the present volume.

Core questions in large-scale studies of social and political elites are linked to elite recruitment, elite cohesion, and the social and cultural distance between elites and the population at large. All of these are relevant to the problem of elites in democracy, and all of them are highlighted in various ways in several articles in this volume.

Elite *recruitment* has traditionally been assessed on a class basis: What are the chances for members of different social classes to enter the elite? It has mostly been taken for granted that normal members of the elite are men. During the last decade questions of recruitment have been broadened to comprise the gender dimension. After the second wave of feminism more women have made it to the top social strata, but there are broad variations between social spheres and countries.

Likewise, variations are found in elite *cohesion* – the degree of cultural and political homogeneity within and between sector elites. A well-functioning modern society has to find a tricky, and mostly unstable, balance of specialization and complementarity between elites, and commonality in their basic worldviews and social loyalties. Too much compartmentalization threatens political governance, whereas too strong unity leads to social inertia.

The *social distance* in attitude and outlook between elites and the population has some paradoxical features as well. Concerning economic inequality, the distance between the highest and the lowest strata in society appears to have increased during recent decades in most modern societies. At the same time, the cultural distance may be significantly diminished, not the least as a consequence of the explosive growth of mass culture, combined with a general increase in income levels. However, the significant variation between countries also points to cultural specificities.

A problematic, but much neglected, aspect of elites is connected to *nationality*. We generally talk about Italian, French, or Brazilian elites. But to which degree does this make sense? Some sector elites are bound up to the national state because their main arena is constituted by national "home markets" such as the civil service, news production, or health services. For others, mostly the business elites, the entire world is their arena. However, all elites are international in the sense that they have a "foreign policy" and take part in large international networks. They are now more dramatically reconstituted at the international level due to the emergence of supranational organizations and institutions. This contributes to increased sociopolitical complexity as demonstrated by Maurizio Cotta in his article in this volume on "Domestic elites in the transformation of the 'European polity'". With Italy as a prime example, Cotta studies the tension between national representation and functioning within the supranational institutions of the European Union. These tensions are not limited to the political sphere, but in varying degrees show their importance within such diverse fields as business, religion, culture, and NGOs. Undoubtedly, this is one of the main fields for future research on elites.

ELITE RECRUITMENT AND CHANGES IN ELITE COMPOSITION IN EUROPE

How the recruitment to elites changes in the long run according to class and gender is one of the core themes of the present volume. If comprehensive elite data sets are scarce, this is even more so for solid longitudinal data. However, the article by Peter Munk Christiansen and Lise Togeby on "Elite transformation in Denmark 1932–1999" is an exception that casts a sharper light on long-term trends. They have collected and analyzed a data set on a broad set of three generations of national elites' cohorts spanning a period of 70 years.

Class Background

Previous studies from Germany and Norway indicate an increase in the equality of chances to reach top positions (Bürklin & Rebenstorf, 1997; Gulbrandsen & Engelstad, 2005). Christiansen and Togeby corroborate and broaden these findings with much more solid data. In Denmark, a significant degree of democratization has taken place in the sense that the chances for persons with a working-class or middle-class background of rising to an elite position have increased dramatically. This is particularly true of the transition from the generation of the 1960s to the present, whereas the patterns of equalization were quite weak in the period from the early 1930s to the early 1960s. The interesting exception to this pattern is found in politics where the equality of chances to attain top positions are much higher than in other sectors, and has remained stable over three generations. Whether these findings can be generalized outside Northern Europe is, however, an open question.

Gender

Politics is that sector which is closest to gender parity in most European countries. In her article "Left – Right – Left?" Verona Christmas-Best takes a long view of the march of the female representatives into European parliaments and the role of leftist party affiliations, and discusses the inclusion of women into national politics over a period of a hundred years. Changes have taken place in all countries after 1970, albeit with varying pace and effects. The pioneering countries – mostly small countries in northern Europe – presently have a level of female parliamentarians around or above 35 percent, whereas the general picture in Europe is a female participation rate between 10 and 20 percent.

There are many factors influencing the inclusion of women in politics. The strength of leftist parties – generally more positive toward feminism – may be one, but definitely not the only one. In "Importance of contacts and women's political representation" Birgitta Niklasson demonstrates the impact of another set of factors, namely the extension of networks in Swedish and Norwegian politics. These show a clear difference between men and women, with men having significantly larger political networks than women. This is true even in countries with a relatively high degree of female participation in politics such as Sweden and Norway.

A significant rise toward gender parity has also taken place outside politics as Munk Christiansen and Togeby point out for Denmark, even though the tendency varies considerably between sectors. Generally, women are closer to the top in the public than in the private sector. In the business elites, the proportion of female members is well below 10 percent. Munk Christiansen and Togeby estimate a rate of just 2 percent in Denmark, which does not differ markedly from that found in studies from Germany, Norway, the UK, and France (Bürklin & Rebenstorf, 1997; Gulbrandsen et al., 2002; Maclean, Harvey, & Press, 2006). In civil service and related spheres including law, women's chances of reaching elite positions are intermediary to those for politics and business.

RELATIONSHIP BETWEEN ELITES AND THE POPULATION

In the present volume two articles focus on the distance between elites and the population in attitudes, outlooks, and modes of behavior. In "Political elites and conspicuous modesty" Jean-Pascal Daloz explores the singular modes of presentation of "self" among political elites in Scandinavia. Strong egalitarian ideals in Scandinavia prescribe that elites do not distinguish themselves in their appearance in public from the population at large, something that is particularly true for politicians. Daloz's article is a sequel to an earlier study which compared ostentatious behavior in Scandinavian politics with that of France and Nigeria (Daloz, 2003), and where Scandinavia and Nigeria came out as extreme contrasts. In Europe there seems to be a general trend of elites appearing more like ordinary people. This tendency is, however, much stronger and has gone further in the Nordic countries than probably anywhere else in the world.

A similar pattern is demonstrated by Anne Krogstad and Aagoth Storvik in their "Seductive heroes and ordinary human beings" on the forms and impact of charismatic power in France and Norway. Traditionally, charismatic power is associated with conquest, be it military, sexual, or oratorical. French politics, with its heritage from Napoleon to de Gaulle, undoubtedly embodies this image. In Norway, a small country without foreign policy ambitions in the past, charismatic appeal is fused with modesty – "human ordinariness" – in a way that would hardly be conceivable in a world power such as France. This does not mean that charisma is absent in Scandinavia; rather, that it is played out on a low key.

Gender

Krogstad and Storvik go on to explore gender differences connected to charisma in the two countries. Their analysis indicates that it is easier for women to appear as charismatic within cultural frames where "ordinariness" and not "conquest" is a key image. Thereby gender specificities are downplayed in a way that makes it easier to combine femininity with political leadership. This observation should be seen in association with the observation in Daloz's article that young women are now the most dynamic group in changing the mode of appearance of politicians in Scandinavia.

COLLECTIVE ACTION AND ELITE COHESION

In the growing literature on "Varieties of Capitalism" (Hall & Soskice, 2001), the main emphasis is put on institutional factors, i.e. varieties in corporatist arrangements and mechanisms coordinating employer behavior. These institutional traits undoubtedly constitute a major frame for distinguishing different types of capitalism. But the dynamics of political–economic systems cannot be well understood without taking into account the people that govern them from top positions, their goals, and how they compete and cooperate across social sectors, i.e. the degree and form of elite cohesion.

"Do elite beliefs matter?" Anton Steen asks as an introduction to his study of political and business elites in the Baltic countries and Russia after the fall of Communism. Among these four countries, Estonia stands out with far greater economic success than the other Baltic countries and Russia. There are strong indications that this is the result of variation in the co-hesiveness of elite orientations. Steen demonstrates that the Estonian elites are the most liberal minded. At the same time they are significantly more consensual in their orientations and political outlooks.

A similar point on variation in elite cohesion is made by Trygve Gulbrandsen and Ursula Hoffman-Lange, when they raise the question of "Consensus or polarization?" in a comparison of business and labor elites in Germany and Norway. Even though both countries are classified as "coordinated market economies" in the "Varieties of Capitalism" scheme, they differ on some central points. In Germany the gap between elite rep-resentatives of labor and capital seems to have widened during recent dec-ades, something that is not visible to the same extent in Norway. These processes may be partly attributed to differences in the economic situation. However, other factors are also evidently relevant, among them varia-tions in the prevalence of political trust across the class divide in the two countries.

ELITES AND DEMOCRACY

The final section of the present volume is dedicated to the basic problems in the relationship between elites and democracy. Presently, John Higley is undoubtedly the most influential researcher active in this field. In "Democracy and Elites" Higley gives an overview of Michael Burton's and his own theory of the historical roots of democracy in elite settlements. The pro-vocative thesis at the core of the theory is that consensually united elites are necessary for the establishment and maintenance of stable democracies (Burton & Higley, 1987; Higley & Burton, 2006). Higley draws his examples worldwide, but concentrates on the Scandinavian countries to illustrate the different mechanisms creating stable elite consensus: negotiated settlements, normative convergence, and colonial opportunities.

In a rejoinder to Higley, "Elites and democracy – are they compatible?," Ilkka Ruostetsaari adds the Finnish case to the analysis of the Scandinavian countries, and takes the discussion of elites and democracy further by un-derlining the distinction between elite cooperation and elite consensus. He places Finland in a group of societies where consensus prevails between elites across sectors, whereas Swedish society is more strongly characterized by the conflict between elites and consensus within them.

Any combination of elites and democracy, or democratic elitism, is necessarily uneasy. Tensions between popular participation and demand for political and social leadership will probably persist and grow in the future. Increasing social complexity owing to internationalization may widen the gap between elites and the population, simultaneously creating greater strains on those filling the elite positions. Higley points out that this does not mean that democracy is threatened in any strong sense. Moreover, one of the main strands of the present volume is that in many ways a democratization of the relationship between elites and the population has taken place, with respect to social class as well as gender. Nevertheless, there is a considerable chance that the modes of operation of democracy will undergo substantial change in the coming decades. In these processes, strengthening political and social participation of the population in central fields is one of the greatest future challenges.

REFERENCES

Best, H., & Cotta, M. (Eds) (2000). *Parliamentary representatives in Europe 1848–2000*. Oxford: Oxford University Press.

Bürklin, W., & Rebenstorf, H. (Eds) (1997). *Eliten in Deutschland*. Opladen: Leske + Budrich.

Burton, M., & Higley, J. (1987). Elite settlements. *American Sociological Review, 52*, 295–306.

Daloz, J.-P. (2003). Ostentation in comparative perspective: Culture and elite legitimation. *Comparative Social Research, 21*, 29–62.

Dogan, M., & Higley, J. (Eds) (1998). *Elites, crises, and the origin of regimes*. Boulder, CO: Rowman & Littlefield.

Gulbrandsen, T., & Engelstad, F. (2005). Elite consensus on the Norwegian welfare state model. *West European Politics, 28*, 899–919.

Gulbrandsen, T., Engelstad, F., Klausen, T. B., Skjeie, H., Teigen, M., & Østerud, Ø. (2002). *Norske makteliter*. Oslo: Gyldendal Akademisk.

Hall, P., & Soskice, D. (2001). *Varieties of capitalism. The institutional foundation of comparative advantage*. Oxford: Oxford University Press.

Higley, J., & Burton, M. (2006). *Elite foundation of liberal democracy*. Boulder, CO: Rowman & Littlefield.

Maclean, M., Harvey, C., & Press, J. (2006). *Business elites and corporate governance in France and the UK*. New York: Palgrave Macmillan.

Mills, C. W. (1956). *The power elite*. Oxford: Oxford University Press.

PART I
ELITE RECRUITMENT

LEFT–RIGHT–LEFT? THE MARCH OF FEMALE REPRESENTATIVES INTO EUROPEAN PARLIAMENTS AND THE ROLE OF LEFTIST PARTY AFFILIATIONS

Verona Christmas-Best

One hundred years ago in 1906, the women of Finland were granted suffrage and eligibility on the same basis as their men folk. This was the first country in Europe and one of the very first in the world to do so. Other European countries followed suit so that by the end of the 2nd World War women could vote and stand for election to their respective national legislatures in the vast majority of European countries.

Following the extension of suffrage to include women, it was generally expected that gender parity in national legislatures would follow quickly and automatically. However, as can be seen in Fig. 1, not only did the expected gender parity in the parliaments of Europe not happen 'quickly and automatically', most recent figures show that the average for women in political positions in Europe, which includes countries with some of the highest levels of female representation in the world, is still only 19.1% (Inter-Parliamentary Union, 2006).

Comparative Studies of Social and Political Elites
Comparative Social Research, Volume 23, 13–34
Copyright © 2007 by Elsevier Ltd.
ISSN: 0195-6310/doi:10.1016/S0195-6310(06)23002-3

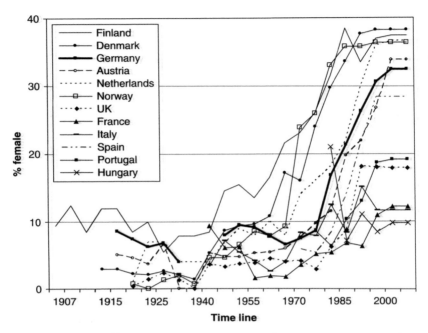

Fig. 1. Percentage of Female Representatives in Parliament in 12 European Countries. Data Cube Dataset Over Time.

The lack of progress for women in terms of gender parity in the parliaments of Europe is all the more notable when seen in comparison to other changes in the social role of women that have taken place over the same period, in particular the expansion of women's (especially married women's) involvement in the labour forces of Europe in the last quarter of the 20th century. This trend for women to move from the private to the public sphere (Walby, 1997) is of particular importance because of the suggested association with changes in their social attitude, political orientation, and level of political engagement. The theory is that as the numbers of women engaged in labour market activity outside of the home have increased so have women moved from a right to a left party orientation and to an increased interest in political matters (Inglehart & Norris, 2000; Togeby, 1994). This political 'lean to the left' has led to the suggestion of a symbiotic relationship whereby women have increasingly associated with parties that demonstrate a greater compatibility with areas of particular interest to them (such as environmental issues and social issues related to the family, health, work, etc.) and that these parties have in turn viewed women's active participation more favourably.

Within the context of labour market participation, women have also made increasing inroads into many areas formerly considered to be a male domain,[1] such as Law and Banking, and have increased their share in leadership positions generally. This has led to an increase in the numbers of women with the higher levels of political and human capital, and thereby to an increase in the supply of potential political candidates among women.

Many researchers have therefore sought to understand why the political arena should have been so resistant to the inclusion of women and, as is evident from Fig. 1, why there should be such international variation. One of the earliest researchers to look at this question was Maurice Duverger (1955), who saw the problem of an under-representation of women in national legislatures as a lack of female candidates, i.e., "few women are elected because few women stand for election" (p. 87), although he noted it was a problem exacerbated by the ideologies and "idiosyncrasies" of the various political parties. Later studies identified other factors as influential in the level of female representation; for example, type of electoral system; level of turnover of incumbents; majority religion; dominant cultural perception of the social role of women; level and type of female presence in the labour force; gender typicality of recruiting base; level of political capital; recruitment processes; demands of selectors; supply of candidates; voter preferences; existence of quota systems; the success of left-oriented parties; and the nature of the political parties themselves (e.g., Caul, 2001; Rule, 1987; Matland, 1998; Norris, 1985, 1997; Lovenduski, 1986; Duverger, 1954, 1955).

PARTIES OF THE LEFT AND THEIR RELATIONSHIP TO LEVEL OF FEMALE REPRESENTATION

In general, factors influencing the level of female representation have been grouped into three broad areas – cultural/historical, socio-economic, and institutional (Matland, 1998). Of those subsumed under the institutional category, one factor has been cited repeatedly as being of particular significance in the success of women as a political representative, i.e., the role played by political parties as gatekeepers to parliamentary access (Rule, 2000; Norris, 1997; Lovenduski, 1993; Duverger, 1955; Christmas & Kjaer, forthcoming).

In the supply and demand model of recruitment posited by Norris (e.g., 1997) political parties are said to form a "structured market place" with party selectors controlling candidate selection and the filter mechanism through which potential candidates must pass on their way to elected office. In other words, although formal barriers to women having access to the parliaments of Europe were abolished with the granting of suffrage and eligibility they have been replaced by others in the form of 'demands' based on ideological fit with party ethos and consideration of "the probable value of the contenders' resources for electoral success" (Best & Cotta, 2000, p. 11). Therefore, as parties vary in their ethos they also vary in their recruitment 'demands', in the types of candidates they prefer for selection, and in the structure of opportunity provided for different groups. In this way, the 'idiosyncrasies' of the different political parties suggested by Duverger (1955) as related to the scarcity of women political representatives are in fact not 'idiosyncrasies' but functional differences based on the 'rational' choices of selectorates as they aim to maximise their party's chances of electoral success (Best & Cotta, 2000).

The long-standing hypothesis, and the one that this article seeks to re-examine, is that a relationship exists between left parties and the level of female representation whereby more women can be expected to be returned to parliament via left than non-left parties. The theoretical basis for this assumption is that parties of the left have always had equality as a core part of their doctrine and have therefore been more committed to women's political inclusion and the promotion of gender-related issues than centre or right parties (Duverger, 1955; Caul, 2001). One reason for testing this hypothesis again is that, while some researchers have found evidence to support the hypothesis (e.g., Caul, 1999) some researchers have questioned the strength of its importance given recent developments in the level of female representation in Europe (Lovenduski & Norris, 1993; Matland & Studlar, 1996). Another reason, however, is that to test such a hypothesis and in order to understand the complexities of such a relationship, "the impact of party ideology on women's representation must be examined over time" (Caul, 1999, p. 82) and to be compared across multiple contexts. To date, although longitudinal data have been used, much of the work that has examined the hypothesis has had to rely on data covering relatively short time periods, and few had access to detailed complete time series. This work is able to draw on such data covering the time women first entered the parliaments of 12 European countries through to the present day. Further, the data not only offer the possibility to look at the question of female parliamentarians from a longitudinal and comparative perspective but all elections can be examined at the party level. This work, therefore, seeks to test the "left party – level of female representation" hypothesis from a longitudinal perspective to see whether the hypothesis holds equally across the one hundred years since the first women in Europe were granted suffrage and eligibility, and whether it is found regardless of national context.

To support this standpoint, and before proceeding to data analysis, it is necessary to look at the relationship between left parties and women's political role over time. First, it was left-aligned theorists and their activism, such as that of the socialists and communists, which championed the equality of women at the turn of the 19th century and which had women's full citizenship as a major part of their proposed social reforms. At this time left parties were "vehemently against any sex discrimination and attempted to give women and men strict equality in political life" (Duverger, 1954, p. 124). However, following the granting of suffrage and eligibility, although they continued to champion equality theoretically, in practice the early left parties associated with these movements did little actively to promote women as political representatives. As Lovenduski (1986) explains, the early socialist movements followed the standpoint of Bebel's socialist treatise, *Women and Socialism* (1879) and Engels' *Origin of the Family, Private Property and the State* (1884) and believed that the full emancipation of women could only be achieved when socialism was fully established. The "central message was that the socialist movement must be more important to its women members than the movement for women's rights" (Lovenduski, 1986, p. 13) which, especially in the case of political reform, was in any case being organised and supported as much by middle-class bourgeois women as by reformers of the Left. Indeed, at this time women were considered to be politically more right-wing and conservative than men (Duverger, 1955) and part of the fears of the early left parties was that an increase in female political participation would in effect mean additional support for parties of the right.

This attitude took an even more extreme stance in some countries, such as France, where the labour movement was openly hostile to the emerging feminism and unsupportive of women workers, and in Britain, where the British Trades Unions (which formed the backbone of the British Labour Party) supported the push for a socialist revolution but based firmly on the maintenance of the traditional gender-roles of the male as breadwinner and the female as carer and nurturer – a position necessary for the wage-bargaining stance of men demanding a family or 'living' wage. In other words, since the early socialist parties were in many cases the political arm of the respective socialist parties, the patriarchialism of the socialist movements was easily translated into a male-dominated political representation. Thus, as noted by Duverger, by the early 1950s left parties had changed their stance with regard to the political role of women so that while not rejecting their original theoretical standpoint on equality they were seen to "stress women's role as wives and mothers and make their women leaders responsible for directing activities for women as such, developing housewives' leagues, or mothers' associations, in preference to encouraging women to join the parties themselves" (Duverger, 1955, p. 124).

This phenomenon of left parties theorising gender equality while maintaining a strong patriarchal stance concerning differences in the social role of women and men held until the second wave of feminism of the 1960s and 1970s (see Nicholson, 1997) when the social context changed and equality (especially gender equality) became the rallying cry of the Left once again. This period also sees the arrival of new 'post modern' left parties, such as the Greens, seeking to break away from the old hierarchical party tradition and having women as a major target group and introducing related affirmative action programs. As already noted, this period was also a time that saw women (married women in particular) entering the labour force in ever increasing numbers, becoming more politically aware and realigning their political orientation to the Left (Lovenduski, 1986).

At the turn of the 20th century it has been suggested that further developments in the "left party – level of female representation" relationship are beginning to be seen. Following Duverger's (1954) contagion theory, whereby the successful election strategy of one party is eventually adopted by others, it has been suggested that the left is beginning to lose the advantage and that convergence among parties in the level of female representation is emerging (e.g., Matland & Studlar, 1996). In sum, the particular relationship between level of female representation and left parties would seem to have been influential at the point when suffrage and eligibility was granted; to have been less effective until the second wave of feminism and associated social change in the 1970s; to have become consequential again with the emergence of new 'post modern' parties of the left towards the end of the 20th century; and to be diminishing in effect in the early part of the 21st century as other parties seek to redress the gender advantage of the Left by appearing more 'female friendly' and appealing to the female vote by adopting more female candidates.

DATA AND METHOD

In order to test this hypothesis longitudinal data from the Data Cube dataset was used. This is an integrated European dataset with countries, time, and variables as its three dimensions. It has been established as part of the Data Cube project (http://www.eurelite.uni-jena.de) which collects and analyses information on the historical transformation of parliamentary elites in 12 European countries (Denmark, Germany, Italy, Netherlands, Norway, UK, France, Spain, Austria, Portugal, Finland, and Hungary) from 1848 to the present day (Best & Cotta, 2000). The Data Cube dataset comprises aggregate data at party level for all elections and includes a wide array of information on the political and social backgrounds of members of national parliaments (for a full description of the current dataset see Best & Edinger, 2005). Such detailed, longitudinal data are particularly important when seeking to test the influence of factors such as those derived from the literature and especially when endeavouring to monitor and compare trends over time. It should be noted, however, that in some countries, such as Hungary, Spain, and Portugal, a continuous series is not available due to the discontinuity of authentic representative institutions and competitive elections. Data on female representatives are held as a percentage of each legislature and of parliamentary parties for each election.

In order to test the "left party – level of female representation" hypothesis across time and across countries, an iterative approach to the analysis of the data is taken. First, using all 12 countries in the dataset, changes in the value of three variables over time are correlated. The three variables are: percentage of female representatives in a legislature; percentage of all left party representatives (male and female) in a legislature; and percentage of female left party representatives in a legislature. The aim is to see whether, given the large degree of variance seen between the countries in the dataset (see Fig. 1) the hypothesis holds in general across the time period under examination i.e., from the earliest time women entered a parliament in Europe (1906) to the present day.[2] In a second step, the party affiliations of all female representatives in the parliaments from eight countries[3] in the Data Cube dataset, namely, Denmark, Germany, Italy, the Netherlands, Norway, UK, Austria, and Finland are analysed and compared. The percentage of female legislators returned by all left parties at each election since the granting of female suffrage in each country is calculated and compared with the overall percentage of female representatives at each election over time. For the purpose of this study the parties classified as 'Left' are Communists, New Left, Socialists, Social Democrats, and Greens. The number of female representatives returned to a parliament by these parties is summed and expressed as a percentage of all female legislators in each parliament for each elective period. These values are then plotted as a time-line for each country starting with the first election following female enfranchisement and continuing to the most recent election for which data are to hand. The percentage of all legislators being female in each parliament is also plotted as a time-line and displayed on the same graph.

Finally, in an attempt to have a better understanding of the relationship between left parties and the level of female representation, one country (Germany) is selected for more in-depth analysis. Germany was selected for several reasons. First, it was one of the earliest countries to enfranchise and grant eligibility to women (1919) and has had a continuous record of female representation to the present day (apart from the disruption of represent-ative government by Nazi rule and subsequent administration by allied forces at the end of the 2nd World War). Second, it has experienced different types of electoral systems (see Best, Hausmann, & Schmitt, 2000) so that what is found can less easily be attributed to a specific electoral system. Also, it has had representatives of parties from across the Left–Right spectrum in its parliament at some time in its history and, of particular use to this work, it has one of the oldest and most consistently represented Green parties in Europe.

RESULTS

When the three variables relating to change over time in the percentage of female left party representatives, all female representatives, and all left party representatives are correlated, as can be seen in Table 1, a highly significant positive correlation is found between all three variables.

Of particular importance is the significant positive relationship found between changes in the level of left party representatives (i.e., percentage increase in level of representatives in a parliament) over time and changes in the success of women as political representatives over the same period. This finding supports the general hypothesis that a positive relationship exists between left parties and the level of female representation but it does not shed any light on the variance seen both between and within countries, nor does it show whether the relationship fluctuates or remains constant over time.

When results of the individual country analyses are examined it is clear immediately that the effect of left party membership has a much greater effect in some countries than in others and that the effect varies within each country over time. Closer examination also shows that the eight countries included in these analyses can roughly be divided into three groups: the first contains countries where the percentage of female representatives returned

Table 1. Correlation between Percentage Change in Level of Left Party Female Representatives, all Party Female Representatives, and all Left Party Representatives (Male and Female) in the Parliaments of Europe as Held in the Data Cube Dataset, Over Time.

	Change in % Female MPs from Left Parties	Change in % Female MPs from all Parties	Change in % all MPs from Left Parties
Change in % female MPs from left parties		0.736**	0.125**
Change in % female MPs from all parties	0.736**		0.250**
Change in % all MPs from left parties	0.125**	0.250**	

**Significant at the 0.01 level

via left parties is rarely below 50%, thus suggesting a continuous relationship in these parliaments between level of female representatives and affiliation to left wing parties. The second contains countries where there are more substantial fluctuations between the level of women returned by left and right parties, but where trends over time suggest support for the hypothesis. The final group comprises countries where the hypothesis has to be rejected in that the majority of female representatives over time are almost continuously returned by non-left parties.

The first group, where a strong continuous relationship between female representatives and affiliation to left parties is suggested comprises Italy, Austria, and Norway (see Figs. 2, 3, and 4). Here the percentage of female representatives returned by left parties almost never falls below 50% apart from the elections of 1922 and 1931 in Norway (when the only female representatives – 1 and 2 respectively – were returned by the Conservatives); the election of 1994 in Italy (where the exceptional level of women representatives returned by the Right Liberals meant the percentage of those returned by left parties dropped to just over 45%); and the election of 1983 in Austria (when left party female representatives accounted for 47.1% of all women in the parliament).

In Italy, the Communist party has typically elected slightly more female legislators than any other party and was particularly influential in the 1970s when it "substantially increased its recruitment of women, thus becoming the strongest vehicle for their global growth in parliament" (Cotta,

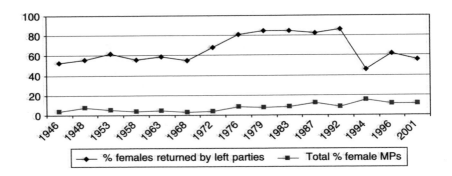

Fig. 2. Percent Female Representatives Returned via Leftist Parties in Italy.

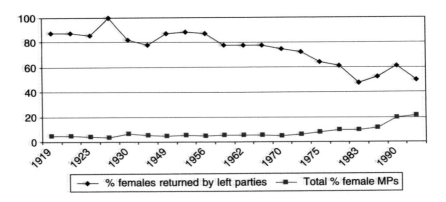

Fig. 3. Percent Female Representatives Returned via Leftist Parties in Austria.

Mastrolpaolo, & Verzichelli, 2000, p. 259). It should also be noted that in Italy the Second Wave of feminism in the 1970s had a particularly strong effect on attitudes towards the recruitment of women. Possibly related to this, the period from the 1970s to the early 1990s is one of an even greater level of female representation via left parties (particularly the Communists or their subsequent successors). It was only then that the main opposition party made an attempt "to ride on top of this new wave by giving more space to the recruitment of women. The other parties followed at a distance." (Cotta et al., 2000, p. 259). This is reflected in the downturn in the percentage of female legislators being returned by left parties from 1994

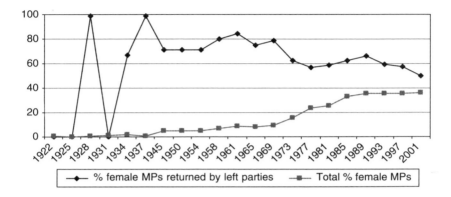

Fig. 4. Percent Female Representatives Returned via Leftist Parties in Norway.

onwards. A similar pattern is seen in Austria where overall the level of female representation is also continuously low. Where women are returned to parliament, however, the majority are nevertheless elected via left party affiliations. At the end of the century, however, as the level of female representatives begins to increase, the share of female representatives is divided equally between left and non-left parties. In Norway, a significant increase in the level of female representatives can be seen from the 1970s onwards. Here, although the majority are still affiliated with parties of the left and the increase is much slower in non-left parties such as the Agrarian and Christian Democrat parties (Eliassen & Sjøvaag Marinao, 2000), the proportion of female representatives returned via the right also increases. This trend continues so that although left-affiliated female representatives still account for the majority for some time, following the election of 2001 the percentage of women returned by left and non-left parties is equal.

In the second group greater variance in the orientation of the parties returning the majority of female representatives to parliament can be seen. At several time-points appreciably more female representatives are returned to parliament via non-left than left parties although overall the "left party – level of female representation" hypothesis is supported. This group includes Finland, Germany, and the UK (Figs. 5, 6, and 7).

In Finland women were from the beginning active participants in the same associations, especially labour movements, as men, and the proportion of women among industrial workers was already high early in 20th century. In 1910 almost one third of industrial workers were women and this early

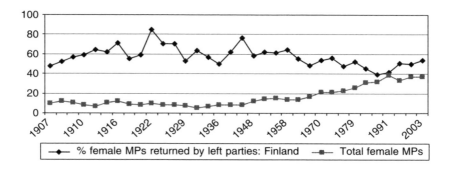

Fig. 5. Percent Female Representatives Returned via Leftist Parties in Finland.

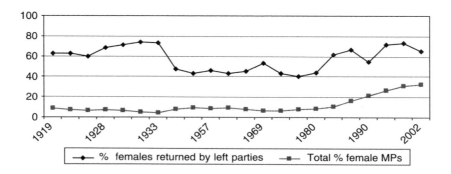

Fig. 6. Percent Female Representatives Returned via Leftist Parties in Germany.

establishment in paid employment gave them "a legitimate position as agents of political change" (Ruostetsaari, 2000, p. 57; Julkunen, 1990). Nevertheless, with regard to political orientation women did not necessarily turn to the Left. The early suffrage movement in Finland was supported by both right-wing and working-class women's movements (Kuusipalo, 1993) and in the first election in Finland in 1907 the majority (albeit small) of female representatives were returned by right-wing parties. For the next 60 or so years, however, although the level of female representation remained very low it was primarily via left parties. From the 1970s onwards the level of female representatives starts to rise. This rise is initially accompanied by an increase in the share of women returned via left parties but following the election of 1975 (when women from non-left parties were just in the

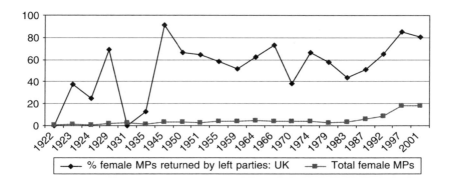

Fig. 7. Percent Female Representatives Returned via Leftist Parties in the UK.

majority − 52.2%), in a reverse situation from countries such as Italy, the majority of female representatives are more frequently returned by non-left parties. In Germany trends of left/non-left party affiliation for female representatives shows three distinct phases and as such mirrors the title of the paper: "Left–Right–Left". In Germany, as explained in detail in the case study, these three phases are related to social change pre and post World War 2. In the UK, as can be seen in Fig. 7, the overall level of female representation has been continuously low and is still one of the lowest in Europe. It took almost 70 years from the time the first women entered parliament to the level of female representatives exceeding 5% (Rush & Cromwell, 2000) and the level did not exceed the 10% mark until the election of 1997 (see Norris & Lovenduski, 1995, for a detailed overview of women in the British parliament). Because of the very low numbers involved an extremely erratic pattern is seen when the level of female representatives is plotted by party orientation. Nevertheless, over time the majority of women in the British parliament have had a left party affiliation and the increase seen at the 1997 election (18.1%), which was almost but not quite maintained in the 2001 election (17.9%), was due to the affirmative action taken by the Labour Party under Tony Blair.

The third group comprises countries where the majority of female representatives over time are not returned predominantly by parties of the left and where the percentage of female representatives returned by non-left parties almost never falls below 50%: Countries included here are Denmark and the Netherlands (Figs. 8 and 9). The Netherlands in particular refutes the hypothesis that female representatives are primarily returned to parliament via left parties – here only in four of the elections since women first entered parliament (i.e., those of 1918, 1972, 1989, and 1998) does the percentage of female legislators returned via a non-left party fall below 50%. This finding is mainly due to the strong affiliation between female representatives and the Christian Democrats and the Liberals.[4] As with most other countries where women first entered parliament at the beginning of the 20th century, no real progress in the level of female representatives is seen until the latter part of the century. By the 1980s, the percentage of women

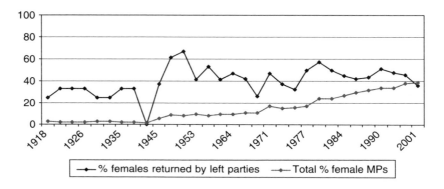

Fig. 8.   Percent Female Representatives Returned via Leftist Parties in Denmark.

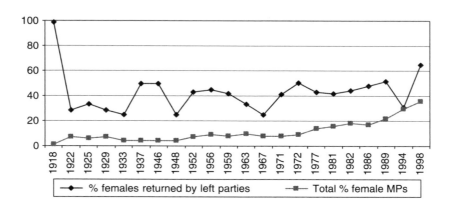

Fig. 9.   Percent Female Representatives Returned via Leftist Parties in the Netherlands.

had more than doubled its level of the 1960s, something seen as a direct result of the "persistent efforts" of the feminist movements (Secker, 2000). These efforts seem to have been advantageous to the Left in that the rise in the level of female representatives is mirrored by an increase in the level of female representatives being returned via left parties.

In Denmark a similar pattern is seen whereby female representatives returned via left parties form the majority in only four legislatures in the whole period from 1918 to 2001. As in most other European countries examined in this paper, the level of female political representatives remained very low in Denmark and did not cross the 30% atypicality[5] barrier until 1988. After this time women formed the majority in some parties, primarily these were the Left Liberals and New Left, but they also formed 50% of the Christian Democrats in the election of 2001 and accounted for almost 45% of the Conservatives, neither of which are parties of the left. In the last election of 2005, the trend away from female representatives in the Folketing having a left party affiliation continues, whilst the overall percentage of female representatives has slightly decreased from 38.3% in 2001 to 37.7% (Folketinget, 2005).

Looking at the country graphs as a whole they show that in the majority of countries findings support the hypothesis that a relationship exists between level of female political representatives and their affiliation to left parties. However, the graphs have also shown that the hypothesis does not hold at all times or in all contexts and cannot therefore be taken as universally given. It would seem that to have a clearer understanding of the processes involved it is necessary to look more closely at the interaction between women, political parties and the context within which the interaction takes place. For this reason one country, Germany, has been selected for closer examination.

THE CASE OF GERMANY, FEMALE REPRESENTATIVES, AND PARTIES OF THE LEFT:

The following looks at the developments of women returned via left parties to the national legislatures of Germany since 1919 when women were first granted suffrage and eligibility.

The Weimar Republic, which "started in troubled circumstances and with inner conflicts after the defeat of World War 1" (Best et al., 2000) can be seen as the result of a progressive revolution of the left that had at its core the ideal of equal citizenship including the extension of full voting rights to women. However, although the Left can be seen as the prime mover behind the introduction of female suffrage, the women's suffragist movement was run primarily by moderate bourgeois women. Nevertheless, as the socialists were the majority party of the 1919 Reichstag (and perhaps as an initial vote of thanks to them for securing women the vote) 62.5% of the women returned to the Reichstag in 1919 were done so on a socialist ticket. During the Weimar Republic, however, women's pattern of voting became one of consistent support for parties of a conservative, confessional bent (Sneering, 2002) although the majority of female representatives were returned by left parties until 1933.

With the failure of the Weimar Republic and the rise of the Nazi party in the 1930s, things became increasingly difficult for women in politics. Hitler proved to be an outspoken anti-feminist arguing that a woman's world should be "her husband, her family, her children, and her home" (Spartacus, 2005a). He went on to say that he detested, "women who dabble in politics ... [and that] ... in no section of the Party has a women ever had the right to hold even the smallest ... post -90% ... of the matters dealt with by parliament are masculine affairs on which [women] can not have opinions of any value" (Spartacus, 2005b). And true to his word, no women ever did hold 'even the smallest post' in the national power structure of National-Socialist Germany between 1933 and 1945.

In the first election following the end of World War II women were again allowed to stand for election but accounted for just 8.1% of all representatives. Over the next 30 plus years, this share remained pretty constant, never exceeding 10% until 1983 when it rose to 10.9%. When this period is broken down by party, unlike the Weimar period when the success or otherwise of women as representatives can be linked to that of the Socialists, very little difference is found between parties of the left or right with regard to share of female representatives. In fact, as can be seen in Fig. 10, in all parliaments between 1949 and 1983 (with the exception of the election of 1969 when 52.9% of female representatives were returned on a left party ticket) more women were returned via a non-left party affiliation (primarily Christian Democratic Union (CDU)) than via parties of the left (i.e. the Social Democrats). The most likely explanation here is that immediately following the end of WWII women were caught by a double-edged sword: On the one (right) side, due to the social climate that heralded a return to Christian values, they were subject to the predominantly Catholic Christian view of a women's place being first and foremost that of housewife and mother supported by a male 'bread-winner'.[6] This social value system was supported by various laws that imposed legal barriers on a (primarily

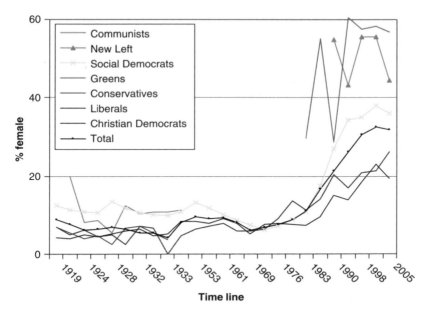

Fig. 10. Percent Female Representatives by Party in Germany Over Time.

married) woman's freedom to choose her own course of action, and although the passing of equal rights laws in the late 1950s changed this legally, in reality attitudes to the role of women, particularly to married women with children, remained strongly conservative, and changed little until the 1970s and the emergence of the second wave of feminism.[7] The other (left) side of the sword, which had previously championed women's involvement in the revolution forcing political and social change, now looked to protect the status of male workers. This resulted in discriminatory attitudes in some quarters of the working-class (socialist) movement that as such no longer seriously championed the equality of women. Thus, in the 1970s we see the German Social Democrats (SPD) only having an average of 6.6% female representatives.

As can be seen in Fig. 10, things changed in the 1980s with the emergence of the Greens, with a strong emphasis on gender politics and policies dedicated to environmental and peace issues. In the election of 1983, 30% of their representatives were women. This pushed the total share of women in Bundestag over the 10% threshold for the first time and meant that for the first time since before WWII the majority of female representatives (61.9%)

were returned on a left party ticket. In the election of 1987 there was another significant increase in level of female representatives overall (from 10.9% in 1983 to 16.9%) and as both the Greens[8] and the SPD had instigated quota systems, it is not surprising that 67% were from left parties. However, the success of the Greens did not go unnoticed and, as can be seen in Fig. 10, the inclusion of women in the other parties also increases at about this time so that in the election of 1990, although the numbers of female representatives continued to rise, only 54.4% of female representatives were returned by left parties. In the following two elections (1994 and 1998), the percentage of female representatives with left party affiliations once again increased, this time reaching a post-WWII high of 73.7% (only exceeded by the all-time high of 74.2% in 1932). Nevertheless, in 2002, the share of female representatives with left affiliations dropped again although the overall share of female representatives increased once more.

In Germany, then, the "Left–Right–Left" of the title of this article would seem to be rather accurate – suggesting only a partial acceptance of the hypothesis that the success of women representatives is predominantly linked to left party affiliation. As has been shown, the importance of parties of the centre and right as a vehicle for women's entry into parliament cannot be dismissed. In particular, although the effect was greater when the overall level of female representatives was still very low, and although the influence of the Greens on the level of female representatives in the Bundestag from the 1980s onwards is irrefutable, the increased role played by non-left parties has to be acknowledged.

CONCLUSION

To recall, the general hypothesis is that gender has always been a rallying cry of left parties and that they are more committed to the promotion of gender-related issues and to women's political inclusion than centre or right parties, so that more women can be expected to be returned to parliament via a left than non-left parties. The purpose of this article was to take advantage of a comprehensive longitudinal dataset to test whether this hypothesis would hold across the one hundred years since the first women in Europe were granted suffrage and eligibility, and whether it would be applicable regardless of national context.

Having correlated three important variables using the whole dataset, and having looked at eight European countries individually from a longitudinal perspective to ascertain whether such a relationship exists or not, the general conclusion has to be that there is evidence to support the basic hypothesis. However, at various time periods in all eight countries the hypothesis is not confirmed. Overall, the data suggests that while left parties provide a highly significant channel through which women are able to enter the legislatures of the countries studied, they do not provide an exclusive route and affiliation with the Left does not fully account for the general success of women as political representatives. Indeed, as the country analyses suggest and the German case study shows, the "left party – level of female representation" hypothesis is highly context dependent. In particular, the data seem to suggest that the mechanism of contagion suggested by Duverger (1954) is already operating in several of the countries analysed. It will be interesting, therefore, to re-visit the 'left party' hypothesis after more elections have been conducted in this new millennium, especially in those countries where to date the hypothesis seems to apply – will the title of that paper perhaps need to be Left–Right–Left–Right?

NOTES

1. Occupations are known to be 'gendered' (Reskin & Roos, 1990) with some viewed as the traditional domain of males or females, while others can be classed as gender-neutral (Anker, 1998; Christmas, 2002).

2. For each country the first election to return female representatives to parliament marks the start of data inclusion.

3. Some countries were not included in the analyses either because the data were not complete for the purpose of testing the hypothesis (France) or because the time span of data including females was too short for useful comparison (Portugal, Spain, and Hungary).

4. In some studies these parties have been classified with left parties (Secker, 2000) but, following the classifications of the Data Cube, for this work they are classed as centre parties and thus not included as the Left for the purposes of the analyses.

5. A measure of typicality/atypicality is used to categorise occupations with regard to the gender concentrations within them. An occupation with 30% or less of either gender is classed as atypical for that gender – breaking through this 30% cut-off point is referred to here as the atypicality barrier. It is also the level recommended by the United Nations Commission on the Status of Women in 1990 as the acceptable minimum, and which is seen as the threshold for women to have an impact on politics (Inter-Parliamentary Union, 2003).

6. Roman Catholicism has been linked to a lesser acceptance of women as political representatives (Rule, 2000).

7. It should be noted that this refers to West Germany. Following the division of Germany in 1945 attitudes to the role of women were very different in the East. Here the ideal was of "heroines of work" working alongside their male comrades to build a new socialist state, being politically active while retaining their maternal role.

However, although women were politically active, for the duration of the GDR there was never a female member of the Politburo, and in the Central Committee of the ruling Communist Party women never accounted for more than an average of 10.6% (Schneider, 1994). For the post WWII period until reunification of Germany in 1991, therefore, only data for the parliaments of the West are included in the Data Cube dataset.

8. In 1987, the Greens are more successful and by this time have introduced a gender quota system ensuring that over 50% of their representatives are female (55.1%).

REFERENCES

Anker, R. (1998). *Gender and jobs: Sex segregation of occupations in the world.* Geneva: ILO.

Best, H., & Cotta, M. (Eds) (2000). *Parliamentary representatives in Europe 1848–2000. Legislative recruitment and careers in eleven European countries.* Oxford: Oxford University Press.

Best, H., & Edinger, M. (2005). Converging representative elites in Europe? An introduction to the EurElite Project. *Czech Sociological Review, 41,* 499–510.

Best, H., Hausmann, C., & Schmitt, K. (2000). Challenges, failures, and final success: The winding path of Germany parliamentary leadership groups towards a structurally integrated elite 1848–1999. In: H. Best & M. Cotta (Eds), *Parliamentary representatives in Europe 1848–2000. Legislative recruitment and careers in eleven European countries.* Oxford: Oxford University Press.

Caul, M. (1999). Women's representation in parliament: The role of political parties. *Party Politics, 5*(1), 79–98.

Caul, M. (2001). Political parties and the adoption of candidate gender quotas: A cross-national analysis. *The Journal of Politics, 63*(4), 1214–1229.

Christmas, V. (2002). *Factors involved in women's atypical career choice: A comparative study of women in East and West Germany before and after reunification.* Doctoral dissertation, Senate House Library, University of London.

Christmas, V., & Kjaer, U. (In Press). Why so few and why so slow? Women as parliamentary representatives in Europe from a longitudinal perspective. In: M. Cotta & H. Best (Eds), *Democratic Representation in Europe: Diversity, Change and Convergence.* Oxford: Oxford University Press.

Cotta, M., Mastrolpaolo, A., & Verzichelli, L. (2000). Parliamentary elite transformations along the discontinuous road to democratization: Italy 1861–1999. In: H. Best & M. Cotta (Eds), *Parliamentary representatives in Europe 1848–2000. Legislative recruitment and careers in eleven European countries.* Oxford: Oxford University Press.

Duverger, M. (1954). *Poltical parties, their organisation and activity in the modern state.* London: Methuen Wiley.

Duverger, M. (1955). *The political role of women.* Paris: UNESCO.

Eliassen, K., & Sjøvaag Marinao, M. (2000). Democratization and parliamentary recruitment in Norway 1848–1996. In: H. Best & M. Cotta (Eds), *Parliamentary representatives in Europe 1848–2000. Legislative recruitment and careers in eleven European countries.* Oxford: Oxford University Press.

Folketinget. (2005). *Folketinget efter valget 8. Februar 2005.* Copenhagen: Folketinget.

Inglehart, R., & Norris, P. (2000). Developmental theory of the gender gap. *International Political Science Review, 21*(4), 381–405.

Inter-Parliamentary Union. (2003). *Political will indispensable for steady progress in women's participation in parliament.* Press Release 155, March 5, Geneva http://www.ipu.org/press-e/gen155.htm.

Inter-Parliamentary Union. (2006). *Women in national parliaments.* Database available on http://www.ipu.org/wmn-e/

Julkunen, R. (1990). Women in the welfare state. In: M. Manninen & P. Setälä (Eds), *Lady with the bow: The story of Finnish women.* Otava: Keururuu.

Kuusipalo, J. (1993). Women's positions and strategies in political arenas. In: H. Varsa (Ed.), *Shaping structural change in Finland.* Helsinki: Ministry of Social Affairs and Health. Equality Publications, Series B: Report 2.

Lovenduski, J. (1986). *Women and European politics: Contemporary feminism and public policy.* Amherst: The University of Massachusetts Press.

Lovenduski, J. (1993). Introduction: The dynamics of gender and party. In: J. Lovenduski & P. Norris (Eds), *Gender and party politics.* London: Sage.

Lovenduski, J. & Norris, P. eds (1993). *Gender and Party Politics.* London: Sage.

Matland, R. E. (1998). Women's representation in national legislatures: Developed and developing countries. *Legislative Studies Quarterly, 23*(1), 109–125.

Matland, R. E., & Studlar, D. T. (1996). The contagion of women candidates in single-member districts and proportional representation electoral systems: Canada and Norway. *Journal of Politics, 53*(3), 707–734.

Nicholson, L. (1997). *The second wave.* London: Routledge.

Norris, P. (1985). Women's legislative participation in Western Europe. *West European Politics, 8*, 90–101.

Norris, P. (1997). Conclusions: Comparing passages to power. In: P. Norris (Ed.), *Passages to power: Legislative recruitment in advanced democracies.* Cambridge: Cambridge University Press.

Norris, P., & Lovenduski, J. (1995). *Political recruitment: Gender, race and class in the British parliament.* Cambridge: Cambridge University Press.

Reskin, B. F., & Roos, P. A. (1990). *Job queues, gender queues.* Philadelphia: Temple University Press.

Rule, W. (1987). Electoral systems, contextual factors and women's opportunity for election to parliament in twenty-three democracies. *Western Political Quarterly, 40*, 477–498.

Rule, W. (2000). Patterns of women's parliamentary representation. Paper presented at the international political science association world congress, Quebec City, 1–5 August.

Ruostetsaari, I. (2000). From political amateur to professional politician and expert representative: Parliamentary recruitment in Finland since 1863. In: H. Best & M. Cotta (Eds), *Parliamentary representatives in Europe 1848–2000. Legislative recruitment and careers in eleven European countries.* Oxford: Oxford University Press.

Rush, M., & Cromwell, V. (2000). Continuity and change: Legislative recruitment in the United Kingdom 1868–1999. In: H. Best & M. Cotta (Eds), *Parliamentary representatives in Europe 1848–2000. Legislative recruitment and careers in eleven European countries.* Oxford: Oxford University Press.

Schneider, E. (1994). Die Politische Funktionselite der DDR: Eine Empirische Studie zur SED-Nomenklatura. [*The political elites of the GDR: An empirical study of the SED nomenclature*]. Opladen: Westdeutscher Verlag.

Secker, I. (2000). Representatives of the Dutch people: The smooth transformation of the
    parliamentary elite in a consociational democracy 1849–1998. In: H. Best & M. Cotta
    (Eds), *Parliamentary representatives in Europe 1848–2000. Legislative recruitment and
    careers in eleven European countries*. Oxford: Oxford University Press.
Sneering, J. (2002). *Winning women's votes: Propaganda and politics in Weimar Germany*.
    Chapel Hill: University of North Carolina Press.
Spartacus (2005a). Speech by Adolph Hitler to the NSDAP women's organisation, September
    1934. Women in Germany, http://www.spartacus.schoolnet.co.uk/GERwomen.htm
Spartacus (2005b). Speech by Adolph Hitler 26th January 1942. Women in Germany, http://
    www.spartacus.schoolnet.co.uk/GERwomen.htm
Togeby, L. (1994). Political implications of increasing numbers of women in the labour force.
    Comparative Political Studies, 27(2), 211–240.
Walby, S. (1997). *Gender transformations*. London: Routledge.

ELITE TRANSFORMATION IN DENMARK 1932–1999

Peter Munk Christiansen and Lise Togeby

In the Danish national elections of 2005, 65 women were elected to the 179-seat parliament. Fifty or hundred years ago, the political elite in Denmark was primarily composed of middle-aged males with lengthy careers in public life prior to entering Parliament. Today, almost 40 per cent of the members of parliament (MPs) are women; many are very young and fairly inexperienced, reflecting the dramatic shift in the perception of the ideal representative.

The political elite differ from all other elites in terms of their pronounced dependence on public opinion. This is also witnessed by the composition of the political elite, which at any time reflects the norms and ideals of the public and consequently changes much more rapidly than the composition of the other elites.

The composition of the other elites does not depend on public opinion to the same degree, but other changes in the recruitment systems have influenced their composition. In this article we deal with the changes in the composition of elites in Denmark in the twentieth century and present information on Danish elites at three points in time: 1932, 1963 and 1999.

Our assumption is that the composition of an elite group is influenced by the specific recruitment system for that particular elite group at a particular point in time. Because recruitment systems differ among elites and recruitment systems change over time, we will find variations among different elites at a given time and variations over time for each elite group.

Comparative Studies of Social and Political Elites
Comparative Social Research, Volume 23, 35–54
ISSN: 0195-6310/doi:10.1016/S0195-6310(06)23003-5

Our basic model is borrowed from classical studies of the recruitment of the political elite (Prewitt, 1970; Norris, 1997), but we generalize the model to cover all the different elites in contemporary society. In addition, we make the model more dynamic by combining the classic recruitment model with theories regarding the transformation of society over time, i.e. the changes from a traditional society over the industrial society to a new kind of society that we refer to, for lack of a better term, as the information society. To understand the changes of the elites in Denmark in the twentieth century, we apply a theoretical framework in which the basic changes of society cause shifts in the recruitment systems, which in turn alter the composition of the elites.

The data for the article come from a comprehensive study of Danish elites, covering all the elites in Danish society (Christiansen, Møller, & Togeby, 2001). To make the analysis more transparent, the paper focuses on only four of the most central elite groups: the MPs, the CEOs of the 200 largest private firms, the top civil servants and the most important judges.

A THEORY OF ELITE RECRUITMENT

Theories concerning the recruitment of the political elite traditionally view the composition of parliament as a result of a multi-phased process, as a kind of an elimination race (Norris, 1997; cf. also Best & Cotta, 2000). In each phase, the candidates who best fulfil the demands of the gatekeepers are selected. Who is selected is the outcome of the interplay of the supply and demand factors, meaning that it depends on the characteristics of the candidates and the priorities of the gatekeepers. Comparative studies reveal that this process varies among countries, meaning that the composition of parliaments also varies. New institutionalism (Ostrom, 1986; Norris, 1997) accounts for this variation in terms of the differences in the national recruitment systems, which create differences in supply and demand.

Building on these theories, we hypothesize that the recruitment process also varies from one elite group to the other, depending on the institutional framework for the selection of elites. The four elite groups chosen for investigation represent three very different recruitment systems. The basic characteristics of the model are illustrated in Fig. 1.

Studies of the political elite generally operate with three different phases: qualification, nomination and election. In the qualification phase, future candidates acquire the relevant qualifications and motivation for entering the more formalized struggle for nomination as party candidates. In

Phases	Institutional rules and norms	Gatekeepers' demands	Incentive for candidates
Qualification			
Nomination (political elite) Appointment (CEOs, civil servants, judges)			
Election (political elite) Advancements (other elite groups)			
Elite position			

Fig. 1. Model for Recruitment of Elites. *Source:* Christiansen et al. (2001).

Denmark these qualifications include party membership and normally some participation in party life, but personal wealth is not a requirement. In the nomination phase, the gatekeepers select the candidates who will appear on the party list. In Denmark these gatekeepers are the ordinary party members and the local party leadership. In the final and decisive election phase, however, the gatekeepers are the entire electorate. It is reasonable to expect that the gatekeepers in the nomination phase select candidates with a view to fulfil the demands of the electorate. In both phases, the gatekeepers are expected to consider the candidate's gender, age, local anchoring, charisma, etc. As Best and Cotta (2000, p. 15) write: "The social makeup of a parliament can in the end be viewed as a 'sediment' of norms, values, interests and opportunities of those involved in the recruitment process and of their respective strategies to achieve their goals". We generally expect that the composition of the parliament mirrors the expectations of the general public to a certain degree.

The contrast to the open and formalized recruitment process of the political elite is the closed and largely unregulated recruitment process for the managing directors of large private firms. In the business sector, we see two different types of directors representing two different types of recruitment processes. The first is the self-made entrepreneur, who personally founded the business and continues to operate it after it has grown in size. The second type of director – the most widespread – has had a relatively long and successful career that has been crowned by a position as CEO in one of the country's major firms. Some directors have advanced in the same corporation from the bottom to the top; however, it has become more common that executives further their careers by jumping from one corporation to another, each time increasing the challenges, responsibilities and salary. The gatekeepers for top positions are the boards of directors, whereas the gatekeepers at the lower levels are the daily management. There are no external demands on the choice of these gatekeepers other than the demand for profit. There is very little – close to none – formal regulation of the recruitment process, and it is not open for public scrutiny. In short, the gatekeepers can choose whoever they want for the position – including the founder's son or daughter.

The state elites, top civil servants and judges represent a third type of recruitment process. The Danish civil service is a merit system established on the Weberian bureaucracy ideal. Advancement is to be based on qualifications and results. There are few formal requirements for entering the civil service or advancing through the system, but a master's degree from a university is a de facto requirement for entering a career as a civil servant or a judge. Traditionally, most civil servants had attended law school; however, contemporary civil servants have a diverse range of backgrounds. Conversely, judges were required to have a law degree.

In the civil service, the normal gatekeepers will be other civil servants, though at a higher level than the applicant; top civil servants are appointed by the government. Denmark does not have politically appointed civil servants who come and go with the government, meaning that the appointment of top civil servants is also governed by the merit system. The composition of the administrative elite is somewhat influenced by changes in society in general, and there is some public interest in the appointment of top civil servants.

There are two main paths to a judgeship in Denmark. One possibility is to start as a civil servant in the Ministry of Justice, while the other is to start directly as a civil servant in the courts. After 10–15 years of employment, it becomes possible for these civil servants to be appointed to a judgeship in a city court. Advancement to more important courts will be based on assessments of the judges' activities in the lower courts. The Supreme Court itself has traditionally had the major say in the appointment of new Supreme Court judges; however, the appointment system was revised in 1999 to make the Supreme Court less self-elective. Appointments to the Supreme Court are now decided in a complicated system in which competence is divided between the Supreme Court, the Ministry of Justice and an independent special appointment board with representatives from the public. It remains to be seen whether the change of the recruitment system will result in changes in the composition of the judicial elite.

For both civil servants and judges, the advancement to top positions is based on a merit system, where appointment to higher positions is decided on accomplishments at a lower level. With the exception of the top civil servants or the Supreme Court judges, the gatekeepers are exclusively people who are already employed within the system. This likely means that the composition of the state elites shifts very gradually, as gatekeepers have a tendency to appoint candidates who resemble themselves – the *Huey, Dewey and Louie effect*, as it is referred to in Denmark.

To make the model more dynamic, we must ask whether elements in these recruitment systems have changed in the twentieth century in a manner that will influence the composition of the four elite groups. We pose four questions in relation to each elite group:

(1) Have there been changes in the way the selection of elite persons is organized?
(2) What are the changes in the incentives for people to enter the elite?
(3) Have there been changes in the supply of candidates?
(4) Have there been changes in the preferences of the gatekeepers?

CHANGES IN THE RECRUITMENT SYSTEMS

We expect the recruitment system to shift in accordance with major changes in – and demands from – the surrounding society. During the twentieth century, Denmark underwent transformation from a traditional agricultural society to an industrial society and eventually to an information society.

In traditional society, the right family background and a higher education constitute significant resources for reaching top positions. Power and wealth are concentrated among the members of the bourgeoisie and the nobility. In the second half of the nineteenth century, a political mobilization of farmers took place in Denmark, followed by a mobilization of workers around the turn of the century. During the first half of the twentieth century, a corporative, industrial society grew stronger and stronger, rendering farming and labour organizations very central players in Danish society. The corporative system reached its peak in the 1950s and 1960s and was gradually weakened during the last decades of the twentieth century at the dawn of the development towards a new kind of society (Christiansen & Nørgaard, 2003). We remain in the midst of the construction of this new type of society, which goes by many names – let us call it the information society. Compared to the industrial society, the information society is generally characterized by demands for improved qualifications, less hierarchical organizations and more reflective and individualized culture. We expect that the different types of societies will be accompanied by different recruitment systems.

Moreover, we expect that periods characterized by rapid social transformation are also characterized by elite groups that differ from the elite groups in periods of stability. The turnover of the elite will be faster in times of rapid social transformation, new social groups will join the elites and persons holding elite positions will be younger. We expect the 1932-elite to be influenced by the transformation from traditional to industrial society, and we expect the 1999-elite to be influenced by the transformation from industrial to information society, whereas the 1963-elite is the result of a long period of stabilization of the classic elites of the industrial society. Of course, major changes took place in the Danish society from the early 1930s until the early 1960s. The recession in the 1930s laid the foundation for the welfare state, the urban population grew and the agricultural sector underwent mechanization. Nevertheless, changes happened within the basic structures of industrial society, and in many respects the 1960s represents the mature industrial society.

We can now ask how these overall transformations have affected the recruitment systems. In general, the institutional framework has not changed significantly. The fundamental principles of the electoral system, with proportional representation and opportunities for preferential voting, were established in 1915. Minor changes have subsequently been made to the system, rendering the preferential voting of the electorate even more important for the selection of candidates. The Danish electoral system allows for the use of either a semi-open list or an open list. Today, however, almost all parties use open lists, meaning that the electorate – as opposed to the party leadership – has the final word in the selection of the specific candidates from the party lists. The recruitment system for the managing directors of private firms has undergone a number of changes. The *managerial revolution* by which the owners and managers of private firms were separated also characterizes the Danish business sector to some extent, even though a larger part of the Danish industry is owned by individuals and families than in the other Western countries (Thomsen, Pedersen, & Strandskov, 2002, p. 51ff). Even if the company boards have had the opportunity during the entire period to choose whomever they want as CEO, changes in the recruitment system increasingly favour professional and well-educated managers. Finally, the recruitment systems for the state elites, top civil servants and Supreme Court judges have remained more or less unchanged during the entire century. The overall principle is that candidates ought to be selected according to their qualifications and achievements. This goes for entrance to the bottom of the hierarchy as well as for advancement towards the upper positions. However, changes are found in the appointment conditions for top civil servants. Today, they are often appointed on temporary 5-year contracts. Since the beginning of the twentieth century, women have in principle had the same rights as men to enter the civil service or to become judges.

What changed during the twentieth century were the incentives for people to enter the elite, the supply of candidates and the preferences of the gatekeepers. The incentives for entering all elite groups are generally high and have been high during the period under examination. However, it is probably fair to say that the incentives for entering the political elite have diminished in comparison to the other elite groups. In the beginning and middle of the century, it was possible for an MP to attend to other duties while serving as an MP. Some members also occupied positions such as CEO in a private firm, editor of a large newspaper, president of an interest organization or university professor. That is not possible today, where being an MP is generally a full-time job. In addition, an MP's salary cannot compete with salaries in other top positions of the society. Consequently, there are few incentives for those who are well established in careers in other sectors to aspire for a seat in Parliament.

In many senses, the supply of candidates has been broadened. The political mobilization of farmers and workers enlarged the supply pool for the political elite and the other elite groups with members from these two classes. Furthermore, even if a social bias remains in the function of the educational system, the system has been democratized, and family background plays a diminished role with respect to succeeding in higher education at the end of the century than was the case at the beginning. At the same time, women have gradually joined the supply pool for elite recruitment.

Most importantly, the gatekeepers' preferences have changed over the last century. This is most striking when the electorate is the direct or indirect gatekeeper, that is, in the case of the political elite, but also to a certain degree of the state elites. In the beginning of the century, the electorate demanded new types of elite persons in addition to the traditional elite consisting of academics and nobles. There was a demand for farmers and workers to represent the upcoming classes. At the end of the century, the electorate again focused on new qualities in future representatives, demanding more women and younger and better-educated people. For the state elites, an academic degree has always been almost mandatory, but in relation to civil servants, the more precise demand for qualifications has changed. In the beginning of the century, most civil servants had a law degree; after WWII, a degree in economics was respected by the gatekeepers, and at the end of the century, new educational disciplines such as political science had become equally popular among the gatekeepers. In addition, top civil servants, for example, permanent secretaries in the ministries, have become more involved in political counselling over the last couple of decades. The recruitment of the state elites is also influenced by changes in public opinion. At all levels the gatekeepers are attentive to the public's demand for elites with a more varied family background and for more women in top positions. Compared to those for the other sectors, the demands of the gatekeepers in the business sector have not changed much – at least not yet. There is very little pressure on the choices of the gatekeepers from the public, and family and network connections remain an important quality. There may be an increasing demand for education and a change in the kind of education demanded. There has been a shift from law over engineering to economics and business science.

We generally expect the composition of the political elite to have changed the most and the composition of the private business CEOs to have changed the least.

DATA

The article is based on a study of Danish elites in 1932, 1963 and 1999 (Christiansen et al., 2001). In principle, the study covers all of the elite groups in the Danish society, i.e. the political elite, administrative elite, judicial elite, military elite, academic or scientific elite, organizational elite, media elite, cultural elite and the business elite. For the sake of clarity, only a selection of these groups – the most important ones – is analysed in this article.

The elite people have been selected on the basis of their formal positions in the Danish society. For example, we have chosen the civil servants occupying the highest positions in the national administrative hierarchy (161 positions in 1999) and the CEOs from the largest private firms and from the biggest consultancy and legal firms in Denmark (463 positions in 1999).[1]

The information about the elite people has been found in works of reference open to the public, i.e. official registers, biographies and databases on the Internet[2]. We have not conducted any interviews or distributed questionnaires. It goes without saying that these data collection methods restrict the kind of information obtained (e.g. preferences, political affiliation and informal networks). Nevertheless, they ensure a rather high response rate, and if we also want data on the historical elites where people are no longer available for interviews, this is the only way to proceed.

CHARACTERISTICS OF FOUR ELITE GROUPS 1932–1999

Gender

The representation of women in four of our elite groups has developed quite differently, cf. Fig. 2. In 1932, hardly any women held elite positions. Only the political elite included women – 3 per cent. The first national election in which women had suffrage was in 1918, when four women were elected to Parliament (Kjær & Pedersen, 2004, p. 94).The increasing proportion of women in the political elite is quite sharp – even dramatic – from 1963 to 1999. The number of women in the political elite does not correspond to the female share of the electorate, but the underrepresentation has decreased sharply. We thus find that the gatekeepers' demand for more women in politics has been met; more women are listed as candidates and more women gain election.

The business elite contrasts sharply to the political elite. The lack of change in the preferences of the business sector gatekeepers produces a near absence of women in the business elite. In 1999, there was only one female CEO in the top 200 Danish firms – the same as in 1963, and there was none in 1932. At least in terms of gender, private businesses have not allowed societal demands to influence the recruitment of directors.

If we dig a little deeper into the recruitment to top business positions below the CEO level, we find an illustration of the *law of increasing inequality* (cf.

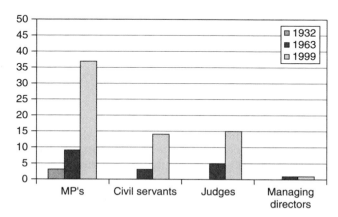

Fig. 2. Per Cent Women among Elites in 1932, 1963 and 1999.

Putnam, 1976). While the female share of CEOs is 0.5 per cent, the share of managers other than CEOs is 3 per cent. If we consider the smaller firms outside of the top 200 group, we also find an increasing proportion of female CEOs, though still at a very low level (Christiansen et al., 2001, p. 148).

In 1932, the number of women with relevant education for the elite positions in the judiciary and the civil service was quite small. Currently, this number is greater, but women continue to hold relatively few top positions in the two sectors. The recruitment systems for civil servants and judges have proven to be more responsive to the demand for female representation in the elite than those of the business sector, but much less responsive than those of the political elite. In 1999, civil servants and judges had a slightly higher proportion of women than the average for all the eight elite groups in the Danish society (12 per cent).

Age

Since it takes time to acquire the necessary qualifications and climb the ladder to an elite position, the members of elite groups tend to be middle-aged; however, there are exceptions. Some reach top positions in politics at a relatively young age. Young people may inherit a large company from their parents, or they may have the skills and good fortune to become successful businessmen at an early age. It is more unlikely for young people to reach top positions in the bureaucracy or in the court system, although there is one example of a 35-year-old male who became the permanent secretary in the Ministry of the Environment in 1973.

Even if the elites tend to be middle-aged, we can expect their ages to vary. We hypothesized that the age of the elite would be responsive to the general development of society and to elite-specific factors. In times of a relatively stable society, elite members will be replaced at a slower rate and the average age of the elites will increase. In times of rapid change, elite members will be replaced more rapidly, and the average age will drop. For each elite group, demands from the gatekeepers may vary over time and differently for each group.

Fig. 3 reveals the development of the average age of the four elite groups. The overall development corresponds well with our understanding of the general state of the Danish society in the three periods. The decades preceding the early 1930s and the late 1990s were periods of rapid societal change, whereas the 1950s and the early 1960s represented the years of the mature industrial society. With the exception of the judges, the oldest elites are found in 1963.

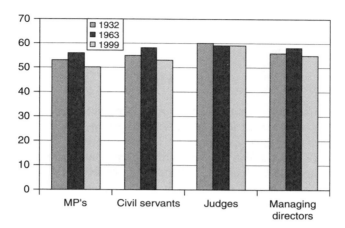

Fig. 3. Average Age of Elites in 1932, 1963 and 1999.

Judges are appointed to top positions through a rather closed system. Until the late 1990s, the Supreme Court itself was the primary gatekeeper. Supreme Court judges are appointed (typically at ages 49–51) to lifelong positions with retirement at age 70. As a consequence of the recruitment system, the judiciary elite is relatively resistant to the general rate of change affecting the rest of society.

The other elite groups may be replaced at a younger age owing to the changing demands from the gatekeepers. In the 1990s, the gatekeepers of the political elite – the local party leadership and the voters – not only preferred more women in the political elite, but they also demanded younger people. Their preferences are reflected in the composition of the political elite. The average age declined from 56 to 50 years from 1963 to 1999. In addition to the changing demands from the gatekeepers, we interpret this drop in the average age as the evidence of declining competition for political posts.

The level of competition for high-ranking civil servants has not decreased, but the demands upon them have changed. Today's top civil servants are highly involved in political counselling and they have replaced the traditional professional bureaucrat (Knudsen, 2000). While top civil servants in the 'good old days' might possibly have been able to spend the final years of their career in a relatively quiet working environment drawing on their career-long body of experience, this is no longer the case. Most of the permanent secretaries in the ministries have 5-year contracts. These contracts – which include an addendum on their hire – can only be renewed once.

Upon the expiration of their contract, they typically receive a retirement post. The declining age of top civil servants is a consequence of changes in institutional rules and increased demands on the bureaucratic elite.

Education

The elite of a society is unavoidably going to be better educated than the population as a whole, at least in those elite groups where a higher education is a *conditio sine qua non* for an elite position. Supreme Court membership requires a law degree. While there is no formal requirement regarding an academic education to become a top civil servant in Denmark as in most other Western countries, it is a de facto requirement. There are exceptions, however. For instance, in the postal service, customs and taxation authorities and railway authorities, there has been a tradition to recruit top civil servants with a vocational education from the authority in question. Nevertheless, as seen in Fig. 4, in all the three periods, few top civil servants lacked an academic education. Candidates for top positions without a university degree are increasingly met with competition from candidates with a university degree in economics, law or political science.

In 1932, very few Danes held an academic degree, and the political elite was significantly better educated than the population at large. In 1999, the educational level of the population had increased dramatically and much more than that of the political elite. The number of well-educated candidates for elite positions has increased significantly. We expected that the gatekeepers of

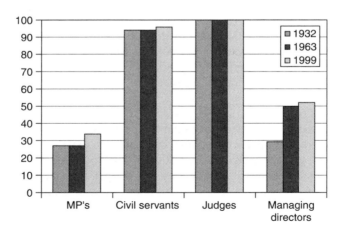

Fig. 4. Per Cent of Elites with an Academic Education in 1932, 1963 and 1999.

the political elite would have become more demanding as regards the educational level of candidates; however, the effect on the political elite is relatively small. Compared to many other Western countries, there are still relatively few highly educated individuals among the political elite in Denmark and the other Scandinavian countries (cf. Aberbach, Putnam, & Rockman, 1981; Narud & Valen, 2000). The political elite remains significantly better educated than the general population, but the distance between the people and the political elite was reduced over the course of the twentieth century.

The business elite is better educated than the political elite. The changes in the recruitment system following the *managerial revolution* are reflected in the sharp rise in the share of business leaders with an academic degree from 1932 to 1963. The share has not grown since then, which has otherwise been the case with the general population. The Danish system of vocational training and on-the-job training allows room for ambitious and bright people to enter top business positions without an academic education.

Social Background

All modern societies are characterized by some degree of inequality. Even if the Scandinavian countries are among the most egalitarian market economies in terms of income distribution (Togeby et al., 2003), the recruitment of elites is marked by inequality. One measure of social inequality is the proportion of elites who grew up in an elite home. Fig. 5 shows the proportion of elites whose father had an elite position. Differences over time are significant, as are differences among four of our elites.

It is hardly surprising that the 1932-elites have a much more privileged family background than the rest of the population. Their social composition reflects the traditional society in which family background was an important prerequisite for the elite. It may be more surprising that, with the exception of judges, the 1963-elite is equally or more privileged than the 1932-elite. It was only after 1963 that the elite's social background became significantly less exclusive. A major explanation – particularly of the two state elites – is that the increasing number of candidates with a non-privileged background did not exist prior to the 1960s and the 1970s, at which time higher education became much more widespread among young people with a middle-class background. These new generations conquered some of the elite positions in the civil service and in the judiciary, even if the social background of the state elites remains biased towards a relatively privileged background. The social background of the business elite has never been highly privileged, and today it is certainly less privileged than that of the state elites.

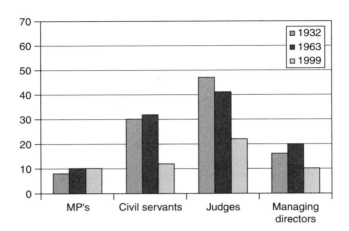

Fig. 5. Per Cent of Elites with Fathers in the elite in 1932, 1963 and 1999.
Note: The Father is Registered as having an Elite Position if he is Mentioned in *Krak's blå bog,* a Danish Equivalent of *Who's Who.*

The social background of the political elite has never been particularly privileged. Contrary to the other three elite groups, the contemporary political elite has the same proportion of fathers with an elite position as in 1963, this being because their fathers had also been top politicians. Birth into a political family has come to play a more prominent role in the recruitment of political elites. Ten per cent of the MPs are sons or daughters of politicians, and an additional 7 per cent of them have close relatives who are politicians. Not less than 25 per cent of the members of the cabinet have close relatives with a political career (Christiansen et al., 2001, p. 51ff). Political clans are a new phenomenon in the Danish political life.

Recruitment Channels

Most elite people have had an occupational career preceding their elite position. The only exception is a small group of MPs with no career prior to their membership in parliament. They are typically university students, some of whom never even completed their university degree. We interpret their presence in the political elite as not only yet another sign of the reduced competition in the political elite, but also of a growing demand for young people.

All the other elite candidates must have some kind of occupational career prior to entering an elite position. Figs. 6 and 7 show the percentage of four

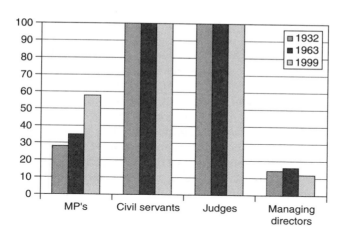

Fig. 6. Per Cent of Elites Currently or Previously in Public Service in 1932, 1963 and 1999.

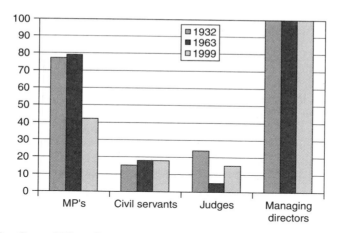

Fig. 7. Per Cent of Elites Currently or Previously Employed in Private Business in 1932, 1963 and 1999.

of our elites with a current or previous position in public service and private business, respectively.

The main conclusion from Figs. 6 and 7 is that three of the elite groups follow separate careers. The two state elites have little experience in private business, and the business elite has little experience in the public sector.

Furthermore, things have not changed very much over the course of the twentieth century.

However, the careers of MPs have changed during the period. In 1932 and 1963, only one-third of the political elite had prior occupation in the public sector, compared to almost 60 per cent of contemporary MPs. In the two early years of measurement, more than three-fourths had previous experience in private business. Currently, this holds for only around 40 per cent of Danish MPs. There are two explanations for this development: first, the public sector has simply increased its share of total employment. One will thus expect an increasing proportion of the political elite to be recruited with a public sector background. Second, a political career is not – any longer – compatible with fulltime employment elsewhere, and the low pay and the (over time) decreasing esteem associated with a political career renders it less attractive for people with a business career.

Elite Networks

C. Wright Mills held that elite groups would participate in different types of cross-sector interrelations and thereby further their common interests (Mills, 1956). Democracy would be endangered by the coherence of elites. Etzioni-Halevy (1993) accepts the inevitability of elites, but points to autonomy and independence as prerequisites for democracy. Elite autonomy and competition are healthy for democracy.

There is a dilemma involved in the cross-sectoral relations between elite groups. On the one hand, elites play a central role in the creation and maintenance of societal coherence. Consequently, they must be able to communicate opinions and coordinate action on a number of different matters. On the other hand, they may communicate and coordinate too much and thus endanger the autonomy of – and competition between – elites.

The transformation of the Danish society in the period under investigation may have consequences for inter-elite networks. Overall, however, we expect networks to be loosened. In the 1930s, the industrial society was still being built; the 1960s were its heyday. The industrial society is related to large-scale production, investments in infrastructure, expansions of the educational system, etc. Coordination is needed through corporatist and other coordination mechanisms. Coordination is also required in post-industrial society, but post-industrial society is a more fragmented society with less coordination required than in industrial society.

Our empirical evidence includes two measures of interdependence and autonomy of elites. C. Wright Mills (1956, p. 288) emphasized that the elites, during their careers, interchanged "commanding roles" in different sectors. As we have already shown in Figs. 6 and 7, the careers of the Danish elites tend to unfold within – rather than across – the main sectors of the Danish society. The careers of the business elite take place within the private sector. And only few top civil servants and judges in Denmark have had posts in the private sector. Except for the political elite, of which a significant part has been occupied in the private or public sector prior to their political career, commanding roles are not interchanged between the public and private sectors.

Inter-elite relations can also be measured in terms of formal posts in political parties, public boards and commissions, economic interest organizations and the boards of private firms. These memberships are shown in Fig. 8. As regards posts in political parties, the figure counts present as well as preceding posts in political parties.

Two main conclusions can be drawn from the figures. First, inter-elite relations through formal posts are not particularly frequent. Many politicians, civil servants and judges hold posts on public boards. These posts are integrated in their elite position. It provides them with opportunities to meet and exchange information and opinions with other elite members, but they rarely meet with the business elite in these forums. Less than one in five top business leaders hold posts on public boards. Very few of the three non-political elites have current or prior political experience.

Second, there are currently fewer interrelations between elites in formal networks than earlier. In 1932 and 1963, more than one out of three CEOs held a post on a public board. Currently, the figure is less than one out of five. MPs and civil servants hold fewer posts as members of boards in

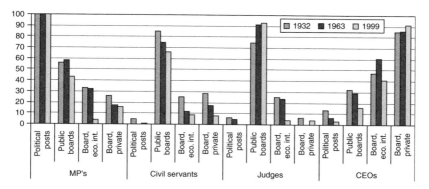

Fig. 8. Elite Membership in 1932, 1963 and 1999.

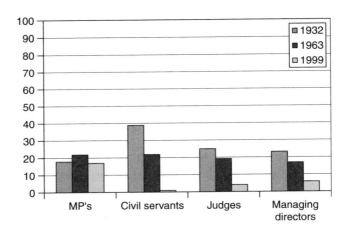

Fig. 9. Per Cent of Elites Holding Board Membership in Non-economic Organizations in 1932, 1963 and 1999.

private business now than was the case in 1932 and 1963. Danish elite groups have become more independent and less cohesive in terms of overlapping membership in formal networks.

They have also been less inclined to engage in activities that do not directly relate to or enhance their own careers. In 1932, almost 40 per cent of the bureaucratic elite was board members in non-economic organizations (religious, charitable, environmental, etc.). Very few are so today, cf. Fig. 9. The same development is found for judges and managing directors. Only the MPs engage in non-economic organizations. The Danish elite has not only become less cohesive, but it also contributes less to activities outside its own narrow interest.

CONCLUSION

After the Danes rejected the Maastricht Treaty in a referendum held in 1992, a 'national compromise' was put together. In 1993, the Danes voted on the compromise, which entailed four exceptions from the Maastricht Treaty, this time voting 'yes'. The course of events triggered much discussion about an elite having taken over the Danish society; the people were not allowed to make decisions that the elite would not accept.

While it is true that the elite is more pro-EU than the rest of the electorate, it is hardly true that Denmark has become more elitist, at least in terms of social background. On the contrary, Denmark has become less elitist. The elite resembles the people more: the number of women in the elite is unprecedented, although they are still not represented according to their share of the population. The elite is better educated than in 1932, but the difference in relation to the rest of the population is reduced significantly. The elite still has a more privileged background than the people, but less so compared to that in the early 1930s. Relatively separate channels of recruitment, particularly between the private and public sectors, characterize the recruitment of elites. In terms of autonomy, the Danish elites have become more autonomous than in the past – to the point where they rarely engage in matters that are not for their own benefit.

NOTES

1. The four elites discussed in this article have the following numbers of elite positions:
The political elite: 1932, 238; 1963, 197; 1999, 199.
Civil servants: 1932, 57; 1963, 107; 1999, 161.
Judges: 1932, 17; 1963, 22; 1999, 27.
Business: 1932, 134; 1963, 272; 1999, 463.
2. The most important are: *Kraks Blå Bog*, multiple editions, the homepage of the Danish Parliament (http://www.ft.dk), Elberling (1949), *Greens*, multiple editions, Weber (1988), Andersen (1939, 1966, 1970); Andersen and Weber (1985).

REFERENCES

Aberbach, J., Putnam, R. D., & Rockman, B. A. (1981). *Bureaucrats and Politicians in Western Democracies*. Cambridge: Harvard University Press.
Andersen, H. (1939). *Hvem ejer Danmark?* Copenhagen: Mondes Forlag.
Andersen, H. (1966). *Hvem ejer Danmark?* Copenhagen: Fremad.
Andersen, H. (1970). *Hvem ejer Danmark nu?* Copenhagen: Fremad.
Andersen, H., & Weber, L. (1985). *Magtens mange mænd*. Copenhagen: Fremad.
Best, H., & Cotta, M. (2000). Elite transformation and modes of representation since the mid-nineteenth century: Some theoretical considerations. In: H. Best & M. Cotta (Eds), *Parliamentary representatives in Europe 1848–2000* (pp. 1–28). Oxford: Oxford University Press.
Christiansen, P. M., Møller, B., & Togeby, L. (2001). *Den danske elite*. Copenhagen: Hans Reitzels Forlag.
Christiansen, P. M., & Nørgaard, A. S. (2003). *Faste forhold – flygtige forbindelser. Stat og interesseorganisationer i Danmark i det 20. århundrede*. Aarhus: Aarhus University Press.
Elberling, V. (1949). Rigsdagsmændenes Livsstilling. In: *Den Danske Rigsdag* (pp. 351–392), bind IV. Copenhagen: J.H. Schultz for lag.

Etzioni-Halevy, E. (1993). *The elite connection, problems and potential of western democracy.* Cambridge: Polity Press.

Kjær, U., & Pedersen, M. N. (2004). *De danske folketingsmedlemmer. En parlamentarisk elite og dens rekruttering, cirkulation og transformation 1849–2001.* Aarhus: Aarhus Universitetsforlag.

Knudsen, T. (2000). Fra bureaukrati til den ny embedsmandsstat. In: T. Knudsen (Ed.), *Regering og embedsmænd. Om magt og demokrati i staten* (pp. 353–366). Aarhus: Systime.

Mills, C. W. ([1956]/1965). *The power elite.* London: Oxford University Press.

Narud, H. M., & Valen, H. (2000). Does social background matter? In: P. Esaiasson & K. Heidar (Eds), *Beyond Westminster and Congress* (pp. 83–106). Columbus: Ohio State University Press.

Norris, P. (1997). Introduction: Theories of recruitment. In: P. Norris (Ed.), *Passages to power. Legislative recruitment in advanced democracies* (pp. 1–14). Cambridge: Cambridge University Press.

Ostrom, E. (1986). An agenda for the study of institutions. *Public Choice, 48,* 3–25.

Prewitt, K. (1970). *The recruitment of political leaders: A study of citizen-politicians.* Indianapolis: Bobbs-Merrill.

Putnam, R. D. (1976). *The comparative study of political elites.* Englewood Cliffs, NJ: Prentice-Hall.

Thomsen, S., Pedersen, T., & Strandskov, J. (2002). *Ejerskab og indflydelse i dansk erhvervsliv.* Aarhus: Magtudredningen.

Togeby, L., Andersen, J. G., Christiansen, P. M., Jørgensen, T. B., & Vallgårda, S. (2003). *Magt og demokrati i Danmark. Hovedresultater fra magtudredningen.* Aarhus: Aarhus Universitetsforlag.

Weber, L. (1988). *Hvem ejer Danmark?* Copenhagen: Fremad.

IMPORTANCE OF CONTACTS AND WOMEN'S POLITICAL REPRESENTATION: A STUDY OF SWEDEN AND NORWAY

Birgitta Niklasson

The importance of having contacts who offer guidance and look after your interests has been recognised in several studies on recruitment in corporations and organisations. For example, Mark Granovetter's (1974) *Getting a Job* describes contacts as playing a central part in the employment process on the labour market. In research on political careers, however, the importance of contacts has attracted curiously limited attention. This may be partly because academics wish to avoid being associated with the kind of journalism which portrays politicians as incompetent swindlers who have obtained their prestigious positions through acquaintances in the political elite (see e.g. Isaksson, 2002).

Nevertheless, the importance of contacts in political recruitment deserves to be taken seriously for several reasons. The most obvious, of course, is that should the journalistic criticism of politicians be correct, this could entail serious consequences for democracy. Not everyone is likely to have contacts who could help start and/or build a political career. Women, for example, tend to have more limited networks within established party organisations (Oscarsson, 2003), a situation which could affect their career

Comparative Studies of Social and Political Elites
Comparative Social Research, Volume 23, 55–75
Copyright © 2007 by Elsevier Ltd.
ISSN: 0195-6310/doi:10.1016/S0195-6310(06)23004-7

prospects negatively if such contacts turn out to be crucial in political re-cruitment. In other words, recruitment based on contacts could constitute a threat to political equality (Dahl, 2000; Phillips, 2000) and consequently this potential career factor deserves our attention. This paper presents data from Sweden and Norway indicating that political careers are no different from careers in business or other kinds of organisations in this respect; contacts may, in fact, be of even greater importance in political contexts.

CONTACTS IN POLITICAL RECRUITMENT

Formal and informal interactions in the political elite and between the polit-ical elite and other actors have attracted a great deal of research (Petersson, 1996; Munk Christiansen, Möller, & Togeby, 2001; Moore, Sobieraj, Whitt, Mayorova, & Beaulieu, 2002). However, such research has mainly been concerned with the contacts of leading politicians once they have already become part of the elite, not the role that contacts might have played in their recruitment.

In studies focusing on political recruitment, contacts have only made a fleeting appearance. When dealt with, they are often discussed in terms of gatekeepers and mentors (Norris, 1996; Best & Cotta, 2000; Vianello & Moore, 2000; Kjær & Pedersen, 2004). Owing to the high status and central position in the recruitment process that these actors enjoy, they are claimed to be the kind of contacts who have the most power to influence somebody's career advancement directly (Knoke, 1990; Brass, 1992; Lai, Lin, & Leung, 1998; Niklasson, 2005), but even people without any part in the actual recruitment may function as career boosters, for example, friends and family (Fredriksson, 2001; Nielsen, 2001; Niklasson, 2005).

Contacts constitute career assets because they supply resources. These resources are often described as being either instrumental or expressive (Stenlås, 1998; Hedin, 2001; Lin, 2001). Instrumental returns are forms of practical support related to the development of skills and the actual acqui-sition of positions. Examples of this kind of support are professional advice about how to act strategically in certain situations, information, and nom-inations to important positions (Burt, 1999; Niklasson, 2005). Expressive returns, in contrast, are forms of emotional support, such as confidence and inspiration, that strengthen a person's will to attempt or continue a career (Matthews, 1984; Teorell, 2000; Karlsson, 2001; Niklasson, 2005).

Different kinds of contacts tend to supply different kinds of resources. Professional contacts like gatekeepers and mentors are more likely to contribute instrumental returns, whereas expressive returns more frequently stem from social contacts like friends and family. It is, therefore, an advantage to have a wide range of contacts instead of just having many contacts of the same kind (Marsden, 1987; Burt, 1983).

To just what extent contacts are important in political careers and how they might affect the political recruitment of different social groups need more thorough examination, though. The hypotheses in this study are that (1) contacts are of major importance to reach leading political positions, and (2) that this requirement has negative consequences to the political advancement of women.

The focus on women in this study stems from the possibility that women run the risk of being disadvantaged in a recruitment process that relies on contacts because of the human inclination towards homosocial behaviour. That is, people normally prefer the company of friends and acquaintances who are similar to themselves with regard to interests, education, social backgrounds, etc. (Mills, 1956; Lipman-Blumen, 1976; Bourdieu, 1996). This behaviour is particularly prominent in recruitment to leading positions (Kadushin, 1995; Lin, 2001; Marsden, 2001; Wahl, Holgersson, Höök, & Linghag, 2001). The uncertain political environment spurs leaders to try to maximise trust and predictability within the elite by recruiting people whom they expect will make the same calculations as themselves in situations when decisions have to be made quickly. As Rosabeth Moss Kanter (1993) somewhat idiosyncratically puts it, they are looking for someone to hang their hat on. Consequently, not everybody has the same access to people in power. Individuals belonging to social groups that are underrepresented in the political elite, for example women, are likely to face greater difficulties when trying to advance through recruitment structures in which contacts constitute an important career asset (see Niklasson, 2005 for a further discussion).

TWO UNLIKELY CASES

There are reasons to believe that having contacts is not of equal importance in all kinds of political recruitment. In central patronage recruitment structures (in which a small number of actors on central positions in the organisation have the power to select the people they want based on unclear criteria) we may expect contacts to have a greater effect on the outcome than in local bureaucratic recruitment structures (characterised by a formalised and decentralised recruitment process involving several actors) (Norris,

1997; Narud, Pedersen, & Valen, 2002). Prewitt and Eulau (1971) observe, for example, that "sponsoring" is widely used when the recruitment process is controlled by individuals in power. There are also other studies showing that contacts are more often used in employment processes in the US, where there are few formal rules regulating recruitment, than in countries where the recruitment process is more bureaucratic (de Graaf & Flap, 1988). In short, if only a few people in the political elite have the opportunity to make their voices heard in the recruitment process, contacts should be more important as a career resource (see also Pettersson, 2001; Holgersson, 2003).

The political contexts in focus in this study are the Norwegian and Swedish national parliaments.[1] The recruitment structures of these two parliaments are local and bureaucratic. All party members have, for example, the right to nominate candidates in their districts and local election committees work independently without having much contact with either the party elite or with the other election committees. Party leaders mainly influence the nomination process through formulating certain goals that have to be fulfilled and they only intervene in the recruitment process in exceptional cases (Norris, 1996; Johansson, 1999; Heidar, Damgaard, Esaiasson, & Hardarson, 2000). Voters also have the power to influence party lists to some extent (Nordy, 1985). Norway and Sweden, then, constitute cases in which contacts should not play a great part in political recruitment. Consequently, if contacts turn out to be important in these contexts (Hypothesis 1) then it is likely that contacts will play an even greater part in others.

The political situations of women in Norway and Sweden are considered to be relatively similar. Both countries are welfare states characterised by openness, corporatism, and pragmatism, in which a fairly large amount of women have been politically successful (Bergqvist, 1999). Should women be disadvantaged by the role contacts play in political recruitment (Hypothesis 2) in these countries, where women are less politically marginalised, it is reasonable to assume that the negative impact of contacts on women's political advancement is stronger elsewhere.

DATA, SAMPLE, AND METHOD

The data used in this paper is derived from two sets of surveys. One of them is *Ledarskap i förändring*, which was carried out by the project "Gender and the social reproduction of elites in a comparative perspective" at Göteborg University in 2001, and the other one is that of the Norwegian Power and Democracy Study, *Lederskapsundersøkelsen*, from the same year. These surveys sampled leaders in different social sectors in Sweden and Norway, such as business, civil service, academia, politics, NGOs, media, and the arts (Skjeie & Teigen, 2003; Göransson, 2005). In Sweden, 169 of these leaders were parliamentarians, in Norway, 165. The response rate among the Swedish parliamentarians was lower than in the Norwegian study (72 per cent compared to 84 percent), partially owing to the fact that the Norwegian survey was not sent by regular mail, but was filled in during an interview (Gulbrandsen et al., 2002). A response rate of 72 percent is slightly lower than normal in studies of Swedish parliamentarians (Holmberg & Esaiasson, 1988; Brothén, 2002), but not any worse than the previous studies of political elites in other countries (SOU, 1990:44; Sansonetti, Lyon, Moore, Neale, & Palgi, 2000).

To what extent contacts constitute important assets in political careers (Hypothesis 1) and what consequences this has for the political representation of women (Hypothesis 2) can be measured through politicians' subjective perceptions. The parliamentarians were asked to consider the importance of different kinds of resources to reach leading political positions. Unfortunately, the questions differ somewhat between the Norwegian and Swedish studies. In the Norwegian study, the respondents were asked to rank contacts in relation to a number of other resources according to importance,[2] whereas the Swedish parliamentarians only considered the importance of different kinds of resources without relating them to one another.[3] The comparison will not, therefore, focus on the exact percentages of responses, but on the stress the respondents put on contacts compared to other resources.

The parliamentarians were also asked to consider the significance of several explanations frequently referred to in discussions on the political underrepresentation of women, for example, that recruitment is carried out through informal networks (contacts). The survey questions are, in this case, more or less identical in the two countries.[4] The only major difference is that the Norwegian study asked about explanations as to why there are fewer women in leading positions in general, whereas the Swedish study focused on explanations related to the field in which the respondents themselves had made a career. This difference may lead to a slight overestimation of how significant an obstacle Norwegian politicians believe that a lack of contacts is to women's political advancement, since respondents seemed to rate the significance of contacts higher in other organisations than in their own (Skjeie & Teigen, 2003). Again, the comparisons between the two cases will, therefore, rely on analyses of the relative significance that Norwegian and Swedish parliamentarians ascribe to the explanatory power of contacts.

IMPORTANCE OF CONTACTS

In the empirical analysis, the importance of contacts will be compared to that of other resources such as professional expertise, the probability that a politician will attract media coverage, and social background variables. These resources are often associated with political careers (Matthews, 1984; Gulbrandsen et al., 2002) and even though there are other relevant resources, for example motivation, political ideology, and political skills (Putnam, 1976; Norris & Lovenduski, 1995), this comparison offers a reasonable starting point to the evaluation of the importance of contacts in political recruitment (Table 1).

When asked to estimate how important contacts are in order to reach a leading position in politics, 27 percent of the Swedish parliamentarians ranked contacts as crucial and 59 percent as of great importance (a total of 86 percent). Contacts, then, are considered at least as important as having good chances of attracting attention in media, which 83 percent ranked of crucial or great importance. In a time when the relationship between politicians and journalists is sometimes described as "a strained cohabitation, in which they [politicians and journalists][5] mutually produce each other's foundations and existence" (Gulbrandsen et al., 2002, p. 210), such a stress on the role played by contacts in political recruitment is quite remarkable.

The relevance of professional expertise and social background is thought to be considerably lower. 22 percent considered professional expertise to be of crucial or great importance, and only eight percent considered social background important at the same levels. The relatively limited importance ascribed to professional expertise could be due to the fact that it was operationalised as "education", which is unlikely to capture all aspects of

Table 1. Swedish Parliamentarians about the Importance of Different Resources (Percent).

	Crucial Importance	Great Importance	Crucial and Great Importance
Contacts	27	59	86
Chances of media coverage	28	55	83
Professional expertise	4	18	22
Social background	4	4	8

Note: 113 parliamentarians have responded. Chances of attracting media coverage were operationalised as "media contacts" and professional expertise as "education".

Table 2. Norwegian Parliamentarians about the Importance of Different Resources (Percent).

	Most Important	Second Most Important	Most and Second Important
Contacts	35	25	60
Chances of media coverage	11	17	28
Professional expertise	3	8	11
Social background	1	8	9

Note: 138 parliamentarians have answered. The figures do not add up to 100 percent, since not all items from the survey are included in this table (see Notes 3 and 7). Social background was operationalised as "gender" and "affiliation to certain professional groups".

professional expertise. It is possible that this item would have scored higher had the survey question used the actual words "professional expertise", which was the case in the Norwegian study. However, as Table 2 shows, the different phrasings of the survey questions do not appear to have caused the Norwegian parliamentarians to rank professional expertise any higher than their Swedish counterparts.

Just like their Swedish counterparts, Norwegian politicians considered that both their contacts and their ability to represent the party in media played a greater part in their nomination to parliament than their professional expertise. 60 percent of the respondents ranked contacts as the most important or the second most important factor in their nomination process, compared to the mere 11 percent who ranked professional expertise this highly. The share of respondents who considered chances of media coverage more important than professional expertise was also noticeably larger; 28 percent believed that their ability to attract positive media attention was one of the two most important factors included in the study.

Thus, the relative stress that Norwegian and Swedish parliamentarians place on different career resources is identical. Contacts are considered to be the most important resource to reach leading political positions in both cases,[6] the probability that a candidate will have media appeal is placed second, professional expertise third, and social background last.

It is hard to say in what way the different operationalisations of the social background variable might have affected this comparison. It is unlikely, however, that changes in either of the surveys with regard to the social background items would have changed the most interesting result here, namely that contacts are the resources most strongly stressed by parliamentarians in both Sweden and Norway.

Comparisons between Elites

While the importance attached to contacts by politicians is striking, perhaps the reason for the limited research attention that this has received compared to research on contacts in other fields is that contacts have been found to be more important to, for example, business elites than to political elites. However, the comparison presented below between Swedish parliamentarians and other social elites in Sweden shows that this is not the case.

Considering the results displayed in Table 3, it is somewhat surprising that contacts have attracted comparatively little attention in studies of political careers since there is no other career in which this resource is claimed to be of greater importance. Only 69 percent of all respondents state that contacts are of crucial or great importance, which is significantly less than that among politicians.[7]

After politicians, contacts were stressed most by those who have made a career in media (76 percent), the arts (74 percent), and NGOs (73 percent). Not even people in business, the kind of career that has most frequently been connected to contacts so far, ascribed to contacts the same importance as parliamentarians. 69 percent of the surveyed business elite claimed that contacts are of crucial or great importance to make a career in their field, compared to 86 percent of the politicians.[8]

Table 3. Swedish Elites about the Crucial and Great Importance of Different Resources (Percent).

Careers	Resources			
	Contacts	Chances of Media Coverage	Professional Expertise	Social Background
Politics	86	83	22	8
Media	76	79	44	7
Arts	74	30	63	6
NGOs	73	33	58	5
Business	69	18	71	3
Civil service	60	8	76	3
Academia	58	15	92	4
All elites	*69*	*32*	*64*	*5*

Note: The number of respondents varied between the different resources, but it is never less than 1,308 (social background). No elite group included less than 113 respondents (politics). Only those who answered "crucial importance" or "great importance" are included in this table. For a definition of the different careers, see Göransson (2005).

The kind of career in which contacts are perceived as the least important is academia. This does not mean that academics think that contacts lack importance entirely; far from it. 58 percent, the majority of this elite group, just like in all elite groups, responded that contacts are of crucial or great importance to academic careers.

Overall, there is a broad agreement on the importance of contacts. The variation in evaluations of other resources, such as media coverage and professional expertise, was greater.[9] As may be expected, professional expertise, which was operationalised as education in the Swedish survey, was strongly emphasised by academics; 92 percent ranked it as crucial or of great importance and in the media group, 79 percent said the same thing about media coverage.[10] In other groups, however, these resources seem to be of little consequence. In civil service, for example, only eight percent ranked media coverage as crucial and among politicians, only 22 percent ranked professional expertise as crucial. In comparison, the importance of contacts is more stable across different careers. For none of the careers did the proportion of people claiming that contacts are crucial or greatly important fall below 58 percent (academia) and it never exceeded 86 percent (politics). In three of the careers (politics, the arts, and NGOs), contacts were considered as the most important resource included in the study and in the other four careers (media, business, academia, and civil service) contacts were placed second.

All respondents, regardless of career, agreed that social background is fairly insignificant. There is a much stronger unity in their view of this resource than on the importance of contacts.[11] The clear message is that you do not succeed in making a career in any profession or organisation just by having the right kind of social background. A politically correct answer, one might think, something, which could decrease the credibility of these results in general. Nevertheless, admitting that contacts are important for a successful career is not really politically correct either, particularly considering that when the issue is brought up in media, it is often insinuated that contacts are prioritised in recruitment processes at the expense of competence (Carlsson, 2003).

An Important Career Resource

So far, the empirical results are in line with my first hypothesis; there is a strong agreement among parliamentarians in both Sweden and Norway that contacts are an important resource for reaching leading political positions. They even ascribe to this resource a greater value than people who have made their careers in other fields, for example, business or NGOs. These results indicate that the role played by contacts in political recruitment deserves further attention.

POLITICAL INEQUALITY: A CONSEQUENCE?

What consequences might the importance of contacts have for the political advancement of different social groups, especially the underrepresented groups such as women? Even though women have been relatively politically successful in Sweden and Norway, men still control a greater proportion of the leading positions in the political elite (Gulbrandsen et al., 2002; Niklasson, 2006). To explore this question, the surveys asked respondents to rank various accounts for women's underrepresentation.

There are two different kinds of explanations regarding women's political underrepresentation that I will compare here. One kind of explanation focuses on the actions and qualities of women themselves, that is, they stress the supply of female candidates. For example, they suggest that too few women apply, that women often have caring responsibilities that limit their work capacity, or that women find it more difficult to handle the pressure that leading positions involve. Other explanations emphasise injustices in the recruitment processes, the demand side. Examples of such explanations are that men have problems cooperating with female leaders, that the recruitment of women is not a prioritised issue, that female applicants are overlooked, or that recruitment is carried out through informal networks (Norris, 1996; Shvedona, 1998; Skjeie & Teigen, 2003). A factor analysis on the Swedish survey data confirms that the explanations empirically divide into these two dimensions related to supply and demand (Table 4).

My focus will be on the career effects of recruitment through informal networks since this explanation implies that women are disadvantaged because they are not a part of these networks, that is, women lack the necessary contacts. However, I will also make comparisons to the importance that politicians ascribe to the other explanations.

According to leading politicians in Sweden, informal recruitment is the most important reason why fewer women make a political career. As Table 5 shows, few of the suggested alternative explanations come even close to the strong support of the explanation regarding contacts. More than one third, 34 percent, of the parliamentarians believed that exclusion from relevant networks is a very significant explanation for why fewer women have political careers and almost one half, 47 percent, thought that it was a

Table 4.   Supply and Demand Explanations to the Underrepresentation
of Women.

Explanation	Supply	Demand
Recruitment through informal networks	0.009	0.737
More women is not a prioritised goal	−0.020	0.789
Women are overlooked	−0.087	0.849
Men have problems with female leaders	0.257	0.696
Women have caring responsibilities	0.751	0.092
Too few women apply	0.620	−0.074
Women cannot handle the pressure	0.745	0.074

Note: This is a varimax rotated (Kaiser normalisation) principal component analysis based on 1,216 respondents. Explained variance of the supply dimension is 22 percent and for the demand dimension it is 35 percent.

Table 5.   Swedish Parliamentarians about Explanations to the
Underrepresentation of Women in Leading Political Positions (Percent).

Explanation	Very Significant	Somewhat Significant	Very or Somewhat Significant
Recruitment through informal networks	34	47	81
Too few women apply	14	61	75
Women have caring responsibilities	14	56	70
More women is not a prioritised goal	20	40	60
Women are overlooked	18	38	56
Men have problems with female leaders	6	35	41
Women cannot handle the pressure	3	16	19

Note: The number of respondents varied depending on the explanation, but was never less than 106 individuals. Explanations focusing on the demand side of the recruitment process have been shaded.

somewhat significant reason. These figures are about the same for the Norwegian study, displayed in Table 6.

90 percent of the Norwegian parliamentarians responded that recruitment through informal networks was at least a significant explanation for why there are fewer women in general in leading positions in society. Lack of contacts, then, was the most strongly supported explanation in Norway as well as in Sweden.

Table 6.   Norwegian Parliamentarians about Explanations to the
Underrepresentation of Women in Leading Positions in General
(Percent).

Explanation	Very Significant	Significant	Very Significant or Significant
Recruitment through informal networks	28	62	90
Too few women apply	23	64	87
More women is not a prioritised goal	19	53	72
Women have caring responsibilities	9	49	58
Women are overlooked	9	35	44
Men have problems with female leaders	3	30	33
Women cannot handle the pressure	0	4	4

Note: The number of respondents varied depending on the explanation, but was never less than 132 individuals. Explanations focusing on the demand side of the recruitment process have been shaded.

The second most credible explanation in both countries focused on the supply of women: that too few women apply to leading positions. 75 percent of the Swedish parliamentarians believed this to be a significant reason why there are more male leaders in politics, and 87 percent of their Norwegian colleagues thought that this was an important explanation to the male dominance in leading positions in general.

Another supply explanation also supported by a large majority of the Swedish politicians was that women have caring obligations preventing them from investing energy into politics. 70 percent of the Swedish politicians believed this to be at least a significant reason why fewer women make a political career. In the Norwegian study, however, only 58 percent responded to this as significant. The Norwegian parliamentarians found it more likely that the underrepresentation of women is caused by a disinterest in prioritising gender equality when recruiting people to leading positions. 72 percent claimed this to be a significant explanation for the enduring gender imbalance.

Neither Swedes nor Norwegians agreed with the explanation that women are unfit to deal with the pressure related to leading positions, though. Not one parliamentarian in Norway ranked this explanation as very significant and only four percent ranked it as significant. The corresponding figures among Swedish parliamentarians were three and 16 percent.

Consequently, apart from the explanations regarding women's caring responsibilities and the priority of gender equality in recruitment, the relative importance that Norwegian and Swedish parliamentarians ascribe to different explanations is identical. Most importantly, politicians in both countries believe that a lack of contacts is the most significant reason why there are fewer women in leading positions in politics and in the society at large.

It is worth noting, however, that there were obvious gender differences in this respect. While almost all female parliamentarians in both countries were convinced that recruitment through contacts is a very significant or a significant reason why fewer women reach leading positions (96 percent in Sweden as well as in Norway), only 69 percent of their male counterparts in Sweden and 83 percent of their male counterparts in Norway agreed.[12] Instead, male parliamentarians put forward the lack of female applicants (76 percent) as a more significant explanation than the role contacts play in recruitment processes. A general result is that men appeared to prefer explanations that focus on the supply of women more than women did overall. The demand explanation that male parliamentarians found the most credible, however, is the one referring to women's lack of contacts. Consequently, the firm belief in this explanation displayed by women and the fact that a convincing majority of the men were also in favour of it make recruitment through contacts the strongest supported explanation.

Comparisons between Elites

To have a perspective on how much trouble contacts are believed to cause women in their political careers, I will compare the answers of the Swedish parliamentarians to those offered by people in other careers in Sweden. Table 7 shows what explanations different social elites find the most credible for the underrepresentation of leading women within their specific fields.

According to the Swedish elite, it is very plausible that women face greater problems in their careers owing to a lack of contacts; 70 percent ranked this as a significant explanation for the lower number of women in leading positions. This is not the explanation that receives the strongest support of those suggested, though; a more important reason is that too few women apply (78 percent).

Only in media is recruitment through contacts perceived to constitute an equal career barrier to women as in politics. Just like the parliamentarians,

Table 7. Swedish Elites about Explanations to the Underrepresentation of Women in Their Own Field (Percent).

Explanation	Sweden							
	Politics	Media	Organisation	Arts	Business	Academia	Civil Service	All
Too few women apply	75	81	78	64	87	84	73	78
Recruitment through informal networks	81	81	76	71	67	62	60	70
Women have caring responsibilities	70	66	64	60	66	67	54	63
More women is not a prioritised goal	60	67	70	62	50	52	47	58
Women are overlooked	56	36	46	41	25	41	31	38
Men have problems with female leaders	41	44	39	34	23	34	27	33
Women cannot handle the pressure	19	23	18	17	13	12	10	15

Note: The number of respondents varies depending on the explanation, but it is never less than 1,255. No subgroup consists of fewer than 106 respondents (politics). Only those who have stated that an explanation is very or somewhat significant are included in this table.

81 percent of the media elite ranked recruitment through informal networks as a very significant or a somewhat significant explanation. Among the civil servants, the corresponding figure was only 60 percent.[13]

This comparison illustrates two things. First, politicians perceive contacts to be a more important career resource than those in other careers. Second, they also believe that the lack of contacts is more damaging to women's career prospects in politics than in other careers.

CRUCIAL CONTACTS: CRITICAL CONSEQUENCES

The data presented here offer only a glimpse of the importance of contacts in quantitative comparison with other career resources, but the results are quite clear. The importance of contacts in career advancement is recognised by people who have succeeded in reaching leading positions in several fields of work, particularly by those who have made a political career and this is equally true in Sweden and Norway. Neither media coverage nor professional expertise is as highly valued as a career resource as having contacts.

The importance of contacts is also believed to have serious consequences for the political advancement of women. Of all the supply and demand explanations suggested in this study for why there are fewer women in leading positions, the one claiming that women lack necessary contacts receives the strongest support by parliamentarians in both countries. In comparison, other social elites in Sweden tend to think that the low number of female applicants is a more important reason for the underrepresentation of women.

Naturally, these results only indicate how the importance and consequences of contacts is perceived. These perceptions may not be related to how recruitment of politicians is actually carried out, or how it is perceived by those who have been less successful in their political advancement. It is possible that individuals who have attempted a political career but failed would have provided a different view of what resources are the most important ones. For example, they might have had plenty of people backing them up; only they were the wrong kind of people. A person who has only experienced support from less influential contacts might ascribe less value to contacts as a career resource than a person whose contacts have been able to play a greater part in his/her career development.

It is also plausible that your contacts can only assist you up to a certain point. The results presented here indicate that contacts are indeed a very important career resource in politics, but it is also possible that this is only true under certain conditions, for example, as long as a person has other resources ready on hand. Strong support from various contacts might not be enough if you totally lack professional expertise or have no prospects at all of attracting positive media attention. A politician who has had plenty of contacts, but who has failed to live up to other possible requirements and therefore has not been recruited to parliament, might therefore perceive those missing resources as more important than the ones to which he/she had access.

Consequently, the ranking of career resources might have turned out differently if candidates who failed to reach parliament had been included in the analysis as well. It can be argued, however, that those who have successfully acquired a seat in Parliament ought to have a clearer idea of what it takes to navigate smoothly through the political recruitment process than those who were lost along the way. Moreover, several of the parliamentarians included in this study do not just base their answers on experiences from their own political careers; they have also actively participated in the recruitment of others. It is reasonable to expect them to have a thorough knowledge and understanding of how political recruitment works in their country.

The fact that such a great majority of those who have experiences of parliamentary careers are convinced of the significance of contacts and the negative consequences that this kind of recruitment has on women's political advancement is, therefore, undoubtedly very interesting. This is particularly the case since the political elites in Sweden and Norway are relatively open. Compared to many other places, it has been easier for new social groups to make their way into the parliamentary institutions in these two countries (SOU, 1990:44). Thus, since contacts appear to have an impact on the recruitment of the political elites there, it is reasonable to assume that they are of even greater importance in other political contexts. The results also indicate, however, that even though informal recruitment through contacts may constitute an obstacle to women's political career, it is an obstacle that can be overcome, since women in Sweden and Norway have been relatively successful in this respect. My claim is, therefore, that further research into what role contacts play in political recruitment is crucial to the scrutiny of power and those who have it. Causal studies of the relative strength of contacts as a career resource and comparative studies between different political contexts may well be a way of improving our understanding of how political representation of different social groups has developed in different countries.

NOTES

1. The Swedish parliamentarians included in the study were those occupying the most prestigious positions in the national parliament: Speakers, the presidency, and the most senior representative from each party in the standing committees and the committee on EU affairs (the two most senior representatives from the two largest parties: the Social Democratic Party and the Moderate Party), the presidency of the parliamentary party groups, members and deputies of the Riksdag Board, members and deputies of the advisory council on foreign affairs, the presidency of the inter-parliamentarian group and members of the parliamentarian ombudsmen, the auditors, the Swedish delegation to the Nordic council, the Swedish delegation to parliamentarian committee of EFTA, and the Swedish delegation to the parliamentarian assembly of the Council of Europe. Compare these with the elite sample of the Swedish power investigation of 1985 (SOU, 1990:44).

No selection of the most prestigious parliamentarians has been made in the Norwegian study; they included all parliamentarians (Gulbrandsen et al., 2002), which might make comparisons between the two countries less reliable. In contrast, all members of the Norwegian parliament are members of a standing committee (Heidar et al., 2000), which is not the case in Sweden. Furthermore, Magnus Hagevi (2000) comes to the conclusion that Norwegian and Swedish standing committees are equally powerful, measured objectively as well as subjectively. Thus, there are no reasons to believe that the career level achieved by the Norwegian and Swedish parliamentarians included in the two studies differ greatly from each other.

The Norwegian study also included party leaders from 10 of the largest (population wise) municipalities (Gulbrandsen et al., 2002), whereas the Swedish study focused on the national level. Because of the low numbers, I do not consider this difference a major problem.

2. The survey question in the Norwegian study was: "On the card, some factors that may have been important in order for you to become nominated to the Storting [the Norwegian Parliament] are mentioned. I am asking you to state which two are the most important ones according to your opinion." The factors included were: party experience, social and professional contacts, possibilities to represent the party in media, professional expertise, affiliation to certain organisations, affiliation to certain professional groups, affiliation to certain fractions within the party, affiliation to a certain geographic region, and gender.

3. The survey question in the Swedish study was: "According to your judgment, of what importance are the following kinds of contacts and resources to the possibilities of reaching a top position within the sphere in which you work?" The alternatives were: "crucial importance", "great importance", "fair importance", "modest importance", and "no importance". The resources included were media contacts, personal contacts, social background, economic assets, and education.

4. The Swedish survey question was: "According to your experience, what are the most important reasons why there are fewer women than men on the absolute top positions in your field? The alternatives were: "very significant", "somewhat significant", "neither significant nor insignificant", "somewhat insignificant", and "completely insignificant".

In the Norwegian survey the same question was: "There are a number of possible explanations to why men continue to dominate top positions on the labour market and in organisations. All of them have been pointed out in the general debate on political equality. In general, how important would you say that each of these are?" The alternatives were: "very significant", "significant", "less significant", or "without significance", and "do not know".

5. Bracketed comment added. My translation from Norwegian.

6. Some factors included in the Norwegian study have been excluded in this comparison, since they were absent in the Swedish survey question (see notes 3 and 4). Even in relation to these factors, however, there is a greater share of Norwegian parliamentarians who think that contacts are the most, or second most important reason why they were nominated to the Storting.

7. $p = .000$ (two-tailed t-test). When politicians are excluded, 68 percent of all respondents ranked contacts as crucial or of great importance.

8. The differences between the parliamentarians and the other kinds of elites are significant in all cases ($p \leq .025$, two-tailed t-test).

9. The standard deviation of the replies concerning the importance of contacts is 0.461, compared to those for media coverage (0.472) and professional expertise (0.487).

10. The operationalistation of media coverage, "media contacts", probably carries a different meaning to people in the media elite compared to other elites. Whereas politicians, for example, are likely to think of media contacts in terms of media coverage, these kinds of contacts may constitute the social and professional contacts of the media elite; to them, media contacts could very well be a resource facilitating their recruitment to powerful positions and not just something that gets them on the news. Consequently, there is a risk that I have underestimated to what extent people in the media elite ascribe contacts as crucial or of great importance.

11. The standard deviation of the replies concerning the importance of social background is 0.212.

12. The difference between female and male parliamentarians in Sweden is statistically significant ($p = .000$, two-tailed t-test).

13. The differences between parliamentarians and civil servants, and the media elite and civil servants are statistically significant ($p = .000$, two-tailed t-test).

ACKNOWLEDGEMENTS

I would like to thank Mari Teigen and Trygve Gulbrandsen for providing data from the Norwegian Power and Democracy Study, and the Bank of Sweden Tercentenary Foundation for funding the Swedish survey.

REFERENCES

Bergqvist, C. (Ed.) (1999). *Likestilte demokratier? Kjønn og politikk i Norden.* Oslo: Universitetsforlaget AS.

Best, H., & Cotta, M. (2000). Elite transformation and modes of representation since the mid-nineteenth century: Some theoretical considerations. In: H. Best & M. Cotta (Eds), *Parliamentary representation in Europe 1848–2000* (pp. 1–28). Oxford: Oxford University Press.

Bourdieu, P. (1996). *The state nobility. Elite schools in the field of power*. Cambridge: Polity Press.

Brass, D. (1992). Power in organizations: A social network perspective. In: G. Moore & J. Allen Whitt (Eds), *Research in politics and society. The political consequences of social networks* (pp. 295–323). London: JAI Press Inc.

Brothén, M. (2002). *I kontakt med omvärlden. Riksdagsledamöterna och internationaliseringen*. Stockholm: SNS Förlag.

Burt, R. S. (1983). Range. In: R. S. Burt & M. J. Minor (Eds), *Applied network analysis. A methodological introduction* (pp. 176–194). Beverly Hills: Sage Publications.

Burt, R.S. (1999). *The Gender of Social Capital*. Selected Paper Series. Chicago: University of Chicago Graduate School of Business.

Carlsson, I. (2003). *Så tänkte jag. Politik & dramatik*. Stockholm: Hjalmarson & Högberg Bokförlag.

Dahl, R. A. (2000). *On democracy*. New Haven: Yale University Press.

de Graaf, N. D., & Flap, H. D. (1988). 'With a little help from my friends': Social resources as an explanation of occupational status and income in West Germany, The Netherlands, and the United States. *Social Forces, 67*(2), 452–472.

Fredriksson, J. (2001). Vägen till politiken. En etnologisk studie av hur det går till när man blir kommunalpolitikt engagerad. In: SOU (2001:48). *Att vara med på riktigt-demokratiutveckling i kommuner och landsting* (pp. 211–256). Stockholm: Fritzes.

Göransson, A. (2005). Bilaga: Enkätundersökningen Ledarskap i förändring. In: A. Göransson (Ed.), *Makten och mångfalden: Eliter och etnicitet i Sverige* (pp. 333–336). Stockholm: Fritzes.

Granovetter, M. (1974). *Getting a job*. Chicago: University of Chicago Press.

Gulbrandsen, T., Engelstad, F., Klausen, T. B., Skjeie, H., Teigen, M., & Østerud, Ø. (2002). *Norske makteliter*. Oslo: Gyldendal Akademisk.

Hagevi, M. (2000). Nordic Light on Committee Assignments. In: P. Esaiasson & K. Heidar (Eds), *Beyond Westminster and Congress* (pp. 237–261). Columbus: Ohio State University Press.

Hedin, A. (2001). *The politics of social networks*. Unpublished doctoral dissertation. Lund University, Lund.

Heidar, K., Damgaard, E., Esaiasson, P., & Hardarson, Ó. T. (2000). Five most similar systems? In: P. Esaiasson & K. Heidar (Eds), *Beyond Westminster and Congress* (pp. 17–47). Columbus: Ohio State University Press.

Holgersson, C. (2003). *Rekrytering av företagsledare: en studie i homosocialitet*. Stockholm: Ekonomiska forskningsinstitutet vid Handelshögskolan i Stockholm.

Holmberg, S., & Esaiasson, P. (1988). *De flokvalda. En bok om riksdagsledamöterna och den representativa demokratin i Sverige*. Stockholm: Bonnier Fakta Bokförlag AG.

Isaksson, A. (2002). *Den politiska adeln. Politikens förvandling från uppdrag till yrke*. Stockholm: Wahlström & Widstrand.

Johansson, J. (1999). *Hur blir man riksdagsledmot? En undersökning av makt och inflytande i partiernas nomineringsprocesser*. Hedemora: Gidlund in cooperation with Riksbankens jubileumsfond.

Kadushin, C. (1995). Friendship among the French financial elite. *American Sociological Review, 60*(2), 202–221.

Kanter, R. M. (1993). *Men and women of the corporation*. New York: Basic Books.

Karlsson, D. (2001). Ny som förtroendevald i kommuner och landsting. In: SOU (2001:48). *Att vara med på riktigt-demokratiutveckling i kommuner och landsting* (pp. 115–210). Stockholm: Fritzes.

Kjær, U., & Pedersen, M. N. (2004). *De danske folketingsmedlemmer-en parlamentarisk elite og dens rekruttering, cirkulation og transformation 1849-2001.* Århus: Aarhus Universitetsforlag.

Knoke, D. (1990). *Political networks. The structural perspective.* New York: Cambridge University Press.

Lai, G., Lin, N., & Leung, S.-Y. (1998). Network resources, contact resources, and status attainment. *Social Networks, 20*(2), 159–178.

Lin, N. (2001). Building a network theory of social capital. In: N. Lin, K. Cook & R. S. Burke (Eds), *Social capital. Theory and research* (pp. 3–29). New York: Walter de Gruyter, Inc.

Lipman-Blumen, J. (1976). Toward a homosocial theory of sex roles: An explanation of the sex segregation of social institutions. *Signs, 1*(3), 15–31.

Marsden, P. V. (1987). Core discussion networks of Americans. *American Sociological Review, 52*(1), 122–131.

Marsden, P. V. (2001). Interpersonal ties, social capital, and employer staffing practices. In: N. Lin, K. Cook & R. S. Burke (Eds), *Social capital. Theory and research* (pp. 105–125). New York: Walter de Gruyter, Inc.

Matthews, D. R. (1984). Legislative recruitment and legislative careers. *Legislative Studies Quarterly, 9*(4), 547–585.

Mills, C. W. (1956). *The power elite.* New York: Oxford University Press.

Moore, G., Sobieraj, S., Whitt, J. A., Mayorova, O., & Beaulieu, D. (2002). Elite interlocks in three U.S. sectors: Nonprofit, corporate, and government. *Social Science Quarterly, 83*(3), 726–744.

Munk Christiansen, P., Möller, B., & Togeby, L. (2001). *Den danske elite.* Copenhagen: Hans Reitzels Forlag A/S.

Narud, H. M., Pedersen, M. N., & Valen, H. (2002). *Party sovereignty and citizen control. Selecting candidates for parliamentary elections in Denmark, Finland, Iceland and Norway.* Odense: University Press of Southern Denmark.

Nielsen, P. (2001). På och av-om uppdragsvillighet, rekrytering och avhopp i den kommunala demokratin. In: SOU (2001:48). *Att vara med på riktigt-demokratiutveckling i kommuner och landsting* (pp. 17–114). Stockholm: Fritzes.

Niklasson, B. (2005). *Contact capital in political careers. Gender and recruitment of parliamentarians and political appointees.* Unpublished doctoral dissertation, Göteborg University, Göteborg.

Niklasson, B. (2006). Den politiska eliten. In: A. Göransson (Ed.), *Maktens kön.* Stockholm: Natur och kultur.

Nordy, T. (1985). *Storting og regjering 1945-1985. Institusjoner – rekruttering.* Oslo: Kunskapsförlaget.

Norris, P. (1996). Legislative recruitment. In: L. LeDuc, R. G. Niemi & P. Norris (Eds), *Comparing democracies. Elections and voting in global perspective* (pp. 184–215). London: Sage Publications Inc.

Norris, P. (1997). *Passages to power. Legislative recruitment in advanced democracies.* Cambridge: Cambridge University Press.

Norris, P., & Lovenduski, J. (1995). *Political recruitment. Gender, race and class in the British Parliament.* Cambrigde: Cambridge University Press.

Oscarsson, H. (2003). Demokrati i nätverkssamhället. In: H. Oscarsson (Ed.), *Demokratitrender. SOM-rapport 32* (pp. 209–239). Göteborg: SOM-institutet.

Petersson, O. (1996). *Demokratirådets rapport 1996. Demokrati och ledarskap.* Stockholm: SNS förlag.

Pettersson, L. (2001). *Genus i och som organisation: Översikt om svensk arbetslivsforskning med genusperspektiv.* Stockholm: Santérus.

Phillips, A. (2000). *Närvarons politik-den politiska representationen av kön, etnicitet och ras.* Lund: Studentlitteratur.

Prewitt, K., & Eulau, H. (1971). Social bias in leadership selection, political recrutiment, and electoral context. *The Journal of Politics, 33*(2), 293–315.

Putnam, R. D. (1976). *The comparative study of politcal elites.* London: Prentice-Hall.

Sansonetti, S., Lyon, D., Moore, G., Neale, J., & Palgi, M. (2000). Methodology. In: M. Vianello & G. Moore (Eds), *Gendering elites; economic and political leadership in 27 industrialised societies* (pp. 11–15). London: MacMillan, Ltd.

Shvedona, N. (1998). Obstacles to women's participation in parliament. In: A. Karam (Ed.), *Women in parliament: Beyond numbers* (pp. 19–41). Stockholm: IDEA.

Skjeie, H., & Teigen, M. (2003). *Menn imellom. Mannsdominans og likestillingspolitikk.* Oslo: Gyldendal Akademisk.

SOU (1990:44). *Demokrati och makt i Sverige. Maktutredningens huvudrapport.* Stockholm: Allmänna förlaget.

Stenlås, N. (1998). *Den inre kretsen. Den svenska ekonomiska elitens inflytande över partipolitik och opinionsbildning 1940–1949.* Lund: Arkiv förlag.

Teorell, J. (2000). A resource model of social capital: Networks, recruitment and political participation in Sweden. *ECPR Joint Sessions,* Copenhagen, Denmark.

Vianello, M., & Moore, G. (2000). *Gendering elites. Economic and political leadership in 27 industrialised societies.* London: Macmillan Press Ltd.

Wahl, A., Holgersson, C., Höök, P., & Linghag, S. (2001). *Det ordnar sig. Teorier om organisation och kön.* Lund: Studentlitteratur.

PART II
ELITES: MOTIVATION AND ACTION

DO ELITE BELIEFS MATTER? ELITES AND ECONOMIC REFORMS IN THE BALTIC STATES AND RUSSIA

Anton Steen

During the 1980s proponents of neo-liberal ideologies argued that state activities had to be downsized and regulation replaced by the market. Think tanks connected to conservative political parties provided systematic critiques of the established social democratic state and paved the way for 'Thatcherism' in the UK and 'Reaganism' in the USA. These ideas had a major impact on elite attitudes, spurred the privatization of previous state responsibilities and introduced market principles into the public administration of Western states. Parallel with the revolution of neo-liberalist ideas among Western elites quite abruptly, the post-communist elites dismissed socialist ideology and embraced neo-liberal economic ideas, vigorously embarking on putting them into effect. However, the speed of institutional change and economic recovery varied considerably among post-communist countries. Do the elites' commitments to liberal ideas explain these outcomes?

The new democratic regimes were intimately connected to expectations for economic growth. Abolishing state regulations and importing neo-liberalist ideas of how to organize the economy became a major ideological

Comparative Studies of Social and Political Elites
Comparative Social Research, Volume 23, 79–102
Copyright © 2007 by Elsevier Ltd.
ISSN: 0195-6310/doi:10.1016/S0195-6310(06)23005-9

force among the new elites. The break with the past was especially abrupt in the Baltic States that saw democracy and market economy as major features of the nation state and independence from the Soviet Union. In Russia, as the dominating republic during the Soviet time, the new technocratic elite enthusiastically embraced neo-liberal ideas of economic recovery. These ideas were intimately connected with democratic liberalization and decentralization, having the unexpected effect of dismantling the Union. In major parts of the population economic reforms became associated with chaos and economic hardship. From 1992 the lack of broad elite conviction forced the small team of neo-liberal top advisers to the Russian president to propel the reform process to achieve anything at all. Patchy reforms could only be made through constant compromises (Gustafson, 1999). In most post-Soviet states the quite small group of western-oriented technocratic liberalists with direct access to the top leadership could not operate in a political vacuum for a long period. In the first phase, small 'change teams' recruited from the ranks of technocrats could be insulated from political pressure inside and outside government. As Nissinen (1999) argues, carrying the initial 'shock reforms' through by a technocratic strategy of secrecy and surprise that characterized the first stage could not continue. To carry economic reforms forward they had to build on elite coalitions ensuing from a common political understanding.

The main question is how the broader segment of elite attitudes in the second phase of reforms may account for the degree of success of economic policies in these countries. The argument is that predominating attitudes across elite groups constitute what Robert Putnam (1973) has conceptualized as an 'elite political culture' which is rather stable over time. Here the term is used to describe patterns of beliefs and attitudes about the economic system following the collapse of the state-controlled economy. Under circumstances of dismantling old institutions and introducing a new economic system, elite configurations and their attitudes are assumed to be the most crucial for instituting or resisting economic reforms.

The countries selected for analysis, Estonia, Latvia, Lithuania and Russia, were previously Soviet republics with centrally planned economies and which introduced market economies in the beginning of the 1990s. However, during the following decade they differed considerably in economic reform and recovery. Quite early, the international community considered Estonia a 'success-story' while the other countries, and particularly Russia, were lagging behind. Thus, the main question is whether the elites' attitudes in 'success-countries' and 'less successful countries' may account for differences in the scope and speed of restructuring the economy.

Elite attitudes do not, however, emerge in a vacuum. The receptiveness of liberal attitudes into the post-communist elite political culture is contingent on historical factors (Hedlund, 1999), international relations (Wedel, 1999), new opportunity structures provided by market-state elite net works (Grabher & Stark, 1997), social effects of economic reforms on electoral cycles (Przeworski, 1991) and degree of elite turnover and interests in 'partial reforms' (Hellman, 1998). It is not possible to delve into all these factors, but one implication of the argument that elite orientations matter for economic reforms is that change of elite from one regime to another is crucial for the elite political culture and ensuing economic transformations.

I argue that the most crucial factor for the ability of new political economic regimes to enact and implement economic reforms is the *content* (preferring liberalist or state regulative solutions), the *level* on which such preferences are expressed (ideological, policy or instrumental) and the *structure* of the statements (conforming or conflicting within and between elite groups). The following hypotheses may be formulated: first, the more liberal and non-conflicting the overall elite attitudes, the more comprehensive and rapid are the economic reforms. Second, attitudes are expected to be more state-oriented among *governing elites* who make policies (parliamentary deputies and bureaucratic leaders) than among *economic elites* (leaders of state enterprises and new private businesses) who are more involved in exploiting market opportunities. Third, ideological orientations have more to do with symbolic, electoral politics than actual policy decisions. Therefore, one may expect elite conflicts to be more widespread on the ideological level than on the instrumental one. As a consequence, I argue, the right-wing ideological rhetoric paving the way for market reforms in tandem with consensual pragmatic solutions on the instrumental level indicates a specific type of elite political culture nourishing an unprecedented form of post-transitional state.

DATA AND METHOD

The descriptions of economic policy reforms and performance in the Baltic States and Russia are based on adapted statistical material collected by the World Bank and the International Monetary Fund.

Surveys of elite attitudes raise the question of which elites shall be included. The validity of the results will depend largely on the sampling of the respondents (Hoffman-Lange, 1987). However, in seeking to cope with the complexities of the real world, elite studies necessarily involve a considerable number of ad hoc choices when it comes to selection (Moyser & Wagstaffe, 1987). In this study, pragmatic considerations of *who it is possible to include in a survey* have been combined with considerations about *which institutions are important* in decision-making processes. The main selection criterion has been to include leaders from institutions with the greatest political, administrative and economic importance. In aggregate, the respondents from different institutions constitute a representative sample of the national and regional elite.

In each country between 280 and 315 top leaders were interviewed face to face with questionnaires. The respondents from the Baltic States include parliamentary deputies, administrative officials, the directors of major private companies and state enterprises and the leaders of NGOs, the judiciary, cultural institutions and local government. The same or comparable elite positions were interviewed regularly after each parliamentary election from 1993 onwards by trained staff members of professional polling organizations. Seventy per cent of the parliamentary deputies, drawn proportionally according to party strength, and about 30 top leaders from each of the other groups, were included. The most recent interviews were made in Latvia and Estonia in the spring and autumn of 2003.

In Russia, structured face-to-face interviews were conducted with 980 respondents in leading positions in 1998 and 605 in 2000. The following eight institutions were included (total respondents in parentheses): prominent politicians from the main factions and parties in the State Duma (100), members of the Federation Council (30), leaders in the federal administration and ministries (100), directors of state enterprises (50), directors of private businesses (50), leaders of educational, cultural and media institutions (50) and political and administrative leaders at the regional level (1998 – 600; 2000 – 225). Fewer members of the regional elite were interviewed in the 2000 survey although it covered the same regional categories as in 1998.[1]

FORCES FOR ECONOMIC LIBERALIZATION

The transition from central planning to a market economy involved a multifaceted process of changes in structures, institutions, actual practices and impacts. The regulated economies of former communist countries have moved along these paths to varying degrees. The huge literature on this topic focuses mainly on policy decisions facilitating liberalization of internal markets, external trade and privatization of state property and consequences for macro-economic performance like growth in GDP, inflation rate and budget balance. These economic-inspired approaches try to answer why some states manage to enact policies that create a fundament for sustainable growth while the others lag behind.

Common to all post-communist countries after the change of regime was a lack of institutional and legal infrastructure underpinning a market economy. Neo-institutionalist-oriented economists saw the rapid enactment of *liberal economic institutions*, in particular laws instituting reliable and predictable exchange relations among market actors, as the main instrument for economic change (Aaslund, 1995). While liberal legislation was introduced at almost the same time and along the same lines in the early 1990s, the effects on the economy varied dramatically among the countries. Others argue that economic recovery is directly related to *political factors*, in particular degree of political competition and individual freedom (de Melo, Denizer, & Gelb, 1996). They find a positive relationship between a composite freedom index and economic progress. A third approach has underscored that political liberalization is a necessary but not a sufficient condition to economic growth. A *legitimate and efficient government* is of the most vital importance to discipline financial oligarchs, encourage the market forces and provide supportive social policies (The World Bank, 2002).

In all these explanations economic, political and government institutions matter for marketization and prosperity, and obviously they do. However, new policy trajectories and institutions do not appear automatically from institutions, they have to be rooted in a prevailing elite culture and decision making. The elite political culture manifests itself through certain configurations of elite recruitment and orientations and amain question is how such configurations relate to the transition of state planning into a market economy. Thus, the *elite political culture* is crucial for the actual decisions shaping liberal reforms. In particular, after a change of regime, institutions are often weak and the elites and their networks are influential not only on policy decisions but also in the implementation stage. The questions of 'why liberal reforms' and 'how do the countries perform' can only be sufficiently answered when the elites' political culture, manifested as their orientations and attitudes, are taken into due consideration.

ELITE POLITICAL CULTURE

In his study of British and Italian political elites Putnam (1973) asks how important their beliefs are for the functioning of the political system. First and foremost, he argues that elites are more important than others in the political process since they possess important positions. However, referring to Robert Dahl's polyarchy thesis, it is less probable that they constitute a unified and self-conscious group who are controlling political processes to their advantage. Accordingly, political influence is a question of establishing more or less stable alliances among various elite groups where, more than direct contact, *common orientations* pave the way for making certain policies viable. Putnam studied 'professional politicians', i.e. the stratum of fulltime employed parliamentary deputies with direct access to decisions. In the Russia/Baltic study four main elite groups are selected from the larger overall elite sample. The parliamentary deputies and the bureaucratic leaders *produce* the authoritative decisions about economic reforms; and the leaders of state enterprises and private businesses who formally are on the *receiving side* of the process – are the employers of policy results, but they are also influential as actors on the political input side.

Referring to Lucian Pye and Verba (1965), Putnam (1973, p. 2) argues that "the development of a political system is conditioned by 'the system of empirical beliefs, expressive symbols, and values that defines the situation in which political action takes place', or less formally, that attitudes matter". The 'elite's political culture', as Putnam formulates it, may be defined as a set of orientations towards society that inform and guide political responses and policy decisions. Some orientations are basic and connected to deep personal values while others are operational and directed towards actual problem solving. Such an individual 'political belief system' may be permanently structured or more pragmatic. Thus, a 'belief system' has a potential for change dependent on how rooted the basic values have become through the socialization process and the pressure from the environment to adapt to new circumstances.

A successful transition from an authoritarian to a democratic regime rests on two main dimensions: some basic 'elite unity' about the rules of the game and differentiation of recruitment (Higley & Burton, 1989). The fundament of elite unity is what Higley, Pakulsi, and Wesolowski (1998, p. 3) refer to as "shared norms of political competition". But such a consensus says little about which policy issues are at stake and the conflicts over priorities and instruments. The other feature of elite unity is defined by these authors as 'elite-interaction and networks'. Interaction is about behaviour and determines if all elite groups have access to the central decision-making process, and may say something about the degree of pluralism among elites. Thus, elite interaction relates to conditions on how the structure of the 'belief system' is working in terms of the association of values and strength of certain elite orientations. The other dimension, 'differentiation', refers to the ability of elites to establish autonomous groups and to distance from mass pressure.

What a belief system consists of, its 'structure' and 'content', is not that easy to entangle. Besides the structure, i.e. the degree of cohesion among the various parts of the belief system, Putnam (1973) argues that there are two basic levels of orientation. One level includes those arising from perceptions of fundamental social justice, like basic preferences for income equality. The other one consists of how such values 'guide political action', i.e. implications for distributional policies, state regulation and the role of private property. By measuring both 'basic' and 'operational' political beliefs and their interrelationships Putnam argues that one may establish a causal effect from the belief system on political actions that sustain a particular type of political regime.

Sabatier and Jenkins-Smith (1999) use the same argument, maintaining that policy decisions, policy stability and policy change are explained by specific policy sub-systems or advocacy coalitions in which actors have important positions and are forming close networks held together by a common 'belief system'. They also underscore the institutional aspect of elite integration where networks constitute quite stable sub-cultures based on special interests. Such a sub-culture consists of 'deep core beliefs' that are very resistant to change and 'essentially akin to religious conviction' (p. 122). The next level, the 'policy core beliefs' among the coalition members, are less rigid but seldom change since the normative implications are very strong. The third level, what these authors refer to as 'secondary aspects', consists of orientations that are assumed to be more adjustable in the light of new information, experiences and strategic considerations. According to Stark and Bruszt (1997) the economic reforms in Eastern Europe created grey zones between the state and private capital that stimulated new networks among leaders from business and state enterprises. One may assume that such policy sub-systems, held together by common liberal orientations among elites in the state and private sectors, is of particular importance for reforming the economic system.

Orientations and attitudes may become manifest on different levels of specification. Here *the ideological level* is measured as self-placement on the left–right scale. This category has much in common with Putnam's 'fundamental social values' and Sabatier and Jenkins-Smith's 'deep core values'. Post-communist elites have been described as opportunistic and non-ideological, but I do not argue that elites are 'ideological' in the meaning that they adhere to a certain ideological system. One may argue, however that elites are well educated and as reflected persons in times of rapid change they need at least some consistency in their basic values. To place oneself to the left or to the right expresses not only essential views about the relationship between individuals and the state, but also a propensity to interpret the world in view of interconnected values. *The policy level* specifies what Putnam names 'operative ideals' that guide political actions. This type of orientation is measured by attitudes to private property ownership. *The instrumental level* refers to the implications of policy choice for specific needs among the population such as state or private responsibility for providing health services, schools or infra structure.

RACE TOWARDS THE MARKET

Mass privatization of state property started in Estonia in 1993, in Latvia in 1994, in Lithuania in 1993 and in Russia in 1992 by issuing vouchers to citizens. However, once vouchers were in private hands several matters were not clear: how should the state companies be sold? And how were the capital market institutions to be organized? And to what extent were the vouchers tradable? Even if the time of enacting privatization policy and the design was rather similar for many countries the consecutive processes varied dramatically.

In the Baltic States reforms were influenced by parallel processes of re-establishing nation-state after the dismantling of the Soviet Union. National elites feared that mass privatization might give the Russian population an opportunity to control industries of national importance. Such concerns induced the governments of Estonia and Latvia, the countries with a large proportion of Russian inhabitants, to rely more on direct government-controlled sales rather than vouchers in contrast to Lithuania, which followed a voucher strategy. In Russia the spontaneous privatization process opened for insider control of old managers, often in cooperation with the employees. Soon powerful financial oligarchs, who at an early stage became the owners of the most profitable industries, established private monopolies and attempted to block the establishment of legal frameworks that would ensure fair competition and reduce their influence (The World Bank, 2002, p. 74).

The design of policies, the sequencing and their speed of implementation vary considerably among the countries, but it has been a broad consensus that the reforms should include macro-economic stabilization (introduced in the Baltics in June 1992 and in Russia in April 1995), price and trade liberalization, budget constraints on banks and enterprises, enabling private sector development, reforming the tax system, legal and judicial reform and reform of public administration and services. The World Bank has developed an index of economic policy reforms based on the main economic indicators mentioned above. Here I summarize in an adapted and compressed form the economic liberalization policies of the four countries (Fig. 1).

In 1990 the reforms were rather modest. As expected, Estonia had made the best start with Latvia and Lithuania in between and Russia still in a very early phase. Five years later the transition to a market economy had accelerated dramatically for all the countries. Estonia was also now in the lead but with rather smaller relative differences compared to the other countries. In 1998 Estonia continued the pace of reforms with Latvia and Lithuania lagging somewhat behind. Russia had at this moment stagnated in its reform efforts. For our purposes this simplification of a very composite reality is useful.

The more rapid progress of economic reforms in Estonia as shown in Fig. 1 obviously had positive effects on productivity and economic growth, while the less ambitious policy changes in the other countries seem to correlate with more modest growth rates (Fig. 2).

An important part of the stabilization programme was to bring the state budget more into balance to counteract inflation. Post-Soviet countries were put under pressure from the international community to cut expenditures in

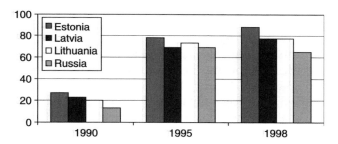

Fig. 1. Progress in Policy Reforms in the 1990s.
Source: Adapted from The World Bank (2002, p. 14.).

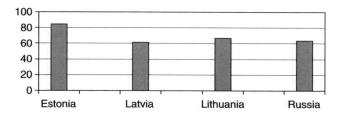

Fig. 2. Real GDP in 2000. (1990 = 100).
Source: Adapted from Table 1.1, The World Bank (2002).

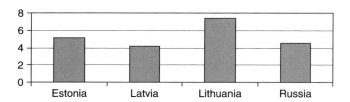

Fig. 3.   Health Expenditures, % GDP, 1998.
Source: Adapted from Fig. 8.2, The World Bank (2002).

state services. Fiscal adjustments were hitting public services like education and health quite directly. In particular, the embedded tradition of universal social rights to free consumption of health services under the previous system became a heavy burden on state expenditures. Privatization of parts of the health services and introducing market prices for drugs contributed to growth in GDP, but hit the populations quite dramatically; many could simply not afford necessary health care. To what extent did the economic reforms affect the states' responsibilities in providing health care? Fig. 3 shows that radical economic reforms did not necessarily lead to more cuts in the health sector.

Following the argument that Estonia is the forerunner of economic liberalization, one could have expected that they had the lowest health expenditures. In 1998 Lithuania used considerably more on health care than the other countries. Estonia was in the second place and Latvia and Russia were on the same level. It seems that to be a predecessor in economic liberalization does not necessarily mean downsizing the public sector.

But, before analysing how elite orientations may be related to the differences in economic liberalization some more specific evidence about country differences in economic and political reforms and performance are presented in Table 1.

After the change of regime in 1990–1991 the GDP declined dramatically. Real GDP increased during the 1990s, but remained at a level lower than that at the end of the central planning period. Despite many problems arising when measuring real GDP in communist and transitional economies (The World Bank 2002, p. 8), Fig. 2 gives an indication of the overall differences between countries. As can be seen, the transition indicators, the liberalization index and the institutional quality index of the IMF are all highly correlated and also correspond to the policy reform index of the World Bank in Fig. 1.

All in all the pattern of economic reforms, quality of political institutions and economic performance in the four countries is quite clear: Estonia has

Table 1. Economic Performance and Institutional Reforms.

Country	Year Transition Started	Starting Date of Stabili- zation	Real Output (1989– 1999)	Inflation Average (1989– 1999)	Transition Indicator Average (1999)[a]	Cumulative Liberalization Index (1989– 1997)[b]	Index of Institutional Quality (1997– 1998)[c]
Estonia	1992	June 1992	0.78	24.3	3.5	5.72	6.1
Latvia	1992	June 1992	0.56	35.1	3.1	5.00	2.6
Lithuania	1992	June 1992	0.70	41.0	3.1	5.39	2.6
Russia	1992	April 1995	0.55	88.0	2.5	4.32	−5.4

Source: Adapted from *World economic and financial surveys. World economic outlook. Focus on transition economies,* Tables 3.9–3.11, International Monetary Fund. October (2000).
[a]The transition indicators include: privatization, governance and enterprise restructuring, price liberalization, trade and foreign exchange system, competition policy, banking reform and securities market reforms.
[b]The index is a weighted average of three indices: market liberalization, foreign trade liberalization and enterprise privatization and banking reform.
[c]The institutional quality index is an aggregate of expert ratings produced by various agencies and organizations and opinion surveys of firms and households compiled by international organizations and other institutions. The index includes five component indicators measuring the extent of democracy, government effectiveness, extent of regulation, rule of law and corruption.

been the forerunner, Latvia and Lithuania placed in between, while Russia has been lagging behind. How then do these success indicators relate to the elites as levers and hindrances for reform? First, I briefly present how national elites imported reform ideas from abroad and how these ideas were moulded in elite turnover and national contexts. I then discuss the elites' political culture in greater detail.

PROCUREMENT AND MALLEABILITY OF IDEAS

Where were the reform ideas coming from and how are they forged? Are countries going through a more basic break with the past and installing alternative elites more amenable to new ideas? It is not easy to dismantle the origins of ideas since they are moulded in history, learning, interests and institutions. In the post-communist reform context it may be useful to differentiate between how the elite are copying ideas from abroad, how the elite use ideas to exploit new opportunities to their own advantage, how ideas may change resulting from learning from how reforms are actually working, and how characteristics about the elite shape their ability to embrace new ideas. The elite political culture is crucial for economic reform, but is also an intermediate variable in which the content of elite orientations may vary according to international circumstances, the elite's self-interest, the impacts of economic reforms, elite turnover and recruitment after a change of regime.

The import of neo-liberal ideas underpinning economic reform efforts in post-communist countries may be seen as an offspring of a Western ideological wave disapproving the state as a competent problem solver. International agencies such as the World Bank and the IMF played an active part in conveying such ideas, particularly during the first period of economic transformation. Later, the EU heavily influenced standards of economic activity as a condition for the Baltic States' membership. These international recommendations were conveyed through direct contacts and in consensus with the national elites. The typical reform package applied in Eastern Europe was sponsored by the IMF, the World Bank and the European Bank for Reconstruction, and had substantial impact on national economic policy since it controlled the flow of credit. It was based on "liberal-monetarist philosophy" and "incorporated in the 'Washington consensus'" (Nissinen, 1999, p. 62). The most prominent adviser to the Russian President and Prime Minister during the first years of reform, the former prominent upper crust communist Egor Gaidar, expressed that "the most important influence on me was Friedrich Hayek. He gave a very clear and consistent picture of the world, as impressive as Marx in his way" (quoted from Gustafson, 1999).

One problem was that the small team of advisers operated as a 'clan'. According to Wedel (1999) the advisers had close connections with neo-liberal economists at Harvard University and used their open access to top authorities in Russia as well as in the United States, the IMF and the World Bank, also to pursue their own individual interests. Paradoxically, the only way to instigate radical reforms was to delegate authority to closed and self-interested 'change clans'. Elites may learn from new opportunities and Aaslund and Dmitriev (1999) explains the failure of the Russian economic reforms during the 1990s with the strength of 'rent seekers' who made money by distorting the market mechanism by preserving clandestine network into the state.

ELITE TURNOVER AND SOCIAL BACKGROUND

After the change of regime in Russia, the old nomenklatura continued to be strong (Szelenyi & Szelenyi, 1995) leading to government compromise in the reforms. In the Baltic States the removal of the old nomenklatura following the demise of the communist regime paved the way for more substantial economic policy changes. But elite changes differed and the turnover among the Estonian top leaders was particularly extensive (Steen & Ruus, 2002). In contrast, a majority of the elites during the mid-1990s still had a background as previous members of the Communist Party (Steen, 1997). However, most of them had been rank-and-file members in the start of their career at the time of regime change while only very few had been top leaders. The major part of the new elite comprised younger persons with little murky luggage from the past. This configuration of the new Baltic elite probably had a major impact on the elite's belief systems and reforms.

Another feature of the Baltic States is the ethnic composition of their populations. The non-indigenous minority had been increasing sharply in Estonia and Latvia during the Soviet period and constituted, according to the 1989 census 38% and 48%, respectively, of the populations. The share in Lithuania was quite stable at 20% during this period. The large minorities, especially in Estonia and Latvia were seen as a threat to national language, culture and independence and had a major impact on ethnic relations and the national elites' willingness to include the largely Russophone group into the political community (Steen, 2000 and 2006). Although the Russophone minority, owing to emigration diminished somewhat during the 1990s, the demographic picture still deviates sharply from the composition of the elites 90–95% of whose leaders are recruited from the indigenous population. In contrast, the multi-ethnicity of the Russian Federation to a larger extent is reflected in the elite's composition. As to social background, almost 100% of the elites have higher education (undergraduate or graduate degree from a university or technical college). Compared to their fathers 30–40% of whom had higher education, a major upward social mobility has occurred (appendix Table A1).

The most important political and administrative positions in all four countries are dominated by men. More than 80% of appointments in the basic institutions are held by men. This is a sizeable proportion and is in fact a break from the tradition during the Soviet period where quota systems secured a more favourable representation of women, especially in governing bodies. One exception is found for leaders of NGOs in the Baltic States. Here the female representation is considerably more common. It seems that when women are barred from state institutions they are advancing their interests through alternative channels outside the male-dominated state.

Around 2000 the post-communist elite were on average between 45 and 49 years old, with Estonia having the youngest, the Russians more dominated by the middle aged persons and the other countries' elite of intermediate ages. The domination of younger men is particularly obvious in the bureaucracy and the business sector. In Estonia, the leaders of state enterprises are also among this group of ambitious young male leaders and they have much of the same geographic background with 66% coming from the cities. A similar pattern is found in Latvia. In the Lithuanian and Russian cases fewer have an urban background and they are older.

ELITE POLITICAL CULTURE

The demise of communism resulted in widespread discrediting of leftist ideology, and shortly after the first free elections a variety of right-wing and nationalist political parties came to the fore. The party programmes expressed beliefs in the deregulation of state responsibilities, privatization of ownership and the virtues of the market economy as the main instruments for economic recovery. The dramatic shift of beliefs in the state towards the market as a problem solver was particularly visible among the elites, but was this shift reflected in a similar trend on the ideological, policy and instrumental levels?

Ideology

A 'political ideology' refers to a coherent system of beliefs, propositions and orientations about the role of the state in society. The left–right scale is often used as an expression of ideological preferences in general, and support for the state and the market in particular. Fig. 4 shows the percentage of all elites and the four sub-groups (parliamentary deputies, top bureaucrats, leaders of state enterprises and business leaders) placing themselves as right-wing sympathisers in 2000 after the economic shock therapy had been working for some time.

In the Baltic states, almost a decade after the economic reforms started, the share of right-wingers is still considerable. As expected, the Estonian elite is the most liberal with about 50% right-wingers, and the other two Baltic states somewhat lower with an average of about 40%. The proportion is much more modest in Russia with <15%. The ideological orientations are fairly well integrated with the exception in Estonia and Russia of business leaders who express considerably more right-wing attitudes than the other groups.

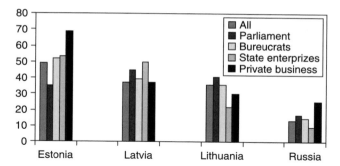

Fig. 4. Ideological Orientations: Right wingers among selected elite groups, per-cent, 2000.

Note: Right wingers are defined as those indicating 8, 9, 10 on a 10-point scale; 'Extreme left' = 1; 'Extreme right' = 10.

Do we observe a change from the exalted rightist orientations in the first transitional years towards more moderate attitudes in the latter period of economic consolidation? And are the elites' attitudes becoming more frag-mented owing to negative social consequences of the economic reforms, for example, sharply increasing income differences? The tendency in the Baltic States, as measured by the mean values for the period 1994–2003, is a three-stage process with changes that are noticeable but not extraordinary (see appendix Table A2). At the start of the economic liberalization in 1993–1994 the elite were less right-oriented than after some years when the right-wing orientations reached a peak between 1997 and 2000. These years of liberal enthusiasm, however, did not last, and in 2003 the right-wing orientations level out or decline, but to a higher level than in the beginning of the transformation. In Russia, the more widespread right-wing orientat-ions in 2000 indicate that the 1998 economic crisis did not have a negative influence on their basic orientations towards the market. The chaotic po-litical and economic situation led to a strong desire among the elites for a change of president but did not undermine the elite's beliefs in the market. The 'wild capitalism' under Yeltsin should not be discarded but disciplined politically with more 'state-led capitalism' (Lane, 2000).

During 1994–2003, the ideological climate, as measured by the standard deviations, became increasingly fragmented in the Baltic countries and Russia. With the exception of business elites in Estonia, Latvia and Russia, the trend is largely the same for all sub-sections and in particular the po-litical elite have adopted more confrontational positions along the left–right axis. On the ideological level, obviously, as the distributional effects of capitalism become apparent, the elite's enthusiasm for the blessing of the market is waning but still a broad vanguard of neo-liberalists dominates those countries that were forerunners in the economic reforms.

Policy Beliefs

The policy level of orientations relates to spheres of policy making in which control and resources are allocated among social actors. Probably, 'type of ownership' is the most important institution for sharing power and distributing wealth among groups. The main issue in the transformation of the state-planned economy was the privatization of state property. Fig. 5 shows the proportion of elites who strongly embrace private ownership.

In 1994, support for privatization was extremely high in all the Baltic States with almost 80% believing strongly in private ownership. The elite attitudes are remarkably parallel during the period. In 1997 the enthusiasm had declined by about 20% and began to level out. The Russian elites were considerably more critical with only about 25% ardent supporters of private ownership under Yeltsin while increasing considerably later after Putin took over as the President.

Although the attitudes are fairly uniform, differences exist among the elite groups. In all countries the political elites are more sceptic than leaders of private business, ministries and state enterprises. This is what should be expected since politicians over time tend to adjust attitudes to a more critical mass public to be re-elected. While the differences among the Baltic elites have remained quite stable over time, a quite dramatic change occurred in

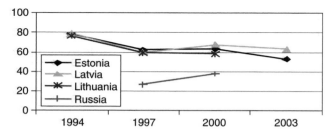

Fig. 5. Ownership Issue: Ardent believers in private ownership, 1994–2003. All elites. Percent.
Note: 'Ardent believers in private ownership' are defined as those scoring 1,2,3 on a 10-point scale.

Russia from splintered elites in 1998 towards tightly integrated elites on the ownership issue after the change of president in 2000.

Although somewhat waning in support for private ownership, after a decade the elite beliefs are on an amazingly high level in the Baltic States, and the Russian elite are catching up. The state is not entrusted as a property owner and with the running of industries. These attitudes indicate that the neo-liberal type of economy has become embedded in a stable pro-market elite political culture. But, do right-wing attitudes and beliefs in the private property imply a dismantling of traditional collective state functions as for example, responsibility for health care?

Instrumental Attitudes

A well-functioning health system is vital to all societies. During the communist period these services were the sole responsibility of the state, and were offered free of charge on a relatively high level of quality. After the change of regime the question of the extent to which health services should be privatized soon came on the agenda (Fig. 6). Obviously, this was an option among the group of radical market liberalists who found their model for organization in the largely privatized health system in the US. But, to what extent did neo-liberalist solutions in this area convince the broader spectrum of elites?

On the instrumental level the elites largely trust the state option when it comes to performing health services. The support is stable or tends to be increasing over time. Estonia is also an exception here with a liberalistic *interludium* during the latter part of the 1990s while later returning to the state option. Comparing the various elite groups, one observes that this

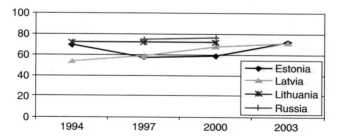

Fig. 6. Responsibility for Collective Problems: Support for state main responsibility in health care, 1994-2003, All elites. Percent.

Note: Those scoring 1 and 2 on a 5-point scale.

u-shaped development is quite clear among several sub-sections of elites in Estonia. An interesting anomaly is that the private business leaders in the Baltic states are among the most positive towards state responsibility for health care while Russian business leaders are more oriented towards private solutions on this issue.

Summarizing the post-communist elite political culture during the 1990s provides a complex but also a clear picture: the elites' *rightist* orientations were strong during the initial phase of reforms and are fairly stable during the 1994–2003 period. The elite support for *private ownership* was extremely high in the beginning among all elite groups but is apparently declining gradually as the effects of capitalism, e.g. income inequality hits the population. The state option for solving traditional *collective problems* has strong support among all elite groups during the entire period.

ELITE POLITICAL CULTURE AND ECONOMIC TRANSFORMATIONS

The main question of this article has been how the orientations of post-communist elites may account for market reforms and restructuring of state functions. During a similar initial period of 'shock therapy' in all these countries, and in cooperation with a closed circle of top political leaders a small group of technocrats introduced Western ideas of stabilizing and liberalizing the economy. While this first period of passing measures to control inflation and prices, restoring fiscal stability and foreign trade liberalization was short and technocratic by nature, a period of 'extraordinary politics' (Nissinen, 1999), the dynamics of the next period was different. The privatization of state property and introduction of a new type of tax system are more complex and "are more vulnerable to dilution, delay and derailment" (Nissinen, 1999, p. 43). The consolidation of the initial achievements of the first reform period and carrying out the more long-term painful efforts of restructuring the state required broad consensual elite coalitions. Not necessarily as formal cooperation but, as I argue, in terms of a common and stable 'belief system' regarding the principal path in which society should be moving.

Comparing various indicators of economic reforms and their impacts for Estonia, Latvia, Lithuania and Russia, one main conclusion is that the reforms, performance and outcomes are highly correlated with the liberalism and consensus of the 'elite political culture', as expected in the first hypothesis. The more comprehensive economic reforms, better performance and faster growth in Estonia seem unlikely if it had not been rooted in a large group of liberal-minded younger, more urban and international oriented elites who were not deeply affiliated with the previous regime. The somewhat slower progress in policy reforms during the 1990s in Latvia and Lithuania fits well with different scores on these elite indicators. Certainly, the extent and manner in which the elites changed from one regime to another has played a major role for the formation of elite beliefs during the 1990s.

Russia's problems with transforming into a market economy and poor performance has many reasons, including 'historical embeddedness' (Hedlund, 1999). Obviously, the elites' closer connections with the previous regime resulted in less willingness to accept and implement rapid economic reforms and may be seen as 'path dependent' behaviour. The Russian elites largely continued from the communist past into powerful positions in the state and private companies. They were quite fragmented during President Yeltsin's period and President Putin's administration from 2000 started to strengthen the power of the federal government, the federal treasury and centralized the management of the large natural monopolies. As Sakwa (2002, p. 291) argues, this was the main strategy of a rejuvenated presidency to overcome the crippling of the market reforms and the 'partial reform equilibrium' supported by the new financial oligarchs identified by Hellman (1998).

However, Putin's fascination for combining market solutions and state regulation not only stems from joining technocratic solutions with the nostalgia of state control. According to the elite survey one-third of the Russian elite sees the Chinese solution to organizing the economy as an example to follow, with Scandinavia and Germany on the next places. The US and UK liberal models are attracted only by a small minority of about 10%. In contrast, a majority of 60% of the Baltic elites sees the Scandinavian model as the best to follow, and also here a surprisingly small group of only 15–20% support the US/UK economic alternative.

One may argue that a more hasty and brutal transformation of the Russian economy would have created a 'valley of tears' with so many negative social consequences that popular uproar and political backlash would have become inevitable. The paradox is that despite slower economic transformation the income differences are much wider than in the Baltic states. The Russian case illustrates that partial economic reforms may create more social problems than a speedy implementation of market institutions. As Hellman (1998) argues, clandestine networks among state and business elites and elite scepticism to substantial reforms are characterizing the Russian situation that generates a few 'winners who take all'. Such winners have an interest in partial reforms that seems to thrive under conditions of 'grey zones' between the state structures and the new business elite (Stark & Bruszt, 1997).

The second hypothesis argues that attitudes will be more pro-state among the governing elites than among the economic elites. As one would expect, the parliamentary deputies and the business leaders are the most polarized on the left–right continuum, and also regarding the property issue. But the business elite are as supportive as the other elites for state intervention in instrumental issues such as the provision of collective goods like health services. The Estonian top bureaucrats, leaders of state enterprises and new business leaders were obviously a vanguard of the neo-liberal economic ideas during the 1990s compared to the other countries, but not to the detriment of basic state social responsibilities. The argument that there exists a causal effect between 'basic' and 'operational' beliefs (Putnam, 1973) is not necessarily correct. Regarding elite groups as policy sub-systems in Sabatier and Jenkins-Smith's terminology elucidates that while the ideological level of orientation may be in conflict, other more operational orientations may coexist between policy sub-systems.

This leads to the third hypothesis, which argues that ideological issues serve the competitive function of electoral democracies while tangible issues relating to basic collective social needs are uniting these societies across elite groups. Policy measures that relate directly to important problems of peoples' lives and positive experiences with a well-functioning health system during the Soviet period seem to encourage consensual politics and state solutions despite the neo-liberal rhetoric. As Aidukaite (2004) argues, when it comes to actual policy instruments the Baltic elites are taking into consideration the historical roots of their social systems and the demands of the population. This illustrates that elite antagonism appears more openly when related to what Putnam (1973) and Sabatier and Jenkins-Smith (1999) refer to as 'ideological' and 'policy core' issues, than to concrete distributions of social services. While electoral volatility, frequently changing governments and economic hardship have challenged the mass population's beliefs in market reforms (Przeworski, 1991), it seems that social responsibility is an important stabilizing element in the politics of economic transitions.

The orientations combining pragmatic state involvement with overall neo-liberal orientations raise the question as to whether a new type of state is emerging. Neither the Scandinavian state-centred, the Anglo-American market-centred and the Continental corporatist model nor the Chinese solution seem to fit well into the post-communist elite's belief system. Lacking the historical roots and institutions of Nordic social democracy, the culture of American competitive individualism, German corporative institutions and Chinese type authoritarianism, the elite political culture and actual reforms in these countries may sustain a specific sort of post-transitional model that rests on a fairly integrated and stable instrumental elite belief system combining in an unprecedented way the neo-liberal principles with substantial state involvement.

NOTE

1. A detailed description of selection of respondents and methods for the Baltic survey is available in Steen (1997), and for the Russian survey in Steen (2003). In Estonia the interviewing was carried out by Saar Poll, in Latvia by Baltic Data House, in Lithuania by Baltic Surveys Ltd. and in Russia by ROMIR (the Russian Public Opinion and Market Research Company).

ACKNOWLEDGEMENTS

I express gratitude to the Norwegian Research Council and the Accommodating Difference Project, University of Oslo, for funding parts of the data collection. A preliminary and extended version of the paper including a comparison with Norway, co-authored by Øyvind Østerud, was presented at a conference in June 2005 organized by IPSA's Research Committee on Political Elites in Balestrand, Norway. The article is a part of the Strategic Institute Project (SIP) 'Politics in the Age of Neo-Liberalism' at the Department of Political Science, University of Oslo.

REFERENCES

Aaslund, A. (1995). *How Russia became a market economy*. Washington, DC: The Brookings Institution.
Aaslund, A., & Dmitriev, M. (1999). Economic reform versus rent seeking. In: A. Aaslund & M. B. Olcott (Eds.), *Russia after communism*. Washington, DC: Carnegie Endowment for International Peace.
Aidukaite, J. (2004). *The emergence of the post-socialist welfare state – The case of the Baltic States: Estonia, Latvia and Lithuania*. Stockholm: Sodertorns Doctoral Dissertations:1.
de Melo, M., Denizer, C., & Gelb, A. (1996). *From plan to market. Patterns of transition*. Policy Research Working Paper 1564. The World Bank, Washington, DC.
Grabher, G., & Stark, D. (1997). Organizing diversity: Evolutionary theory, network analysis, and post-socialism. In: G. Grabher & D. Stark (Eds), *Restructuring networks in post-socialism. Legacies, linkages and localities*. Oxford: Oxford University Press.
Gustafson, T. (1999). *Capitalism Russian-style*. Cambridge: Cambridge University Press.

Hedlund, S. (1999). *Russia's "Market" economy: A bad case of predatory capitalism*. London: UCL Press.

Hellman, J. S. (1998). Winners take it all: The politics of partial reforms in post-communist countries. *World Politics, 50*(1), 203–234.

Higley, J., & Burton, M. G. (1989). The elite variable in democratic transitions and breakdowns. *American Sociological Review, 54*, 17–32.

Higley, J., Pakulsi, J., & Wesolowski, W. (1998). Introduction: Elite change and democratic regimes in Eastern Europe. In: J. Higley, J. Pakulsi & W. Wesolowski (Eds), *Postcommunist elites and democracy in Eastern Europe*. London: Macmillan Press.

Hoffman-Lange, U. (1987). Surveying national elites in the Federal Republic of Germany. In: G. Moyser & M. Wagstaffe (Eds), *Research methods for elite studies*. London: Allen & Unwin.

International Monetary Fund. (2000). *World economic and financial Surveys. World economic outlook. Focus on transition economies*, October.

Lane, D. (2000). What kind of capitalism in Russia? A comparative analysis. *Communist and Post-communist Studies, 33*(4), 485–504.

Moyser, G., & Wagstaffe, M. (1987). Studying elites: Theoretical and methodological issues. In: G. Moyser & M. Wagstaffe (Eds), *Research methods for elite studies*. London: Allen & Unwin.

Nissinen, M. (1999). *Latvia's transition to a market economy. Political determinants of economic reform policy*. London: Macmillan Press Ltd.

Przeworski, A. (1991). *Democracy and the market: Political and economic reforms in Eastern Europe and Latin America*. Cambridge: Cambridge University Press.

Putnam, R. D. (1973). *The beliefs of politicians. Ideology, conflict, and democracy in Britain and Italy*. New Haven: Yale University Press.

Pye, L., & Verba, S. (Eds) (1965). *Political culture and political development*. Princeton: Princeton University Press.

Sabatier, P. A., & Jenkins-Smith, H. C. (1999). The advocacy coalition framework: An assessment. In: P. A. Sabatier (Ed.), *Theories of the policy process. Theoretical lenses on public policy*. Boulder, CO: Westview Press.

Sakwa, R. (2002). *Russian politics and society*. London: Routledge.

Stark, D., & Bruszt, L. (1997). *Postsocialist pathways. Transforming politics and property in East Central Europe*. Cambridge: Cambridge University Press.

Steen, A. (1997). *Between past and future: Elites, democracy and the state in post- communist countries*. Aldershot: Ashgate.

Steen, A. (2000). Ethnic relations, elites and democracy in the Baltic States. *The Journal of Communist Studies and Transition Politics, 16*(4), 68–87.

Steen, A. (2003). *Political elites and the New Russia. The power basis of Yeltsin's and Putin's regimes*. London: RoutledgeCurzon.

Steen, A. (2006). Accessioning Liberal Complinace? Baltic Elites and Ethnic Politics under New International Conditions. *International Journal on Minority and Group Rights, 13*, 187–207.

Steen, A., & Ruus, J. (2002). Change of regime – continuity of elites? The case of Estonia. *East European Politics and Societies, 16*(1), 223–248.

Szelenyi, I., & Szelenyi, S. (1995). Circulation or reproduction of elites during the postcommunist transformation in Eastern Europe. *Theory and Society, 24*(5), 615–638.

The World Bank (2002). *Transition: The first ten years*. Washington, DC.

Wedel, J. R. (1999). Rigging the US–Russian relationship: Harvard, Chubais, and the trans-identity game. *The Journal of Post-Soviet Democratization, 7*(4), 469–500.

APPENDIX

Table A1. Background of Baltic and Russian Elites (Total) in 2000 (in %).

Country	Gender – Male	Mean Age (Years)	Place of Birth[a]– Urban Born	Ethnicity – Indigenous	Education[b] – With Higher Education	Education of Father[b] – With Higher Education	N
Estonia	83	45	66	94	96	31	281
Latvia	76	47	66	90	96	40	285
Lithuania	80	48	51	95	96	30	315
Russia	84	49	48	83	99	42	605

[a]Urban: the capital, city, city/regional centre.
[b]Higher education: undergraduate higher, graduate higher, scientific degree.

Table A2. Self-Placement on the Left–Right Scale 1994–2003 (Left = 1, Right = 10, Mean and (Standard Deviation)).

Country	1994	1997	2000	2003
Estonia				
Total elites	6.60 (1.76)	6.86 (1.79)	6.94 (1.86)	6.70 (1.85)
Parliament	6.88 (1.96)	7.02 (1.76)	6.35 (2.04)	6.49 (2.05)
Bureaucracy	6.65 (1.48)	7.12 (1.82)	7.03 (1.78)	7.38 (1.37)
State enterprise	6.47 (1.84)	6.52 (1.75)	7.13 (1.53)	6.97 (1.63)
Private business	7.24 (1.77)	7.45 (1.62)	7.53 (2.18)	7.47 (1.48)
N	303	271	279	269
Latvia				
Total elites	6.02 (1.46)	6.34 (1.69)	6.65 (1.68)	6.65 (1.76)
Parliament	5.99 (1.59)	6.64 (1.82)	6.54 (2.13)	6.43 (2.22)
Bureaucracy	6.04 (1.31)	6.52 (1.67)	7.06 (1.44)	6.77 (1.43)
State enterprise	6.19 (1.05)	6.00 (1.48)	7.03 (1.59)	6.77 (1.63)
Private business	5.67 (1.80)	5.89 (1.23)	6.62 (1.39)	7.07 (1.53)
N	279	288	282	279
Lithuania				
Total elites	5.71 (1.83)	6.72 (1.96)	6.43 (2.08)	
Parliament	5.33 (2.11)	6.97 (2.03)	6.78 (2.05)	5.19 (2.53)
Bureaucracy	5.63 (1.71)	6.37 (1.61)	6.27 (1.82)	

Table A2 (*Continued*)

Country	1994	1997	2000	2003
State enterprise	5.55 (1.40)	6.14 (1.60)	5.79 (1.77)	
Private business	5.96 (1.50)	6.29 (1.80)	6.13 (2.05)	
N	270	294	286	108
Russia				
Total elites		5.23 (1.50)	5.47 (1.77)	
Parliament		4.44 (1.87)	5.33 (2.12)	
Bureaucracy		5.58 (1.90)	5.51 (2.01)	
State enterprise		5.29 (1.40)	5.38 (1.47)	
Private business		5.68 (1.18)	6.19 (1.61)	
N		942	591	

CONSENSUS OR POLARIZATION? BUSINESS AND LABOUR ELITES IN GERMANY AND NORWAY

Trygve Gulbrandsen and Ursula Hoffmann-Lange

The conflict of interest between capital and labour is a basic characteristic of capitalist economies. In several West European countries, as for instance Germany and Norway, this conflict has been contained and regulated through labour legislation, agreements and cooperation between organizations representing capital and labour. The organizations have cooperated in several areas – rules for regulation of conflicts, wage determination, improvement of the work environment and introduction of new technology. Cooperation has taken place on the national level as well as within individual enterprises, and has been extended into a large number of public boards and committees. On many occasions the government has joined the employer and labour organizations as a third party in the negotiations.

The regulation of the class conflict has produced economic results beneficial to the parties involved and to the respective nations. But have the compromises and cooperation also affected the ideological orientations of the involved elite groups?

Within previous literature on neo-corporatism and within elite research it has been suggested that corporatist arrangements and national elite networks can promote consensus and create ideological and political moderation among the organizations and parties concerned. The industrial

Comparative Studies of Social and Political Elites
Comparative Social Research, Volume 23, 103–135
Copyright © 2007 by Elsevier Ltd.
ISSN: 0195-6310/doi:10.1016/S0195-6310(06)23006-0

relations regimes are important pillars in the corporatist systems in Germany and Norway, and the top leaders of the employer and labour organizations are significant participants in the elite network in the two countries. The general ideas about moderating effects should therefore be particularly relevant for the industrial relations elites.

Consensus within corporatist structures and national elite networks may be a result of collective processes unfolding over many years. Repeated compromises and the accumulation of experiences of concrete cooperation between labour and capital may gradually create mutual trust and convince more and more leaders about the necessity of ideological and political restraint. The quality, direction and speed of such collective processes are influenced by nation-specific institutional and structural factors. Historical traditions, national economic conditions, the strength of the organizations involved and the character of the labour legislation determine what actions are possible and influence the outcomes of chosen solutions. Accordingly, the degree of consensus or polarization between the business and labour elites may vary between countries.

Collective processes creating political consensus are difficult to study and document. In this article we have instead chosen to focus upon mechanisms that foster ideological moderation and conciliatory attitudes among the individual business and labour leaders. By ideological moderation is meant that the leaders hold beliefs which are more ideologically centrist or which are closer to the opinions held by the other side. Conciliatory attitudes are measured by the degree of trust in the adverse party in the Norwegian study, and by the business and labour leaders' evaluation of the other side's influence in the German case. The hypotheses that are developed below are subsequently tested with data from unique national survey studies of elites in Germany and Norway.

In previous research it has been suggested that the ideological beliefs of individual leaders are affected by the frequency of their contacts with representatives of the other side that in turn, fosters an understanding of the interdependence of interests of business and labour. Following up on this assumption, we examine first whether the top leaders in business who are involved in wage bargaining hold more moderate ideological views than the other business leaders. Second, we study whether business and labour leaders who have much personal contact with representatives of the other side are more centrist in their political outlook than leaders with less contact.

Other circumstances and mechanisms influencing the views of the individual top leaders in the various labour and business organizations are examined as well. Their political affiliation is taken into account measured by membership in a political party. In the Norwegian case we also analyse the effects of previous occupational experience in politics and the public sector. For both labour and business leaders and the leaders of the employer organization, finally, we also look for the effect of membership on public boards and committees.

THEORY AND HYPOTHESES

Several scholars have maintained that corporatist arrangements may contribute to a national consensus between groups with opposing interests (Katzenstein, 1985; Siaroff, 1999). Some have even described (neo) corporatism as a strategy for consensus building (Woldendorp, 1995). These general viewpoints seem to imply that participation in the various channels and networks in a corporatist system may influence participants to moderate their ideological attitudes, to become more centrist. Participation has a "civilising" effect. In a study of the Swedish industrial relations system Öberg and Svensson (2002) concluded, however, that there is not much trust across the class borders, a finding which questions the validity of these assumptions. It seems therefore appropriate to test these assumptions empirically in a variety of national settings.

Elite researchers have, similarly, claimed that participation in national elite networks is conducive to a greater appreciation of the interests and attitudes of adverse groups, which in the next round may pave the way for political compromise and consensus. In a study of national elite networks Higley, Hoffmann-Lange, Kadushin, and Moore (1991) found that elite people located in the centre of the national elite network of the USA were more inclined to forge a political compromise than the leaders located in the periphery. Studying business leaders in the USA, Barton (1985) found that leaders who were active in national organizations for political discussions held more liberal (in the American meaning) economic policy attitudes than the others . The mechanisms or factors behind such consensus building are operating both on the macro-level through the specific national institutions and structures, and on the level of the individual business and labour leaders.

On *the level of the individual business and labour leaders* one significant mechanism behind more centrist ideological attitudes is the personal contacts between the leaders. According to general theories about trust (Blau, 1964; Coleman, 1990), this gradually evolves and is extended the more frequently two individuals or partners see each other, and the longer their relationship lasts. Possibly, the sheer encounters with people representing the other side may also foster a greater tolerance for other beliefs. An implication of this idea is that the more frequently top leaders of opposite organizations see each other, the more similar their views on significant political issues will become.

Both within the employers and the labour organizations' leaders who are directly involved in negotiations see representatives of the opposite party more frequently than those without such assignments. Moreover, some of the leaders occupy informal liaison or broker roles in the network or relationships between the different labour market organizations. In addition, on both sides some leaders may have a preference for frequent contact with the other side. For instance, in some enterprises the CEO and the union representatives engage in regular interactions while in other enterprises they meet less frequently. It is reasonable to believe that business and labour leaders with much contact show more understanding for the attitudes of their opponents than their counterparts in the second group. Controlling for the organization they are representing we therefore hypothesize that the ideological and political views of the industrial relations elites are tempered *the more frequently they see their partners on the other side* of the capital/labour divide.

Hypothesis 1. The more frequently business and labour leaders interact with each other the more centrist their ideological views and the more positive their perceptions of each other will be.

The attitudes of the business and labour leaders can also be affected by the particular roles they hold and the institutional assignments and duties that they shoulder. There is reason to believe that those leaders who participate actively in central wage negotiations develop an *understanding for the interdependence of interests between business and labour.* We suggest that this understanding also promotes ideological and political prudence.

A basic distinction is between organizations that are supposed to enter into negotiations and agreements with the other party to find concerted solutions and organizations that one-sidedly promote the interests of their clientele or members. This distinction is exemplified by the difference between employers' and business associations in Germany. Similarly, it can be expected that the top leaders of the individual enterprises first and foremost pay heed to the profitability of their firm and to the interests of their owners. As a result, they will be less inclined to taking national concerns into consideration than the top leaders of the employer organizations.

Accordingly, we hypothesize that top leaders in business and employer organizations exhibit more centrist ideological attitudes than the top leaders in the individual enterprises. In addition, in Germany it can be expected that the elites of employers' associations are more moderate than the representatives of business associations.

Hypothesis 2a. The top leaders in the employer and business associations in Norway hold more centrist ideological opinions than the leaders in the individual enterprises. In Germany the top leaders in the employer associations hold more centrist attitudes than the elite of the business associations and the enterprise leaders.

Being actively involved in preparing and implementing public policies can also instil into the business and labour leaders a feeling of responsibility for the common interest. Being or having been *members of advisory bodies, boards and committees in the public sector* may for instance give the leaders a better understanding and sympathy for the complexity and functions of the state. This should be particularly valid for business leaders who initially held a negative view of the public sector. Accordingly, we expect that having or having had such posts will result in a better appreciation of politics. That is, we expect these business leaders to be ideologically more moderate than those without this experience. Similarly, we expect that labour leaders with posts on public boards have more centrist attitudes than labour leaders without experience from such corporatist bodies.

Hypothesis 2b. Business and labour leaders who are or have been member of advisory bodies, boards and committees in the public sector hold more centrist ideological beliefs than leaders without such posts.

In both countries, labour leaders may have served as *representatives of labour on the boards of private corporations.* Such assignments imply regular contact with private business leaders and also require these labour representatives to deal with the challenges of running a company. Both these experiences probably create more understanding for the necessity that businesses operate profitably, not only for the sake of their management and shareholders, but for the employees as well. We suggest therefore that labour leaders with such posts hold more centrist ideological and political views than labour leaders without such experiences.

Hypothesis 2c. Labour leaders who are or have been representatives on the boards of private corporations are ideologically more centrist than labour leaders without such experience.

Two additional factors can also be presumed to affect the attitudes of business and labour leaders. First, some of the top leaders are *members of political parties*. Becoming a member of a political party is an indication of deliberate support for well-defined ideologies or policy positions. Leaders who are members of a political party can therefore be expected to be loyal to the opinions advocated by their party. Gulbrandsen and Engelstad (2005) have shown that the political parties in the Norwegian parliament have a wider range of attitudes and are located more towards the extremes than the elite groups that are usually their allies and sympathizers. Similar findings have been presented in other countries as well. This is in accordance with "the directional theory" of voting (Rabinowitz & McDonald, 1989). According to this theory, the electorate will vote for the political party that most clearly shows them the direction in issues of particular importance to them. As a result of their role as political "guides", the political parties take more extreme positions than the voters, including members of the various elite groups. This theory is relevant for Germany also (Hoffmann-Lange, 1992, p. 256). In line with the theory we expect to find that labour and business leaders who are members of a socialist or bourgeois political party, respectively, are less moderate than their counterparts without party affiliation.

Hypothesis 3. Labour leaders who are members of a socialist party are more leftist in their ideological orientation than labour leaders who are non-members. Similarly, business leaders who are members of a bourgeois party are ideologically located more to the right than business leaders without such membership.

Second, *experience* from a particular sector or institution may also affect a leader's political attitudes. According to Putnam (1976), having worked in a particular institution usually involves a socialization with the values dominating in the institution. It is to be expected that such a socialization can foster an ideological outlook that supports the institutions concerned. Information about previous occupational experience is only available in the Norwegian study. We have concentrated the attention on previous experience in politics and public administration. Several of the top leaders in the Norwegian sample have previously worked or been active in these two sectors. In both sectors the participants are trained to balance competing interests and considerations, to find broad-based compromises and to have an eye for more general values and goals. It can be assumed that this training fosters more moderate political views among business as well as labour leaders. We expect to find that the longer they have had a position in politics or within the public sector the more they express centrist political opinions.

Hypothesis 4. The longer business and labour leaders have been active in politics or worked in the public sector the more they hold centrist ideological beliefs.

This hypothesis is in contrast to Hypothesis 3 which maintains that political affiliation through membership of a political party promotes more "extreme" opinions.

GERMANY AND NORWAY: TWO VARIANTS OF "COORDINATED MARKET ECONOMIES"

A particular characteristic of coordinated market economies (CMEs) (Hall & Soskice, 2001) is that employers as well as unions are organized in strong national associations. Nevertheless, within the group of "coordinated market economies" there are significant varieties. In addition to the wage bargaining systems, there are differences with respect to their national systems of corporate governance (van den Berghe, 2002) and welfare state regimes (Esping-Andersen, 1990).

Germany is the prototype of and the most frequently discussed example of a CME. There is extensive coordination among private businesses through widespread crossholdings of shares, interlocking directorships and bank control based on fiduciary holding of shares (Kogut & Walker, 2001). Germany's economy has for decades been dominated by advanced industrial production (for instance cars, electronics and machinery) concentrated in large and powerful transnational enterprises. Since the early 1990s, the German economy, though still successful in terms of exports, has, however, been sluggish. Increasing strains on public budgets resulting from generous welfare services and from huge costs incurred by the German unification have put severe pressures upon the economy. High unemployment, particularly in the former GDR and declining employment are witnesses to the problems in the German economy (Jacobi, Keller, & Müller-Jentsch, 1998; Hassel, 1999; Streeck & Hassel, 2004).

In contrast, Norway is a small country on the periphery of Europe. It is not even a member of the EU. It has an open economy as witnessed by high import and export ratios. The Norwegian economy has traditionally been based upon extraction and processing of natural resources, as for instance, paper, pulp, fish and oil. A unique feature of the Norwegian variety of capitalism is that the state traditionally has been an active participant in the economy and remains a large owner to the present time. For instance, in 2003 the state owned 40 per cent of the total stock listed at the Oslo stock exchange. The Norwegian state is richer than most states. There is a positive balance of trade, no public debt and substantial state investment in firms abroad. The major key to this economic bliss is Norway's development of successful strategies for acquiring, exploiting and controlling offshore oil and gas deposits since the 1960s.

The state's role as a "senior partner" to private business can be traced back to the beginning of the industrialization in the second half of the 19th century. At that time the Norwegian economy lacked large, dominating firms in production and credit supply and the bourgeoisie was weak, characterized by many small and medium-sized enterprises. In spite of a liberal orientation the state had to step in to safeguard the emerging industries, investing heavily in the infrastructure and assisting the establishment of a national banking system. The state had thus to compensate for the absence of an "organized capitalism". This model has been characterized by a leading historian as "democratic capitalism" (Sejersted, 1993), a state-dominated capitalism tempered by small-scale enterprises and strong norms of popular legitimacy.

INDUSTRIAL RELATIONS SYSTEMS IN GERMANY AND NORWAY

Germany

The bulk of the German enterprises is organized into numerous *branch associations and specialized associations*, e.g. the influential association of the automobile industry (Bundesverband der Deutschen Automobilindustrie). Peak association is the Federal Association of Germany Industry (Bundesverband der Deutschen Industrie, BDI) that represents more than 90 per cent of all German private enterprises – not counting mostly the small farms, crafts businesses and self-employed professionals such as lawyers, doctors, architects and others – and is politically very influential. It represents the political interests of the German business community and traditionally maintains close relations with the Christian Democratic and the Free Democratic parties.

Business interests in Germany are also represented by *employer associations* that are the ones directly involved in wage negotiations with labour unions. Traditionally very strong, the organization ratio of enterprises in employer associations has declined since the mid-1990s, especially among smaller enterprises and in the East German states. In East Germany, it declined from about 60 per cent of all enterprises to only 24 per cent. The peak association is the Federal Union of German Employers Associations (Bundesvereinigung der Deutschen Arbeitgeberverbände, BDA).

The German Trade Union Federation (Deutscher Gewerkschaftsbund (DGB)). The German work force is organized by branch rather than by profession. The DGB is the peak association of currently 8 branch unions (down from 17 owing to several mergers), representing altogether 7.4 million individual members (2003).

Declining membership is a serious problem for the DGB member unions. While they initially profited from German unification since the membership figures were traditionally much higher in East Germany, membership has declined precipitously in the East, from 4.2 million in 1991 to 1.8 million in 1998. The decline in West Germany started much earlier and has been much slower instead. Here, membership declined from 7.6 million in 1991 to 6.5 million in 1998. The organization ratio of all employees declined from 35 per cent in 1990 to 22.5 per cent in 2004.

The federation of public officials (Deutscher Beamtenbund (DBB)) with 1.25 million members is another important association of the labour side. The DBB represents the tenured public officials (Beamte). The bulk of these officials are professionals with specialized training which explains the political clout of the DBB. The salaries of public officials are determined politically, and public officials do not have the right to engage in organized strikes. The DBB is therefore not directly involved in wage negotiations, but still serves as an effective lobby for its clientele.

Wage negotiations are held for the entire branches and *wage agreements* (*Tarifverträge*) specify regulations for different categories of employees according to their professional expertise and job description. Owing to the German federal system, such negotiations are held at the regional level (*Tarifbezirke*), and the agreements reached are only valid for that region. The series of wage negotiations for a branch will usually start in one region and the agreements reached in that region will then be taken over by the other regions, thus reducing the time and effort that have to be invested in wage negotiations.

Two different laws govern *labour representation at the level of individual enterprises.* The *Industrial Democracy Act* (Betriebsverfassungsgesetz) that has been in existence since the early 1950s and has been amended several times, requires that elected works councils have to be set up at the floor level of all enterprises with more than 5 employees if a formal request is turned in by a fraction of the employees. The size of these works councils depends on the number of employees in the enterprise and ranges from 1 (in small enterprises up to 20 employees) to 39 (7,000–9,000 employees) and more (another 2 for every 3,000 additional employees). Works councils have to be involved in all management decisions regarding working conditions, hiring and dismissals. They are very influential at the plant level. Owing to the mass layoffs that have taken place in most large German corporations in recent years, one major activity of the works councils has been devoted to negotiate the so-called social plans regulating the criteria for dismissals and compensations for employees who lose their jobs.

The law of codetermination (Mitbestimmungsgesetz) has been in existence since 1951 in the mining, iron and steel industry and since 1976 in all German corporations with more than 2,000 employees. It requires that half of the members on the supervisory boards of corporations are representatives of labour (mostly belonging to the DGB). This implies that labour interests are represented directly at the level where the fundamental management decisions are made (e.g. investments, mergers and mass layoffs). Usually, the deputy chair of the supervisory board is a labour union representative. Moreover, the law requires that in large corporations the managerial board member in charge of personnel affairs has to come from the ranks of the labour union representatives within the corporation.

Membership in political parties is common among the industrial relations elites in Germany, but less prevalent in Norway.[1] In this sense, the industrial relations in Germany are more politicized than the ones in Norway.

Norway

The Confederation of Norwegian Business and Industry (NHO) is the largest *employers' confederation* in the private sector. NHO comprised about 16,000 firms with approximately 490,000 employees in 2001 (Stokke, Evju, & Frøland, 2003). The firms are members of the NHO as well as one of the 21 branch associations, which combine the roles of employers' associations and industrial interest organizations. NHO exerts strong central authority over member associations on bargaining strategies, industrial action and the conclusion of collective agreements. The confederation is the strongest in manufacturing. Its density is particularly high in the chemical and metal sectors (Dølvik & Stokke, 1998).

The other major employer confederation in the private sector is HSH (the Federation of Norwegian Commercial and Service Enterprises). In addition, there are significant employer organizations in financial services, insurance, private health and welfare services and agriculture. In 2001, organized enterprises in total covered ~58 per cent of private sector employment, up from about 50 per cent in 1995 (Stokke et al., 2003).

In an international context, the *union density* in Norway is fairly high, 53 per cent in 2000 (Stokke et al., 2003). This is a slight decrease from 1990 and 1995 when the union density was 57 per cent and 56 per cent, respectively. The Norwegian Confederation of Trade Unions (LO) has always been and is still the dominant union force. It has a traditional hegemony among the blue-collar workers in core manufacturing industries and organizes a substantial proportion of employees in the public sector. Twenty-five LO-affiliated unions covered 51 per cent of the unionized workers in 2001.

The other confederations are The Union of Education (UNIO) with 9 unions and 255,000 members, The Federation of Norwegian Professional Associations (Akademikerne) representing 122,000 members organized in 15 unions and the Confederation of Vocational Unions (YS) consisting of 22 unions with 197,500 members.

Union density in Norway has been relatively stable over the whole post-war period. LO's share of members has, however, fallen. Despite the relative decline in membership, LO unions are still able to dominate the bargaining rounds. LO itself has a centralized power structure, exerting strong central authority over member unions. The centralized power is, however, partly offset by a strong tradition of direct democracy, whereby decisions regarding agreements and mediation proposals are taken by a ballot of members (Dølvik & Stokke, 1998).

In 1973, through amendments to the Company Act, employees were given *the right to elect* one-third of the *members of the board of directors* on industrial companies employing more than 50 people. The system has since been expanded to cover also other sectors of the working life in Norway. In companies employing more than 200 employees a *company assembly* was to be established with a minimum of 12 members, one-third of whom were to be elected by the employees.

LO and NHO have been actors in a multi-tiered *bargaining system* in which centralized negotiations have been complemented by workplace structures of participation, negotiations and cooperation in productivity growth and industrial restructuring throughout the post-war period. The concerted action between the main organizations has been extended several times to include the state in tripartite income policy agreements with elements of fiscal and social policy.

A national mediator is almost always called for in bargaining rounds. There is also a strong tradition of compulsory arbitration. Such arbitration is initiated by ad hoc decisions in parliament and carried out through a standing National Wage Board. This system is quite unique to Norway. Mediation and compulsory arbitration have successfully exerted a "police function", directed against potential free riders inside or outside the NHO–LO area (Dølvik & Stokke, 1998).

DATA AND METHOD

The German Elite Study

The German Elite Study of 1995 is the fourth comprehensive elite survey carried out in West Germany since 1968 and the first elite study after the German (re)unification. The study was directed by Wilhelm Bürklin, University of Potsdam (Bürklin, Rebenstorf et al., 1997). The study included 2,341 respondents, of whom 272 were of East German background, i.e. had lived in the GDR until 1989. Among these respondents, 58.8 per cent were politicians, whereas only a few East Germans held elite positions in the business sector (3.6 per cent) and in German labour unions (12.4 per cent). The response rate in the business sector was below average. It was, however, about the same as in the previous German elite studies.

The German Elite Study of 1995 included a set of attitudinal questions related to political issues and economic policy actors. To measure the business and labour leaders' ideological views and their attitudes to each other we selected:

(1) Self-placement on a left–right scale ranging from 1 (left) to 10 (right).
(2) Perceptions of the degree to which various policy goals are realized in Germany. The items for the realization of social justice, equal opportunities and social security were included in the present analysis. Since the answers for these three items were highly intercorrelated, they were combined into one additive index. The scale values range from 1 (not at all) to 7 (fully realized).
(3) Respondents were asked to assess the influence of various organizations and to indicate whether they thought that the influence of those organizations should remain as it was or rather be higher or lower. From this question, two dummy variables were created, one for labour unions and one for business (big business, banks or business associations). A code of 1 indicates that either business or labour should have less influence in Germany.
(4) The questionnaire included two questions that allowed respondents to express their preference for a political party.[2]

(5) The most important independent variable for the following regression analyses is membership in one of the subgroups within the business and labour elites. The following *subgroups* were defined:

Business ($n = 192$). This subgroup of respondents includes holders of top leadership positions in the largest German enterprises, mostly corporations (Aktiengesellschaften). German corporations have both a managerial board (Vorstand) responsible for running the day-to-day business and a supervisory board (Aufsichtsrat), elected by the shareholders, which in turn appoints the members of the managerial board and oversees its activities.

Two hundred enterprises were selected from rankings – based on turnover – of the most important enterprises in industry, commerce, banking and insurance. The selection of elite positions within the enterprises depended on the size of the enterprise. In the 14 largest corporations, all members of the managerial board plus the chair and deputy chair of the supervisory board were included. In the other enterprises only the chairs and deputy chairs of the managerial board and the chairs of the supervisory boards were included.

Business associations ($n = 93$). This subgroup includes the board as well as the two chief executive managers (Hauptgeschäftsführer) of the Federal Association of German Industry (BDI) plus the presidents and chief executive managers of its member associations. Additionally, the top representatives of the German Association of the Chambers of Industry and Commerce (DIHT) were included. Representatives of the Association of Farmers (Deutscher Landwirtschaftsverband) were excluded.

Employer associations ($n = 41$). This subgroup includes the members of the board plus the chief executive managers of the Federal Union of German Employers Associations (BDA). All major branch associations are represented on the board of the BDA.

Labour board members ($n = 38$). As mentioned before, the German law of codetermination requires equal representation of labour on the supervisory boards of the large corporations and also that one member of the managerial board is drawn from the ranks of labour representatives. It can be assumed that these labour representatives differ in their outlooks from the representatives of capital and should therefore be treated as a separate group for analysis. From a theoretical point of view, this should be a particularly interesting group since its members are subject to strong cross-pressures. As board members of a major enterprise, they are responsible for the economic health of their enterprises, but at the same time they have to represent the interest of labour in board decisions. Labour union membership was used to identify the members of this subgroup.

Labour unions ($n = 97$). This subgroup includes board members and top executive officers of the German Association of Trade Unions (DGB) and its major member unions as well as the chief representatives (chair, deputy chair and chief executive officer) of the other member unions. At the time of the survey, a second major labour union of employees (German Union of Employees), still in existence, had meanwhile merged with the DGB. Sixteen top officials of the DAG are also included in this subgroup.

The other *independent* variables are:

- Membership in policy advisory boards of federal ministries.
- Contact with labour unions. This and the following two contact variables take the value 1 when the leader reports that he or she has *regular* contact with the organizations concerned and 0 when they do not have such contact.
- Contact with business associations.
- Contact with business enterprises, i.e. banks, insurances, industrial corporations and other business enterprises.
- Membership in bourgeois parties: Christian Democratic Party (CDU/ CSU), Free Democratic Party (FDP).
- Membership in leftist parties: Social Democratic Party (SPD), Green Party and Party of Democratic Socialism (PDS).

We included the following *control variables*:

- Level of formal education: low (up to lower secondary, i.e. < 10 years), intermediate (10–11 years; "Mittlere Reife") and high (12–13 years; "Abitur"). This last category also includes holding a university degree.
- Age/generation: born before 1931, 1931–1945 and after 1945.

The Norwegian Leadership Study

The sample originally included 1,969 persons. Personal interviews based on a questionnaire were obtained with 1,710 of the leaders, a response rate of 87.3 per cent.

To measure the top leaders' political preferences and ideological attitudes we selected the following questions:

(1) Attitudes towards the "Norwegian welfare state", i.e. the public–private cleavage.[3]
(2) Institutional trust that was enquired into in the following manner: "How much trust do you have in the institutions listed on this card. Please rank the institutions on a scale from 0 to 10, where 0 is no trust and 10 is very high trust".

(3) Which political party they voted for in the parliamentary election in 1997 (the last election prior to the survey).[4]

The following *subgroups* were defined:

Business ($n = 297$). This subgroup includes CEOs, presidents, vice-presidents and chairmen of the boards of the largest private enterprises in Norway. We included the CEO (or president) and the chairman of the board in all firms with more than 400 employees and also the vice-presidents in enterprises with more than 4,000 employees.

Employer and business associations ($n = 74$). This subgroup includes the presidents and vice-presidents in The Confederation of Norwegian Business and Industry (NHO) and The Federation of Norwegian Commercial and Service Enterprises (HSH), the chief executive manager in each of the branch organizations of NHO and HSH and the presidents of the employer organizations within financial services, insurance, private health and welfare services and agriculture.

Labour unions ($n = 100$). This subgroup includes the then top leaders of three confederations LO, YS and AF and the top leaders of the member unions.

The response rate among the enterprise leaders was 75 per cent. The response rate among the leaders of the employer, business and labour associations was closer to 90 per cent.

The other *independent variables* included are:

- Contact with labour union leaders
- Contact with enterprise leaders[5]
- Contact with leaders of business organizations
- Membership in political party, three dummy variables: (i) not member in any party, (ii) member in a socialist party and (iii) member in a non-socialist/bourgeois party
- Occupational experience in politics[6]
- Occupational experience in public administration
- Membership in public advisory boards

In addition, four *control variables* are included:

- *Class* of origin is constructed on the basis of information about the father's occupation or mother's occupation where there is no information about the father. The class variable has three categories: (1) the upper and upper middle classes, (2) middle class and (3) working class.
- *Age* is a continuous variable.

- *Level of education* has eight values, and is likewise treated as a continuous variable.
- *Gender*

PROBLEMS OF INTERPRETATION

The analyses presented in this article are based upon data from two different elite studies that were conducted in different years. The studies were not designed to be directly comparable. As a result the questions in the German and the Norwegian elite studies are not identical. Nevertheless, the two studies address similar research questions, which imply that the data nonetheless give ample opportunities for comparison. For instance, a core topic within elite theory and elite research is whether national elites or particular sector elites are cohesive and integrated or, alternatively, fragmented. The issue addressed in this article – consensus or polarization between business and labour elites – can be seen as a variant and a specification of this more general topic. One indication of elite integration has been the degree of similarity or difference between political beliefs. In the German as well as the Norwegian elite studies there are therefore several questions measuring the elites' attitudes towards ideological and political issues, an important purpose of which is to measure how close or distant the elites are in relation to each other.

Given the differences between the two data sets, in the interpretation of the reported findings we concentrate on the robust differences between the two countries.

FINDINGS

Tables 1 and 2 present information about the contact patterns between the business and labour elites in Germany and Norway. In general the two tables reveal quite extensive contacts between the two elite groups. The extent of contact does not seem to be significantly different in the two countries. Not surprisingly, on both sides of the capital/labour divide the leaders have the most frequent contact with leaders within their own camp. But the frequency of contacts across the class divide is, nonetheless, quite impressive. Notice for instance that as much as 76 per cent of the German labour leaders report regular contact with leaders in employer associations. In Norway 70 per cent of the leaders of employer and business associations see labour union leaders at least once a month.

Table 1. Contact Patterns among Business and Labour Elites in Germany (Per Cent of the Leaders who Report Regular Contact).

	Enterprise Leaders	Leaders of Employer Associations	Leaders of Business Associations	Labour Representatives on Boards of Large Enterprises	Leaders of Labour Unions
Contact with major private corporations	81	66	65	32	57
Contact with business associations	52	97	92	42	76
Contact with labour unions	38	83	60	84	95
N	191	41	92	38	97

Table 2. Contact Patterns among Business and Labour Elites in Norway (Per Cent Reporting Weekly/Monthly Contact.

	Leaders in Private Enterprises	Leaders in Employers' and Business Associations	Union Leaders
Contact with leaders in private enterprises	50/90	46/86	8/38
Contact with employer and business associations	8/49	57/90	35/65
Contact with labour unions	13/40	36/70	78/94
N	297	70	94

In both countries leaders of employer associations have more regular contact with labour unions than the other business leaders. Moreover, in Germany it is more common among labour union leaders to have regular contact with the other party than among the labour representatives on the boards of large enterprises.

The business and labour elites also meet each other as representatives in the many state boards and committees. According to the Norwegian elite study 56 per cent of the top leaders in the Norwegian employer associations and 52 per cent of the labour leaders have had posts on such boards. In the German elite study it appeared that only 34 per cent and 29 per cent of the

German employer and labour leaders, respectively, report the same. In other words, the business and labour elites in Norway are much more involved in the activities in the state sector than their German counterparts, a reflection of the more developed corporatism found in Norway compared to Germany.

Next, to check the validity of the hypotheses formulated above, the results of a series of multivariate analyses are presented.

Table 3 exhibits the results of regression analyses of the views of the German business leaders on the left/right dimension, on the accomplishments of the welfare state and of their evaluations of the influence of capital and labour in the society.

The first column shows that the top leaders of employer as well as business associations place themselves ideologically more to the right than the

Table 3. Ideological and Political Attitudes of German Business Leaders (Regression Analyses (OLS)).

	Left–Right Scale	Attainment of Welfare Goals	Capital Too Much Influence	Labour Too Much Influence
Intercept	7.127**	5.565**	0.438*	0.441*
Employer association leaders (compared with enterprise leaders)	0.433*	−0.023	−0.069	−0.147
Business association leaders (compared with enterprise leaders)	0.355*	−0.225*	0.045	−0.035
Membership left parties	−1.597**	−0.347	0.286*	−0.192
Membership bourgeois parties	−0.102	0.011	0.015	0.035
Contact with labour unions	−0.192	0.031	−0.013	0.014
Membership on political advisory boards	−0.040	0.057	0.040	0.058
Education	−0.094	0.092	−0.139*	−0.045
Generation	−0.262*	−0.137	0.065	−0.006
R^2 adjusted	0.06	0.02	0.03	−0.01
N	316	318	324	324

**Significant at the 1 per cent level.
*Significant at the 5 per cent level.

leaders of the individual enterprises. This is contrary to the expectation formulated in Hypothesis 2a. The formal representatives of capital are more conservative than the leaders of the firms that they represent. Second, and not surprisingly, the few business leaders who are members of a leftist political party are ideologically more leftist than their business counterparts without membership in a political party. Contrary to expectation, membership in a bourgeois party does not influence the business leaders to become more right wing. In addition, the younger generation of business leaders are ideologically somewhat more moderate than those of the older generation.

The second column focuses upon the business leaders' evaluation of the welfare state's attainment of significant goals. The top leaders of business associations appear in this analysis as less conservative than the leaders of the individual enterprises. In their opinion justice has not yet been sufficiently achieved in the German society, indicating that they shoulder a stronger responsibility for central welfare goals than the other business leaders. Furthermore, this finding is contrary to Hypothesis 2a. No other variables affect the leaders' views on this issue.

Column 3 in Table 3 gives information about what factors affect how the business leaders assess the influence of capital. The analysis demonstrates that business leaders who are members of a left party more frequently think this influence is too large, while leaders who have higher education are less concerned with this influence than the less educated leaders.

In column 4 we can see that none of the variables is significantly related to the business leaders' views upon labour's influence.

In the theory section above we hypothesized that frequent contact with labour leaders (Hypothesis 1) and membership on state advisory boards (Hypothesis 2b) would induce the business leaders to hold more moderate political views and more conciliatory attitudes towards labour unions. It is striking that none of the four models presented in Table 3 lends support to these hypotheses. There seems to be no moderating effects of meeting representatives of the other side or participating in public advisory bodies with corporatist representation.

Table 4 presents the results of regression analyses of how the labour leaders relate to the four attitudes or issues.

In Table 3 we saw that the top leaders of the individual enterprises are ideologically more moderate than the business leaders who represent the general business and employer interests. In this table it appears, in accordance with Hypothesis 2c, that labour representatives on the boards of the large German enterprises are ideologically and politically more moderate than the

Table 4.   Ideological and Political Attitudes among German Labour Leaders (Regressions analyses (OLS)).

	Left–Right Scale	Fair Distribution	Capital Too Much Influence	Labour Too Much Influence
Intercept	4.709**	4.489**	0.612*	−0.013
Labour members on boards of co-determination corporations (compared with labour union leaders)	0.706*	0.953**	0.398**	0.126**
Membership left parties	−0.692*	−0.166	0.027	−0.024
Membership bourgeois parties	1.161*	0.592*	−0.091	0.021
Contact with business enterprises	0.239	0.369	−0.148	−0.042
Contacts with business associations	0.335	0.149	−0.076	0.053
Membership on political advisory boards	−0.068	0.138	0.023	0.021
Education	−0.331*	−0.248*	0.011	0.000
Generation	−0.067	−0.319*	0.124	0.008
R^2 adjusted	0.21	0.32	0.15	0.06
N	130	130	132	132

**Significant at the 1 per cent level.
*Significant at the 5 per cent level.

union leaders, even when we control for the labour leaders' education and generation. They are more centrist on the left/right scale. They believe more frequently that significant welfare goals have been attained. Compared with the labour union leaders they are less concerned with the influence of capital and somewhat more concerned with the influence of labour.

Second, membership in a political party independently affects the labour leaders' ideological and political opinions. Members of left parties place themselves more frequently to the left, and they are less satisfied with the accomplishments of the welfare state. In contrast, labour leaders who are members of one of the bourgeois parties are ideologically more conservative and more content with the attainment of welfare state goals than their counterparts with no membership in any political party. There are, however, no effects of party membership upon how the labour leaders judge the influence of capital and labour in the German society.

Moreover, columns 1 and 2 show that labour leaders belonging to younger generations are more moderate and centrist than those belonging to the older generation and the higher educated labour leaders are more radical than the labour leaders with less education. This last finding is exactly the opposite of what we found among the business leaders.

Furthermore, in none of the models did we find any significant effects of amount of contacts with business leaders of participation in public advisory boards.

Table 5 focuses on the Norwegian business leaders. Column 1 in the table shows to what extent the business leaders' opinions about the private/public issue are related to the various explanatory and control variables. Contrary to Hypothesis 2a, there is no difference between enterprise leaders and

Table 5. Ideological and Trust Attitudes among Norwegian Business Leaders (Regression Analyses (OLS)).

	Views on the Private/ Public Issue	Trust in Labour Unions
Intercept	1.234**	4.496**
Top leaders of employer organizations (compared to top leaders of business enterprises)	0.061	−0.261
Contact with labour union leaders	0.035	0.281**
Member of a political party (compared with non-members)		
Member of a socialist party	0.371*	−0.151
Member of a bourgeois party	−0.111	0.324
Previously worked within politics (number of years)	0.049**	−0.054
Previously worked within public administration (years)	0.002	−0.017
Post on a state advisory board	−0.032	−0.087
Class background (compared with upper and upper middle class)		
Middle class	0.054	0.152
Labour class	0.035	0.0003
Education	−0.023	−0.101
Age	0.008*	0.022*
Gender (man = 1)	0.017	0.193
R^2 adjusted	0.04	0.02
N	345	343

**Significant at the 1 per cent level.
*Significant at the 5 per cent level.

leaders of the employer and business associations. Next we see that business leaders who are members of a socialist party are more supportive of the welfare state than those who are not members of any political party. Being member of a bourgeois party has, however, no significant effect upon their opinions. This pattern is similar to the one we found among German business leaders.

Moreover, in accordance with Hypothesis 4 work experience from politics seems to foster a more positive attitude towards the public sector. Furthermore, this variable is significantly related to the leaders' ideological views independent of their leadership position and party membership. Several business leaders have had previous experience from political work. It seems then as if this experience induces them to become ideologically more moderate.

In addition, column 1 reveals that older business leaders are more positive to the role of the state and to the welfare policies than the younger ones, a pattern that is opposite to what we found among the German business leaders.

Column 2 gives information about the business leaders' trust in labour unions. Only two of the variables are significantly related to their trust attitudes. Business leaders who have frequent contact with labour union leaders have more trust in labour unions than those with little contact with representatives of the other side. This finding seems to corroborate the hypothesis presented in the theory section. However, this result can also be explained to be a consequence of self-selection, i.e. those business leaders who already had trust in labour unions find it more easy to involve themselves with labour leaders.

Second, compared with younger business leaders, the older business leaders appear to have more trust in labour unions.

Table 6 presents the results of similar analyses among top leaders in the Norwegian labour unions. In column 1 we can notice that labour leaders who are members of a socialist party are much more in favour of the present welfare state model than union leaders who are non-members. Second, supporting Hypothesis 2c, union leaders who previously have been members of the board of a private business enterprise are more in favour of privatization and less involvement of the state in the economy than those without this experience. This finding is quite similar to what was found in the German analyses – that labour representatives on the boards of large private enterprises are more centrist in their ideological views than the regular union leaders.

Column 1 also demonstrates that male union leaders are less supportive of the public sector than their female counterparts. In other words, male union leaders are ideologically somewhat more conservative than their female counterparts.

Table 6. Ideological and Trust Attitudes among Norwegian Labour
Union Leaders (Regression Analyses (OLS)).

	Views on the Private/ Public Issue	Trust in Private Business
Intercept	3.738**	7.511**
Contact with leaders in private business enterprises	−0.047	−0.164
Contact with leaders of business and employer organizations	−0.020	0.024
Member of a political party (compared with non-members)	0.813**	0.012
Member of a socialist party	0.300	0.120
Member of a bourgeois party		
Previously worked within politics	0.010	−0.182
Previously worked within public administration	0.006	0.019
Post on a state advisory board	0.312	−0.090
Post on the board of a private business enterprise	−0.442**	0.300
Class background (compared with upper and upper middle class)		
Middle class	−0.001	−0.057
Labour class	−0.025	0.416
Education	−0.092	−0.160
Age	0.0006	−0.030
Gender (man = 1)	−0.420**	−0.012
R^2 adjusted	0.38	0.02
N	91	91

**Significant at the 1 per cent level.

It is also noteworthy that the model presented in column 1 explains as much as 38 per cent of the variation in the attitudes of the union leaders towards the private/public issue.

In the analysis presented in column 2 it appears that none of the independent variables is significantly related to the union leaders' trust in private business.

DISCUSSION

In the theoretical section we suggested that frequent contact with representatives of the other side could be one significant mechanism through which the industrial relations system fostered ideological moderation. The reported findings give only scant evidence in support of the theoretical ideas mentioned. As demonstrated above, neither in Germany nor in Norway is there any such effect of frequent contact with the other side. The business and labour leaders keep their ideological attitudes intact even if they may become familiar with the leaders of the adverse organizations and respect their positions. Moreover, they are not tuned to more conciliatory attitudes towards their adversaries.

The only exception here is that business leaders in Norway who have frequent contact with labour leaders have more trust in labour unions than the business leaders without such contact. This isolated finding gives some reason to conclude that if the Norwegian system of industrial relations is not producing any consensus, at least it promotes some trust.

As shown above, neither did we find any significant relationship between the attitudes of the business and labour leaders and their having had posts on public advisory boards. In other words, meeting representatives of other interest groups and taking part in the political deliberations in these corporatist bodies does not tune the leaders to more tempered ideological opinions. The reason for this is probably that they are meeting in these bodies with limited mandate, expected by their principals to represent and advocate the interests of their respective organizations.

We suggested above that another mechanism for encouraging ideological moderation could be a feeling of national responsibility for economic stability that we assumed would accompany the roles of top leaders in the main organizations of the labour market. Among the Norwegian elites we found no evidence for the operation of such a mechanism. There were no differences between the two groups of business leaders as to how they looked upon the private/public issue.

In the German case, we found the opposite pattern. The leaders of the employer and business associations appear to be more right-wing oriented than the enterprise leaders, with respect to party preference as well as their placement on the left/right scale. It was also demonstrated that the top leaders of the German labour unions generally have an ideological orientation more to the left than the labour representatives on the boards of the large enterprises.

The overall conclusion of the empirical results of our analyses is that, contrary to the hypotheses derived from theories on neo-corporatism and elite theory, leaders who represent capital and labour on national level are not ideologically tempered by frequent contacts with the other side or by occupying roles with nationwide responsibility. The previous findings seem rather to lend support to Therborn (1992) and Pekkarinen, Pohjola, and Rowthorn (1992). Following these scholars, the basic conflict between capital and labour is still a significant divide in the "coordinated market economies" of Germany and Norway, even if this cleavage has been attenuated as a result of the extensive changes in the occupational structures of both societies. The several historical compromises between capital and labour and the establishment of a set of supportive institutions have tamed the conflicts and channelled them into regulated negotiations and compromises. But the conflicting interests are still present and operative. The top leaders of the organizations on each side of the capital/labour divide are selected and socialized to be conscious about what interests they are representing. They are expected by their respective principals to achieve results in accordance with these interests, an expectation which motivates the leaders at any time to consider the option of reviving the conflict to acquire better results (Wright, 2000).

These conclusions do not rule out the possibility, however, that regular contacts between the business and labour elites can promote ideological moderation on a collective level. This can come about in two different ways. First, influential leaders on each side may be convinced about the necessity or wisdom of less partisan attitudes. Through their example and influence their beliefs may gradually be followed by and spread to the other leaders. As a result, there will be a sway of opinion in favour of more ideological temperance. Second, collective moderation may also be a result of a relatively rapid change of mentality within a particular organization or elite group, precipitated by instances of good will or benign commitments from the adverse party. In addition, interest groups in the labour market can also adopt ideologically more balanced views as a result of accommodation to legal regulations that originally appeared to be threatening to their interests.

The findings in the German study indicate that, at least in Germany, it is rather the working together in the individual enterprises to solve operational problems and meet strategic challenges that fosters ideological and political moderation among the individual business and labour leaders. These local leaders are free of the obligations of representing the general interests of capital and labour which are inherent in the roles as top leaders in the business organizations and the labour unions. This freedom gives them the opportunity to be flexible with respect to finding local solutions to economic and labour problems. In the wake of this flexibility it seems that they are on both sides prone to become ideologically somewhat more pragmatic. The more centre-oriented attitudes of Norwegian labour leaders who have had posts on the boards of private enterprises confirm the effect of this factor.

The analyses of the Norwegian data offered clues to yet another factor that may be favourable to ideological moderation. In Norway there has for some time been a tendency within the employer and business associations to recruit top leaders with experience from politics. The reason for this recruitment policy is that such experience is seen as a vital asset when the employer and business associations attempt to influence decisions taken by politicians and senior public officials. We demonstrated above that business leaders with occupational experience from politics are ideologically less "extreme" than the business leaders without such experience. Moreover, this effect is the same regardless of the political party in which this experience was acquired.

This finding indicates, in accordance with Putnam (1976), that the socialization which guarantees that incumbents of leadership positions perform their tasks to the satisfaction of their principals, also assure that the ideas, experiences and outlook which they acquire are not lost when they change jobs. These ideas and the lessons learnt in previous positions influence how they understand their new tasks and how they shape their new roles. Previous experience in politics fosters the development of a better understanding for the overall concerns which responsible national leaders must pay heed to, and this understanding seems to foster more centrist political views among business leaders. We can therefore conclude that *mobility* of individual leaders across sectors is more important for promoting ideological moderation than personal contacts with representatives of adverse groups and organizations.

Inspired by Rabinowitz' and McDonald's (1989) "directional" theory of voting we expected to find that those business and labour leaders who were members of a political party (on the same side) would hold more "extreme" ideological attitudes and be less conciliatory than the non-members. This is indeed the case for labour leaders in Germany as well as in Norway. Labour leaders who are members of a socialist party have a stronger leftist orientation than those without such political affiliation. Among business leaders membership in a bourgeois party does not have the same effect however.

COMPARISON BETWEEN GERMANY AND NORWAY

As demonstrated above, the top leaders of employer associations and in trade unions in Germany are ideologically more divided than the business and labour representatives in the individual enterprises. There were no similar differences among the Norwegian business leaders. This finding

Table 7.   Party Political Preferences[a] of Business and Labour Leaders in Germany (Per Cent).

	None	PDS	Grüne	SPD	FDP	CDU/CSU
Other elites	4.5	2.7	15.3	25.7	11.5	40.3
Business leaders	4.2	0.0	1.6	5.2	20.8	68.2
Top leaders in employers associations	0.0	0.0	4.9	4.9	24.4	65.9
Top leaders in business associations	5.4	0.0	0.0	3.2	20.4	71.0
Labour members of the boards of private businesses	2.6	2.6	5.3	50.0	5.3	34.2
Top leaders in national labour unions	4.1	0.0	17.5	67.0	1.0	10.3

[a]Party preference was measured by rank ordering the sympathy ratings for the different parties and taking the party that had received the highest rating. In case of ties or missing values, vote intention was taken instead. This operationalization can be considered as a more reliable measure of party preference than vote intention because the German electoral system encourages tactical voting and vote intention may therefore not reflect the true party affiliation of a respondent.

Table 8.   Party Voting among Business and Labour Leaders in the 1997 Norwegian Parliamentary Election.

	SV	AP	SP	Krf	Venstre	Høyre	Frp	Andre
Top leaders in private businesses	0.4	20.6	2.8	3.2	4.9	62.3	4.4	1.2
Top leaders in employer- and business associations	4.8	24.2	4.8	5.7	5.7	51.6	0.0	1.7
Top leaders in national labour unions	16.3	48.8	0.0	7.5	5.0	17.5	1.3	2.5

indicates that there is a wider gap with respect to political attitudes between the elites of business and labour organizations in Germany than in Norway. It seems that the peak business and labour organizations are more politicized in Germany than in Norway.

In the following we explore this difference in the quality of the relationship between the representatives of capital and labour in the two countries somewhat further. In Tables 7 and 8 we compare the political party preferences of the industrial relations elites in Germany and Norway, respectively. Table 7 is mainly based upon the reported party preferences of the German leaders. The Norwegian study asked about the vote of the top leaders at the parliamentary election in 1997. Despite the different measures of political party affiliation, Tables 7 and 8 reveal some interesting differences between the two countries. First of all, Norway is distinguished by a relatively large number of business leaders who reported voting for the Labour Party in 1997. Nearly every fourth top leader of an employer or business association voted for the Labour Party in 1997. Twenty per cent of the top leaders of the individual business enterprises did the same. In Germany support for the Social Democratic Party was much weaker among the business leaders: only 5 per cent of the enterprise leaders and 5 per cent of the leaders of the employer associations expressed preference for the Social Democratic Party.

Another remarkable finding is that a much higher percentage of the top leaders of the German labour unions feel politically close to the leftist parties. Eighty-five per cent of the German labour leaders expressed sympathy for either the Social Democratic Party or the "Grüne". Only 65 per cent of the labour union leaders in Norway voted in 1997 for the Labour Party or the Socialist Left Party. As many as 31 per cent of them voted for one of the bourgeois parties. In other words, the political gap between the business and labour elites, as measured by political party preference or voting, is undoubtedly smaller in Norway than in Germany.

However, we must be careful not to overstate these differences. Despite the higher party political polarization found in Germany, the elite respondents share a consensus on the present political order. In the elite study of 1995, 88 per cent of the respondents stated that they were satisfied with the workings of the democratic political system in Germany. More than four out of five leaders also supported a statement that rather than insisting on one's own right, one should always try to reach for a compromise.

Conversely, the seemingly smaller ideological cleavage between capital and labour in Norway may be called into question. It cannot be ruled out, for instance, that the peculiar voting pattern among the top leaders of the Norwegian employer associations in 1997 was primarily due to the pragmatic expectation that a Labour government was better able to promote macro-economic stability at that particular point of time. Such stability was a collective good that was much in demand within the private business at that time. It is therefore conceivable that their more conservative attitudes towards the Norwegian welfare state are a more reliable indicator of their true ideological positions.

Given that the ideological split between business and labour elites in Germany is wider than in Norway, how can we explain this difference? One possibility is that there has been a stronger tradition of mutual trust and awareness of mutual dependence between the main organizations of labour and capital in Norway than in Germany. The relationship between business and labour elites in Norway has been distinguished by a sense of community and complementarity at the same time as there have been tensions and conflicting interests. Early in the 20th century the main employer and labour associations came to realize that coordination and centralized wage setting

was necessary to avoid devastating conflicts and protect the export industries from unfortunate wage increases. According to Bowman (2002), early
centralization was even established as a result of employer initiative, and it
has persisted because employers have pursued strategies to preserve it. Since
then the business and labour elites, first and foremost in NHO and LO, have
shared the same understanding of the macro-economic challenges facing
Norway and have repeatedly managed to enter into agreements to the benefit of all parties and the nation as a whole. They have frequently met
resistance from the rank and file within their own organizations or from
competing organizations. But their dominance in the labour market and the
centralized power within both confederations has guaranteed that their
shared understanding has come to mark the industrial relations in Norway.

In Germany as well, there has been a widespread consensus on a commonality of interest among the business and labour elites. Relations between
organized labour, organized business and the government were characterized by mutual recognition, institutionalized co-operation and regulation of
conflict during most of the (West) German post-war history. Cooperation
between labour and capital was institutionalized in the particular German
model of extensive workplace participation combined with the employers'
investing extensively in skills, advanced technology and quality-competitive
products. In many firms or industries the close cooperation between the
employers and the unions and work councils has continued up to the
present.

According to Hassel (1999) and Streeck and Hassel (2004), this stable
industrial order has gradually eroded during the last two decades, however,
a development which was already under way at the time of the German elite
study in 1995. More severe macro-economic conditions, increasing fragmentation and decentralization of the industrial relations system created a
more precarious situation for employer as well as labour associations. Significant losses of members on both sides and a shrinking coverage of collective agreements put pressures on the leaders of these associations. This
seems to have influenced them to choose different courses of action and to
support different political solutions. The business leaders moved to the
right, embracing neo-liberal ideas. The union leaders encapsulated themselves in traditional left positions. During these processes the leaders on each
side appeared to have become more antagonistic towards each other. The
business leaders resented the unions' inability to adapt to the new and more
severe economic environment. The union leaders on their part felt that
business in collaboration with bourgeois parties attempted to dismantle
significant welfare rights which labour had struggled for.

At the same time, business and labour elites in Germany may have been less consensual than business and labour elites in Norway even before these changes in the German industrial relations system took place. There are some aspects of the industrial relations system in Germany that probably have not been conducive to the development of a sense of community across the capital/labour divide. First, the institutionalized cooperation between capital and labour in Germany was to a large extent a post-war construction initiated from above. It did not emerge to the same extent as in Norway from the partners' gradual learning to accommodate each other. It is quite conceivable that the relationship between business and labour is therefore less rooted in mutual trust in Germany than in Norway.

Second, the extent and form of corporatism differs in the two countries, and this difference may as well have been a source of more divergence in the German industrial relations system already in the first decades after World War II. As mentioned above, one significant difference is that the state has been more directly involved in the wage setting process in Norway than in Germany (Siaroff, 1999; Høgsnes, 2002; Traxler, 2004). The Norwegian state has on several occasions presented substantial financial incentives to help the parties come to an agreement. The state has for instance increased the budgetary grants to an active labour market policy in exchange for wage moderation on the part of the trade unions. It has also used compulsory arbitration to stop strikes that had gone out of control. In other words, the state has several times relieved the employer and labour associations of the burdens or sacrifices that were necessary to reach a final agreement. In these ways the state has lifted some of the pressures off the shoulders of the organizations and thus removed reasons for antagonism between the business and labour elites.

CONCLUSION

At the outset we raised the question whether the extensive cooperation between capital and labour in Germany and Norway affects the ideological attitudes of leaders who are personally involved in this cooperation. The answer is that frequent personal contacts between the business and labour leaders do not instil more moderate or centrist political beliefs, at least not on the individual level. Neither does an extensive involvement in tripartite cooperation with the state through participation on state advisory boards affect their attitudes. The basic class conflict is still operating and is influencing ideological positions of the representatives of labour and capital.

At the aggregate level, we have seen that in the mid-1990s the balance between consensus and polarization leaned somewhat more towards polarization in Germany than in Norway in 2000. Whether the relationship between labour and capital is distinguished by moderation and conciliatory attitudes or polarization seems first and foremost to be determined by institutional and structural factors. We have emphasized a historical legacy of compromises and mutual trust as one such institutional mechanism. In addition, the German case has indicated that national economic problems and an erosion of the power basis of the main organizations in the labour market may be other factors that may have negative influence upon the cooperative climate.

NOTES

1. In Germany 51 per cent of the top leaders of employer organizations, 33 per cent of the leaders of business organizations and only 18 per cent of the enterprise leaders are members of a political party, most of them in a bourgeois party. Eighty-seven per cent of the labour elites and 55 per cent of the labour representatives on the boards of large enterprises are members of a political party. Twenty-two per cent of the Norwegian business leaders were members of a political party and 37 per cent of the labour union leaders.

2. Respondents were first asked to rate the degree of their sympathy for the German parties on a scale ranging from $+5$ to -5. Additionally, they were also asked for their vote intention. Both questions yielded different distributions. Since vote intention in Germany – as elsewhere – not only depends on feelings of closeness to a political party, but also on the current performance of the political parties and on tactical considerations, we decided to create a variable "party preference" based on the sympathy ratings and indicating the party to which respondents had assigned their highest sympathy rank. Respondents who had not assigned a unique first rank or who did not give ratings for all parties were coded as "no first rank".

3. They were asked to express their opinions regarding the four following statements: (a) "It is more important to extend public services than to reduce taxes"; (b) "In Norway one should put stronger emphasis upon privatization and a smaller public sector"; (c) "State influence on private business should be reduced"; and (d) "In Norway we have gone far enough in the reduction of income inequalities". The leaders were given four response alternatives: (i) strongly agree, (ii) agree somewhat, (iii) disagree somewhat and (iv) strongly disagree. The coding for item (a) had to be reversed since it was phrased in the direction opposite to that of the other items. The index is based upon the mean of the leaders' evaluation of the four statements and has values from 1 to 4. Value 4 indicates that the leaders fully back the public sector and policies for levelling of incomes. Value 1 indicates that the leaders favour a smaller public sector, more privatization and a curtailing of the state power over private business. Cronbach's α for the index is 0.83.

4. Only 8 per cent declined to provide this information; 5 per cent had not voted at all and 3 per cent could not remember which political party they had supported. In the following analyses these three groups – a total of 16 per cent of the respondents – are treated as "missing data".

5. Each contact variable had four values: "weekly or more frequently", "monthly", "less frequently" and "never". In the models the variables were used as continuous variables.

6. Both experience variables were constructed as continuous variables, each of them measuring the number of years of fulltime work in each sector.

REFERENCES

Barton, A. H. (1985). Determinants of economic attitudes in the American business elite. *American Journal of Sociology, 91*, 54–87.

Blau, P. (1964). *Exchange and power in social life.* New York: Wiley.

Bowman, J. R. (2002). Employers and the persistence of centralized wage setting. The case of Norway. *Comparative Political Studies, 35*, 995–1026.

Bürklin, W., Rebenstorf u.a., H., (Eds.). (1997). *Eliten in Deutschland.* Opladen: Leske + Budrich.

Coleman, J. (1990). *Foundations of Social Theory.* Cambridge, MA: The Belknap Press of Harvard University Press.

Dølvik, J. E., & Stokke, T. A. (1998). Norway: The revival of centralized concertation. In: A. Ferner & R. Hyman (Eds), *Changing industrial relations in Europe.* Oxford: Blackwell.

Esping-Andersen, G. (1990). *The three worlds of welfare capitalism.* Cornwall: T.J. Press.

Gulbrandsen, T., & Engelstad, F. (2005). Elite consensus on the Norwegian welfare state model. *West European Politics, 28*(4), 899–919.

Hall, P., & Soskice, D. (2001). *Varieties of capitalism. The institutional foundations of comparative advantage.* Oxford: Oxford University Press.

Hassel, A. (1999). The erosion of the German system of industrial relations. *British Journal of Industrial Relations, 37*, 483–505.

Higley, J., Hoffmann-Lange,, U., Kadushin, C., & Moore, G. (1991). Elite integration in stable democracies: A reconsideration. *European Sociological Review, 7*, 35–53.

Hoffmann-Lange, U. (1992). *Eliten, Macht und Konflikt in der Bundesrepublik.* Opladen: Leske + Budrich.

Høgsnes, G. (2002). Organisasjonseliter – makt og avmakt? *Sosiologisk tidsskrift, 10*, 308–331.

Jacobi, O. B., Keller, B., & Müller-Jentsch, W. (1998). Germany: Facing new challenges. In: A. Ferner & R. Hyman (Eds), *Changing industrial relations in Europe.* Oxford: Blackwell.

Katzenstein, P. J. (1985). *Small states in world markets: Industrial policy in Europe.* Ithaca, NY: Cornell University Press.

Kogut, B., & Walker, G. (2001). The small world of Germany and the durability of national networks. *American Sociological Review, 66*, 317–335.

Öberg, P., & Svensson, T. (2002). Power, trust and deliberation in Swedish labour-market relations. *Economic and Industrial Relations Democracy, 15*, 455–475.

Pekkarinen, J., Pohjola, M., & Rowthorn, B. (Eds) (1992). *Social corporatism: A superior economic system?* Oxford: Clarendon Press.

Putnam, R. D. (1976). *The comparative study of political elites.* Englewood Cliffs, NJ: Prentice-Hall.

Rabinowitz, G., & MacDonald, S. E. (1989). A directional theory of issue voting. *American Political Science Review, 83*, 93–121.

Sejersted, F. (1993). *Demokratisk kapitalisme*. Oslo: Universitetsforlaget.

Siaroff, A. (1999). Corporatism in 24 industrial democracies: Meaning and measurement. *European Journal of Political Research, 36*, 175–205.

Stokke, T. A., Evju, S., & Frøland, H. O. (2003). *Det kollektive arbeidslivet. Organisasjoner, tariffavtaler, lønnsoppgjør og inntektspolitikk*. Oslo: Universitetsforlaget.

Streeck, W., & Hassel, A. (2004). The crumbling pillars of social partnership. In: H. Kitschelt & W. Streeck (Eds), *Germany. Beyond the stable state*. London: Frank Cass.

Therborn, G. (1992). Lessons from "Corporatist" theorizations. In: J. Pekkarinen, M. Pohjola & B. Rowthorn (Eds), *Social corporatism: A superior economic system?* Oxford: Clarendon Press.

Traxler, F. (2004). The metamorphoses of corporatism: From classical to lean patterns. *European Journal of Political Research, 43*, 571–598.

van den Berghe, L. (2002). *Corporate governance in a globalising world: Convergence or divergence? A European perspective*. Boston: Kluwer Academic Publishers.

Wright, E. O. (2000). Working-class power, capitalist-class power, and class compromise. *American Journal of Sociology, 105*, 957–1002.

Woldendorp, J. J. (1995). Neo-corporatism as a strategy for conflict regulation in the Netherlands (1970–1990). *Acta Politica, 30*, 121–151.

DOMESTIC ELITES IN THE TRANSFORMATION OF THE "EUROPEAN POLITY": THE CASE OF ITALY

Maurizio Cotta

THE PROBLEM: DOMESTIC POLITICS OF NATION STATES IN A MORE INTEGRATED EUROPE

What has happened, after 50 years of persistent (deepening, expanding) European integration, to the domestic politics of the nation states involved in this increasingly dense institutional net (whatever its ambiguous nature, inter-governmental or supra-national or both at the same time) is a question of growing importance. This environment, within which the politics of European nation states takes place, has undoubtedly gained a growing importance in itself and a stronger relevance for crucial aspects of domestic political life. More precisely, it must be asked what has been altered in the traditional "setting" within which domestic politics used to develop, how domestic political actors bring into their political calculations the new conditions and how they are affected by them.

Those who study the politics of European countries cannot avoid such questions any longer. I will try here to move some steps in the direction of elaborating a general scheme for the interpretation of this situation.

Comparative Studies of Social and Political Elites
Comparative Social Research, Volume 23, 137–170
Copyright © 2007 by Elsevier Ltd.
ISSN: 0195-6310/doi:10.1016/S0195-6310(06)23007-2

The point of view adopted is that of domestic politics and of political and representative elites. With regard to the first point we must remember that nation states maintain their importance as the dominant arenas of democratic politics. In spite of the growing importance of the European Parliament, it is national elections that decide who governs in the member states and thus also (directly or indirectly) who governs Europe. As for the second aspect, I will follow the predominant interpretation of contemporary democracy as a regime based on the competition among elites for the support of the electorate (Schumpeter, 1942; Downs, 1957; Sartori, 1987). This interpretation, which for all its possible qualifications has not been so far seriously challenged, means that in our understanding of the working of this regime we have to pay special attention to the behaviour of relatively restricted groups of (professional) politicians, and to their motivations (Field & Higley, 1980). This obviously does not deny the importance of the voters in deciding the competition and of other actors (such as interest groups, social movements, etc.) in influencing the game. In fact the competitive strategies of elites continuously take into account these elements as constraints and resources for their actions. Yet it can be easily granted that political elites have the central and most active place in the democratic game.

It is surprising however that whereas the role of political elites in the establishment, consolidation and working of national democracies is sufficiently well researched (see for instance, Higley & Gunther, 1992), their position in the current transformation of European politics has received little specific attention.

To reach a better understanding of the present situation I propose to compare it with a sort of "point zero" in contemporary politics, what we

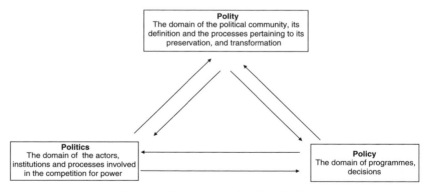

Fig. 1. Three Faces of Political Life.

might call the "pristine" or ideal-typical nation state. The whole discussion will be conducted having on the background a three-dimensional interpretation of political life centred on the concepts of *politics, policy* and *polity* (Fig. 1).

EUROPEAN POLITICAL ELITES IN THE OLD (DANGEROUS) WORLD OF SOVEREIGN NATION STATES

Politics in the "golden age" of democratic sovereign nation states had typically the following characteristics (which are still very much what analysts have in mind when they study political life):

- a relatively well-bounded and coherent political community which (although with some variations) had fairly clearly defined boundaries and a distinctive identity (*polity dimension*);
- a constitutionally defined system of institutions pertaining to that polity where political power and authority over that community (to a great extent) resided; competing national political elites deriving popular support and legitimacy at the national level as a more or less direct consequence of their performances in the fields of internal and international policies (*politics dimension*);
- a set of country-specific policies (i.e. having a space of validity coinciding with that of the polity) (*policy dimension*);
- stronger or weaker external constraints deriving from the position of the polity in the international system (*international dimension*).

This reality could be observed from many different points of view. For the reasons previously specified I will focus on national political elites and their behaviour.

National or domestic political elites are defined here for operational purposes as the group of top politicians who are in government or, even if not being formally part of the government, de facto guide its action (this may be the case of some party leaders who from their position as the head of the membership parties exert their influence over the executive) (Cotta, 2000). This group will typically include the prime minister, the main ministers and the top leadership stratum of the parties in office. To this should be added the leadership stratum of the opposition parties that have a reasonable perspective to take, sooner or later, the place of the incumbents in the government.

In democratic regimes political elites have to compete for the support of the demos, as defined by the boundaries of the polity (but also of particularly important groups within the polity because their control of crucial resources might positively or adversely affect that relationship). In sovereign nation states success in this competition was in the end dependent on the (real or perceived) performances of elites in the two principal domains of political action: the international and the internal arenas.

Performance in the international arena could be measured on the basis of a variable mix of yardsticks: gaining influence in the world, protecting national territory from external encroachments, winning back territories defined in the prevailing political discourse as part of national territory and extracting the best conditions from international commerce. These goals could be achieved either through peaceful or military competition among nations both in Europe (competition for national boundaries and influence) and overseas (the imperialistic competition of the 19th century and of the beginning of the 20th century) or through cooperation with other countries.

This domain of political action proved extremely risky for European states and for their political elites. The lack of an overarching authority made the possibility of war a serious one (Waltz, 1979). Gains and losses to be faced in this domain were (perceived as) extremely significant. If war could bring about expansion and conquest, it could also entail very serious damages to the polity (severe losses of human and material resources, of territories, even the destruction of the polity itself). In this sphere trade and security aspects would often end up being coupled and this meant that opportunities of international economic cooperation were often neglected because of the pre-eminence of the imperatives of security.

There is a large empirical evidence for the fact that results in the international competition could affect domestic political elites: the cases of governing elites being displaced through electoral defeats or even of regime breakdowns because of unfavourable international events are far from rare.[1]

Performance in the internal arena could be measured on the basis of a mix of the following aspects: maintenance of the internal order, promotion of economic development, ability to control social tensions, re-equilibration of social inequalities, distribution of resources to particularistic interests, etc. In fact the ability to build broad coalitions of supporters for redistributive purposes has been a major challenge for political elites throughout the 20th century. Political radicalisation and regime disruption have been a significant risk in the internal domain of politics if the incorporation and mediation of the main societal interests (business, workers, etc.) could not be achieved (Linz, 1978). Considerable empirical evidence can also be found for the impact of this dimension of political action on the success of political elites.

The importance of competition for influence and security among national states in the international arena (to which should be added the difficulties in defining uncontested borders) in the era of national states, proved disastrous in Europe. Total or partial destruction of existing polities and creation on a major scale of new ones were the results of the turbulent international environment prevailing during the first half of the 19th century on the old Continent.[2] In this environment interactions among states could not produce sufficiently significant international institutions with pooled sovereignty or empowered with delegated authority and capable of providing, on a stable basis, cooperative answers to the economic preferences of the states. Given a situation characterised by limited trust among major players and unrestrained competition, sub-optimal solutions typical of the prisoners' dilemma prevailed.

THE "CIVILIANISED" NEW WORLD OF EUROPE AFTER WWII

The crucial step that altered significantly this situation was the political earthquake brought about by the Second World War and the deep restructuring of the international arena which soon after that event, with the freezing of the "two blocks system", produced in Europe a strong and stable international regime. In this new political environment most European countries fell directly under the protective/directive umbrella of the great powers; a few others remained neutral, but even they could not avoid being affected by the new order and found themselves as the former countries in a much more constrained international condition than in the past. This meant that in spite of some remaining differences – colonial vs. non-colonial powers; winners vs. losers, big vs. small countries, etc. – there was for all European countries a fundamental loss in terms of freedom of action in the international arena. Persisting differences among countries were relevant more for the impact they had upon the speed in perceiving change than for their effects upon the real conditions of the new situation.[3]

In a situation where security was fundamentally assured through the participation in one of the two blocks (or by a sort of self-exclusion from action on the international arena via neutrality), the performances of domestic political elites in the international arena lost a good part of their uncertainty[4] and thus also much of their importance for domestic competition (unless a political party wanted to question affiliation and loyalty to the block its country belonged to).[5] International performances remained important mainly for what concerned trade matters (that is for the external projections of internal economic problems and interests).

To a much greater extent than in the past domestic political elites were left to deal with internal affairs only. It is probably no coincidence that the great development of the welfare state happened in Europe after the Second World War (Flora & Heidenheimer, 1981): welfare took the place of warfare as the dominant preoccupation of political life. This phenomenon can be interpreted not only as a consequence of the ability to shift resources from external security to internal affairs, but also as a compensation for the loss of a domain of political action: once that there was not much to be gained for political elites out of promoting and boosting national influence in the world in front of the internal public, it became more important to pay attention to internal successes. The diminished importance of the international domain obviously did not apply to the leading countries of the two blocks, for which the "imperial" dimension (both in its civil and military aspects) remained a fundamental component of politics.

An important consequence of the new world order is what we might call the "civilianisation" of the politics of Western Europe under the umbrella of American authority (and of Eastern Europe, albeit in rather different forms, under the rule of the Soviet Union). The chances of military conflicts among the countries of each block were drastically curtailed: the case of Greece and Turkey shows that if the potential for conflicts on sovereignty matters was not totally erased, yet the possibility of a war was strongly constrained (it is easy to imagine what could have happened if NATO had not existed).

The two blocks, often defined by international relations theory as "international regimes", can in fact be conceptualised as two new *meta-polities*, overshadowing the persisting nation states and downgrading them and their political leadership to what we might define as a semi-sovereign status. For the purpose of this analysis we can leave aside the Eastern block and focus on the Western one. With its creation the nation states of Western Europe became part of a new *Atlantic polity*. We can define it as a polity as it entailed well-established borders (and rules deciding who belonged to it and who did not); a reinvention of political geography (the cleavage line between Western and Eastern Europe relegated the concept of *Mitteleuropa* to the field of literature only); an articulated cultural identity (the "Western World") with institutions designed for reinforcing it (elite exchange programs, etc.) and for sustaining *we/they* feelings vis-à-vis the other meta-polity; rights and duties attached to being part of it.

We can detect also some important elements of a *new Atlantic politics*. This comprised a system of legitimate political authority residing in the political institutions of the US and of NATO (whose legitimacy was not based on electoral democratic processes, which obviously did not exist for an Atlantic polity as such, but on their ability to preserve democracy from the Soviet threat) and governing over that polity in some crucial policy domains (all matters linked to international security); constraints on some outcomes of national politics (anti-NATO parties excluded from government); the legitimation of national political elites reinforced through proper mechanisms of the new polity (approval from and regular visits to Washington). National politics was fundamentally downgraded to "internal/low politics".

With regard to the policy domain the new order entailed that some crucial *policies* (the hard core of foreign and security policies) were "coextensive" with the new polity, while the other ones remained within the borders of the old national polities.

I have spent a few words on this reality, because the process of European integration (with its successes and its limitations) probably cannot be explained without the Atlantic umbrella (Lundestad, 1998). The existence of an overarching external authority (and organisation) in the field of security made it easier to reach agreements in the other fields of international matters (essentially commercial questions) among European countries. As these questions could now be decoupled from security imperatives, it became easier to reach Pareto optimal economic agreements, as suggested by Moravcsik's (1999) analysis of European integration. At the same time this situation seriously restricted the domain of "European only" agreements and integration to fields that did not touch security matters. To move in that field would have meant for European institutions to face a powerful and successful competitor (the American-European NATO).

European integration can be viewed therefore as an initially small seed, slowly and gradually developing within an internationally protected niche and in the realm of policy areas that were not dominated by political conflicts as dramatic as the security ones. It can be suggested that Europe was nurtured, but at the same time pre-empted and prevented (in the domains of security policy) by the existence of the Atlantic block and NATO. The two views do not seem to be contradictory. "Low politics" integration (in the field of trade and economic cooperation) was made easier because of a protective security environment (not dominated by European nation states). "High politics" integration (in the field of security) of Europe was on the contrary made impossible by the existence of a more effective contender.

Because of the timing and paces of the two processes of supra-national integration (the Atlantic and European ones) the meta-polity within which European nation states developed after WWII was for some time more Atlantic than European. Public opinion data collected in European countries in the 1950s show for instance that attitudes towards the US were generally more positive than those towards the other European nations, and that those who supported Europe were very much those supporting the Atlantic alliance.[6] For a long time, thus, Westernisation counted more than Europeanisation.

A SYSTEM OF PARTLY NESTED AND PARTLY CONCURRENT POLITIES AND ITS DEVELOPMENT

For the core of Europe the political landscape of the second half of the 20th century was thus defined by three different polities: the nation states, the Atlantic alliance and the European Union. At the borders of this system existed "partial members" (i.e. members of NATO only, such as Greece and Portugal until the end of the 1970s, Norway and Turkey to this day, or members of the European Union (EU) only, as Ireland and then Austria, Finland and Sweden), "excluded countries" (Spain until the 1970s) and states we might call "free riders" since they profited from this international order without being institutionally part of it (Sweden until 1994, Switzerland).

The three polities have different borders (but for a long time never crosscutting) and work on the basis of a rather clear division of labour with regard to policy areas, and of specific patterns of authority. Political elites, which have basically maintained their national bases, have adapted to this complex environment. This has meant that through institutionalised mechanisms of cooperation national political elites act also in some way as the political elites of the two meta-polities. As a consequence, they have been increasingly involved in "two levels games" (Putnam, 1988), as in many fields decisions have to be ratified both at a national and at a supra-national levels. This entails also that elites can use the constraints imposed at one level to their freedom of action as instruments for strengthening their positions at the other level.

Within this peculiar political environment the most striking phenomenon of the last decades is obviously the growth of European integration along two main dimensions – the scope of its competencies on one side, the extension of its membership on the other (what is currently called deepening and widening). We must then discuss what have been its effects upon domestic politics.

Both developments are clear indicators of the success of European integration. Whether the increasing number of policy areas where the EU has acquired powers to intervene is just the result of repeated but unconnected convergences of national preferences as some interpretations would put it (Moravcsik, 1998), or is the effect of the institutional mechanisms at the European level and of their progressive (and sometimes unintended) buildup, as others would prefer to say (Pierson, 1996; Dyson & Featherstone, 1999), it is in any case an undisputable sign of the vitality of the European polity and of the growing predisposition it produces in its members to reach agreements among themselves (owing to growing reciprocal confidence, a greater convergence of interests, the success of its institutional mechanisms).

As for enlargement, although it is common to underline the problems created by it to the cumbersome decision-making processes of the Community, it should also be seen as an important proof of the success of this polity. The new entries have been a repeated favourable plebiscite for the Community, as it has been shaped by its development, and for its institutional arrangements. The consequence of this has also been the reduced bargaining powers of the newcomers and the growing costs of exclusion for the countries left outside.

Extension of competencies and widening are to an extent linked together. New countries have raised new policy demands thus stimulating a broadening of the scope of the European Community. This in turn has produced a greater ability to accommodate the interests of different member countries through different policy programmes.[7]

The result of these developments (to which we should add changes in the international environment) is that in the last years the balance between the three types of polities relevant in Europe has changed significantly. I will not discuss here its possible consequences for the Atlantic polity but only for the national polities. The policy and the polity dimensions are directly involved, but it is easy to understand that the politics dimension will also be affected by this transformation.

CONSEQUENCES OF THESE TRANSFORMATIVE TRENDS FOR THE DOMESTIC POLITICS OF EUROPEAN STATES

After WWII the *Atlantic polity* had to a great extent "extracted" matters of international security from the scope of responsibility of European nation states thus creating: (a) a security community (polity dimension); (b) a superior political authority in this field (politics dimension) and (c) an area of policies specific to the new polity (policy dimension). Nation states had consequently been deprived of this responsibility and national political elites had lost (to a great extent) the ability to perform effectively in this domain, but also the risk to fail dramatically (successes and failures were shifted to the shoulders of the US political elites).[8]

The internal domains of policy-making (economic growth, employment, levels of inflation and social redistribution) were thus left as the main domains with respect to which performances of domestic elites had to be evaluated at home. Even if constrained by international economic factors, domestic elites maintained a wide array of instruments (manipulation of exchange rates, controls over the labour market, variations in welfare expenditures, recourse to public borrowing and expansion of debt, subsidies to domestic firms and patronage, public monopolies, etc.) for enhancing/protecting their performances at home.

The deepening and widening of Europe has produced some important consequences for this equilibrium. The most obvious aspects concern the policy dimension, but the politics and polity dimensions are also significantly involved.

The fact that an increasing number of policy areas have been upgraded to a "European size" has meant that decisions concerning them are taken at the supra-national level and that their sphere of application and enforcement has become the European Union rather than the nation state (Fig. 2). The policy repertoire which was previously typical of nations states and of their domestic political processes has been significantly depleted. A crucial turning point in this development was undoubtedly the deliberation first and then the implementation of the European Monetary Union (EMU) coming on top of the completion of the Single Market. With the EMU and its practical consequences, such as the Stability Pact, some major instruments for manipulating internal economic performances have been lost by domestic elites or have been severely curtailed for them (as far as they are playing the political game individually at home, not of course when they play it collectively in the European arena).

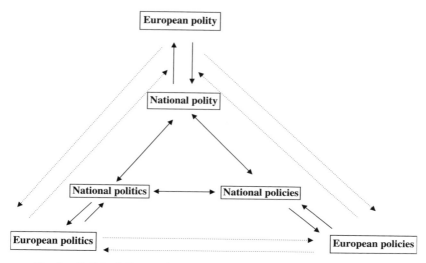

Fig. 2. Political Connections between European and National Level.

Besides its obvious relevance for the policy dimension of political life, this phenomenon has had implications also for the polity and the politics dimensions. On the polity level, it has increasingly contributed to defining a common European space, which has become internally more homogeneous (EU countries share many common policies) and differentiated from the external space (non-EU countries adopt different policies). If it is true that policies contribute significantly to the self-definition of a polity, the extension of Europe-wide policies must have strengthened the interpretation of national states as "parts" of a European polity rather than as independent units. On the politics level, since these policies affect the control over the allocation of substantial amounts of collective and individual goods, there is also an important shift of political resources originating from this control from the domestic to the European level of politics.

There is no doubt that European integration has also progressively created something that can be defined as "a European politics". Europe is not just an unstructured terrain where unrestrained national actors meet and confront each other, but an arena where rules, procedures, institutions and their policy competencies are defined by "constitutional" norms that pose rather serious hurdles to modification. True enough, these institutions work according to different principles which the European jargon distinguishes as "supranational" or "intergovernmental". But this vocabulary could be to a good extent converted into one, more familiar in domestic politics, that distinguishes between majoritarian and consensual rule, direct and indirect delegation, accountable and non-accountable authority, etc. European institutions are clearly distinguishable from national institutions even when their members are drawn from domestic institutions. Significant (and increasing) amounts of power and authority are legitimately located in Brussels (or in the other capitals of Europe). Important decisions are taken there and therefore it can be said that there is a new significant power game going on at the European level. Even if there are some European-specific actors – the Commissioners and their staff, the directorate of the European Central Bank (ECB) etc. – and other national actors (such as interest group representatives) who are able to reach the European arena directly without the intermediation of their national governments, this game is predominantly played by national governments (i.e. government heads, ministers, high bureaucrats and diplomats), but acting on a political arena that is different from the one on which they normally operate.

Summing up, over the last 50 years, the environment within which (most) European national states work has undergone major changes, which have also significantly altered crucial aspects of domestic political life (and touching upon its three main dimensions – policy, polity and politics). The creation first of the Atlantic alliance has produced an enhanced security but also reduced the international capacity of European states and civilianised national politics. The development then of a common market and a unified monetary system governed by European institutions have greatly strengthened the common economic chances of European countries, but have also increasingly reduced the scope of internal decisions by member states and domestic elites. At the same time, a European political arena has become increasingly significant.

National political elites are faced with this new situation and its evolutionary trends. At least in part they have lost control over the policies that in the past had been crucial for them in the playing of the democratic game. They are faced with new actors, new ways of deciding and with a new polity, which is not the same as the one within the boundaries of which they have won their position of authority. At the same time, not much has changed with regard to the bases of their political authority: they are still determined by national elections. We must now explore what can be the consequences of these changes for them.

DOMESTIC ELITES' STRATEGIES VIS-À-VIS EUROPE: EXIT, VOICE OR ACQUIESCENCE?

It could be objected that no serious problem exists since domestic elites have obviously agreed to the new situation and have maintained strong control over it. This answer however is not fully convincing. It is true, with regard to the first point, that Europe as it is was produced essentially through unanimous agreements (the treaties). Yet, because of the large amount of pooling of sovereignty and even more of delegation of authority to European institutions involved, an agreement on each step does not mean also the ability to foresee all the cumulative effects (which are also determined by changing conditions at home and abroad). Each agreement may have been the best possible for domestic elites as Moravcsik (1998) would put it, but the same is not guaranteed for all of its consequences (Pierson, 1996). Moreover, the preferences of elites who were part of an agreement can change; and new elites who were not part of a past agreement may have come to power. As for the second point, strong controls (robust veto powers) over European policy-making do not ensure that each national elite can always obtain its most preferred deal (mainly because the costs of a no-deal are often substantial). This means that, in any given moment, the existing equilibrium point between European and domestic politics is not necessarily the optimal one for domestic elites and, at the same time, cannot easily be changed.

When is it that such a situation can become a serious political problem for domestic political elites? The answer that we can suggest is that as far as they are able to obtain what is needed to satisfy their electorate at home via Europe and its policies, nothing should happen. Things will turn differently if domestic elites "underperform" (or foresee a risk of underperforming) at home because of European constraints. Underperforming can mean any of the following things: not being able to deliver enough economic growth and employment or to obtain the preferred exchange rates on the international markets because of the conditions produced by the monetary union and its management; being forced to cut social expenditures to uphold the budgetary standards imposed by the Community; being prevented from delivering patronage to domestic interests because of restrictions imposed by European market rules or being deprived of the use of symbolic goods that had previously proven helpful in mobilising internal consent, etc. It is not unreasonable to assume that these risks can increase significantly when the direct control of national political elites upon policy-making decreases as in the present European situation.

When faced with such situations national political elites might pursue a number of purely internal strategies, such as rebalancing their score by improving their performances in other fields, putting the blame on globalisation, etc. Yet there are probably serious limits to this, also because some of these strategies might be forbidden by existing European regulations. Domestic elites have then to address more directly the problem at the European level where it was produced. If they do not take steps in this direction they could soon be facing internal trouble: the dissatisfaction of voters and the challenge of alternative elites.

There are different "European" strategies national elites may adopt in this situation. To analyse them I will use as a point of departure the seminal discussion of Hirschman (1970) in his book *Exit, Voice and Loyalty* regarding the dilemmas faced by social actors within economic firms or political communities.[9] The two first concepts – exit and voice – which Hirschman uses to indicate the different answers that members of a social group can choose when not satisfied by its performances, can be adopted to designate also two alternative strategies available to national elites to cope with the problems raised by the new advances in European integration. To these I will add a third option – that of acquiescence – which, although in part inspired by the Hirschmanian concept of loyalty, does not fully coincide with it.

Exit (Total or Partial; Opting Out)

Leaving aside the refusal of entry, which is obviously the most extreme reaction in anticipation of the possibility of negative effects deriving from the European polity and its policies, the first possible strategy, when a country belongs to the European Community, to cope with its possible negative effects is to exit. Through full exit, that is to say by abandoning completely the European polity, domestic elites would extract themselves fully from a possible negative impact of European policies, and regain their original freedom of action. Unless we consider the case of Norway that twice, after having negotiated the entry into the Community, decided immediately to leave, so far, such a radical reaction has never taken place, which says a lot about the consolidation of the European polity and the price to be paid for leaving it. A less strong, but also more easily adoptable strategy is that of partial exit, which entails leaving just one (or more) policy domain(s), or not entering into a new one that is in the making (opt out). In fact instances of opting out have become a significant outcome of some recent processes of European integration: one or more countries, without preventing the majority of members to move ahead, have decided not to follow them. Such decisions suggest the existence of potential conflicts between the developmental dynamics of the European core and the domestic requirements of some national elites. The Euro has obviously produced the most important example of opting out: Britain, Denmark and Sweden have preferred not to renounce their currencies and to preserve for the time being a national control of monetary policies.

If the meaning of this strategy is clear what is the balance sheet of benefits and costs deriving for domestic elites from its adoption? Given the fact that national elites play an internal game, but are also involved, because of their role in the institutions of the Union, in a European one we can distinguish between internal and external benefits and costs. With regard to *internal benefits* the consequences of (partial) exit are that political elites will maintain the control at home of a (larger) repertoire of policy instruments which they can use in their governing action and supposedly for building/maintaining electoral support. Moreover, they can capitalise on anti-European feelings that might exist among the voters. As for *internal costs*, it must be reckoned that if the Union develops successfully in the new areas (from which the option of exit or opt out has been decided by a country) the risks of being marginalised may become significant. To this should be added that, even when opting out, the danger of losing control over internal policy instruments is not entirely excluded, especially when the size of the country makes it difficult to isolate its domestic policies from the impact of European policies. Finally, it may happen that some internal sectors of society might feel the need to be integrated in the community and therefore challenge the choices of the national elite. We must also consider the possibility of *external costs*. Partial exit will obviously determine the exclusion of national elites who have adopted this strategy from taking part in the decisions regarding the policy area concerned. But if these areas are significant, it may end up also reducing their ability to play a more global leadership role in the Union and to be at the centre of its dominant coalitions. This is probably what has happened to the British leaders as a result of the exit strategies adopted by them in some important fields of European policy-making.

The balance sheet of costs and benefits will be obviously affected by the specific conditions of the country and by the internal standing of its elites. The possibility of appealing to public opinion in defence of national sovereignty against European encroachments (linking thus more tightly policy, politics and polity) varies significantly among European countries. The access to the resources required for sustaining an exit strategy also differs from country to country: the British pound alone can fare better than the Italian lira or the Greek drachma; oil puts Norway in a situation different from that of Sweden, etc. It is reasonable to assume that with the combined deepening and enlargement of the EU, the costs of exit (and opting out) will tend to increase. Moreover, the ability to maintain control over internal performances even when adopting an exit strategy will diminish. Domestic elites will then have to devise new balancing strategies. At the same time, it is foreseeable that increasing anti-European feelings among (part of) the population, originating from the fear that European integration might endanger special country standards acquired with great sacrifice over the years, could enhance the internal benefits of exit.

Voice

The second strategy – voice – consists of actively promoting national demands at the European level. Elites, faced with the problem of losing control over domestic policy resources, may try to redress the balance by exerting their influence in the European arena with the aim of obtaining European policies that will produce favourable domestic effects. National preferences would thus be transformed into European preferences and, if this strategy succeeds, "domestic underperformance" will be balanced by a European positive performance of national elites. Contrary to the previous strategy by which domestic elites played a defensive game oriented to preserve their national freedom of action in the European arena, with this strategy they play an active game in the political arenas of the Union, trying to use the opportunities offered by the participation in the larger polity to reach their internal goals.

For a voice strategy to be successful domestic political elites must, first of all, have the ability to influence the European agenda and then have the political skills to build and guide at the supra-national level the large coalitions required by Community rules and practices to have their (substantial or institutional) policy proposals passed. Given the peculiar features of European politics, this will normally entail very substantial side payments and prolonged efforts.

With regard to the benefits and costs of this strategy we can propose the following observations. As for the *internal benefits*, national elites opting for voice will regain, by way of the European policy-making process and European policies, at least some amount of the political resources lost at home. They may thus sell to the voters the idea that they can now assure through their influence in Brussels the policy results that they previously managed to produce through the internal policy-making process. They may add to this an increased internal prestige owing to their prominent European role. For example, German elites, when it came to monetary integration in the 1990s, have been able to impose at the European level an institutional model and a policy for the central bank very close to those previously adopted at home. In this way, they could reassure their voters that the stability that would not be safeguarded anymore through domestic institutions would be guaranteed by the European ones that they had to a great extent contributed to shape.

Yet, also with this strategy, *internal costs* are not to be excluded. For the purpose of obtaining a European agreement domestic elites will need to coordinate their action with that of other countries and thus to compromise, at least in part, national preferences. This might trigger internal accusations of betrayal of some national interests. To go back to the previous example the German leadership had to face significant internal criticisms for abandoning such a strong symbol as the D-Mark and for accepting to take on board of the European currency also less rigorous countries (as Italy). To this we should add that a voice strategy might require, for the country adopting it, the need to embark on costly "prestige" policies (French nuclear policies could be one example) to enhance its voice capacities vis-à-vis the other member states.

Under what conditions can we expect domestic elites to adopt voice instead of exit strategies? This should happen when exit strategies are comparatively less convenient: both because the country would lose significantly from being left out of the European process; and because the country is in the position and has the resources to mobilise a favourable coalition on the European front. A crucial condition is also the ability to keep the "domestic front" united behind this choice.

Acquiescence

In Hirschman's treatment loyalty is not a third strategy of action, but a condition pertaining to the relationship between individuals and the collective entity (firm, political community, etc.) to which they belong. The strategies considered are only two. Loyalty is a condition that affects their choice of strategy. The higher the loyalty the greater the chances of selecting voice against exit. Yet in our case (as in others) it seems relevant to discuss a third possible option after the two already mentioned. This option is based on loyalty (and refusal of exit), but does not entail an active role of demand vis-à-vis the supra-national community. This third option is that of accepting decisions taken at the European level even if they are not those preferred by domestic elites and curtail the policy resources they used to control at home.

To stress the passive role of domestic elites I propose to call this option *acquiescence*.

The potential *internal costs* of this option are pretty obvious: acquiescence will mean the acceptance of policies promoted by other European actors which will deprive the domestic elites of resources traditionally used by them to win internal support and which might be significantly different from those preferred by them and by the voters. It is less clear what could be the *internal benefits*. If we compare with an exit strategy they probably consist of the avoidance of internal disapproval from public opinion (or from significant interest groups), which, sharing a strong pro-European orientation, would have been seriously antagonised by the adoption of an exit strategy.

Why should national elites adopt this option? The answer is because they are neither able to push through their agenda in the decision-making arenas of Europe, nor can they accept to see their country excluded from the European process; the only solution left to them is that of adopting a passive position. Under what conditions do we expect such a position to be taken? On one side national political elites must lack the resources and the ability required for pursuing with enough determination a voice strategy in Europe. They are not in a pivotal position for building a favourable coalition in Brussels. They do not have good bargaining chips to put on the table. In contrast, they face internally a strong pressure to pursue a European path because there are rooted and diffuse pro-European feelings among the mass public and crucial groups, and this majority opinion is not seriously challenged by any significant anti-European counter-mobilisation of similar important groups. The need to be part of the European process prevails then over policy matters.

From the point of view of domestic elite, this option is clearly the weakest of the three. Contrary to the other two strategies, it can neither restore nor compensate the resources lost by domestic elite as a result of the process of European integration.

So far I have discussed the possible choices faced by domestic elites as if they were three fully independent options. It is reasonable however to ask whether it is possible for domestic elites to adopt a mix of the different strategies sketched here. The answer should be positive: to a certain extent voice, (partial) exit, acquiescence can be combined; but there are probably some limitations to this. Exit or the threat of it can be used as a bargaining chip to strengthen voice positions, but in the end such a strategy may undermine voice if the country using it ends up being left out of the dominant European coalition. If the strategy of voice does not succeed, the elite of a country might resort to exit or fall back into acquiescence. But typically, a political elite geared for exercising voice will not easily take into consideration the possibility of abandoning the game through exit. Furthermore, when acquiescence is the prevalent attitude, it will probably be difficult to find the instruments to sustain voice; at the same time it will be difficult to explain exit.

CONSEQUENCES OF THE DIFFERENT STRATEGIES FOR NATIONAL ELITES IN THE DOMESTIC AND IN THE EUROPEAN ARENAS

What are the foreseeable consequences of the adoption of the different strategies by domestic elites? In assessing them we must obviously start from their effects at home: in the end it is at home that the political future of democratic elites is decided. There will also be implications for politics at the European level: we should not forget that the domestic elites of the member states put together constitute the political elite of the European Community.

Elites adopting an *exit strategy* will see their national role reinforced or at least maintained: by managing to protect or restore a broader area of policy-making from external encroachments they will preserve their freedom of action at home. They will thus continue to be able to use some of the traditional policy instruments for building electoral support in the national arena. If exit is not complete but only partial their role will be that of "filtering" europeanisation, that is of selecting out of the European menu what is more acceptable for their internal strategies and discarding what is more threatening. This strategy will be domestically rewarding up to the point when the isolation of the country from supra-national integration becomes a liability. If the advantages produced by integration prove to be more substantial than expected for the other member states, the choice of going alone may turn out to be short sighted. This will be compounded by the fact that the elites of a country adopting this strategy will be weakened in their ability to influence the developments of the European polity unless they are able to put together a sufficiently large blocking group.

Domestic elites adopting a *voice strategy* will reinforce, if they are successful, their national role through the acquisition of a stronger European role. In fact the second will become for them an important instrument for playing the first. Material and symbolic resources won in the supra-national arena will be put to work in the domestic one. Domestic elites can then boast to national voters about the prestige gained in the European arena and show that they can satisfy their demands in a way that is different, but not less successful, than that of domestic policy-making. The crux of the matter is whether what is gained "in Europe" is enough to compensate what is lost at home.

This strategy has an important collateral effect at the European level: because of their strong projection in the supra-national arenas national elites adopting it are in the best position to become the real core of the political elite of the European polity even while maintaining their national role. To reach their (domestic) goals, they have to devote very substantial efforts to the participation in the decision-making processes at the European level (trying to define the European agenda, working in the institutions of Brussels, building coalitions with other national elites, etc.). Through this activism they will gain a more central role in the supra-national arena than the other national elites and this will, in turn, put them in a better position to succeed in their voice strategy.

This is not to say that this strategy is devoid of risks. It may in fact happen that national elites, fully engaged in their European voice strategy with all its bargaining complexities, may lose touch with public opinion at home and find out, at the end of the game, that what they have won in the supra-national decision-making arena is not exactly what voters at home expect. This is perhaps what happened recently to the French leadership that after having significantly contributed to steer the European constitutional convention, was faced at home with an astonishing rejection in the referendum of the results achieved.

Elites adopting the *acquiescence option* run a bigger risk: that of being downgraded to "subordinate" elites. They have little weight and autonomy at the European level and are strongly constrained internally because they are not able to influence European decisions and to deflect the unwanted effects of these upon the domestic system. As a consequence, the domestic system will be more permeable to European influences and, to a greater extent than in the two other situations, national elites will stand to lose control over its functioning. There will be greater incentives for domestic interest groups to try to bypass national elites (who are perceived as not able to protect their interests and to promote effectively their demands) and to look for direct access to European authorities. A serious crisis of the domestic elite and the rise of internal challengers pushing either in the exit or in the voice direction could be the extreme consequences of such a situation. At the European level these national elites will have a role of followers rather than leaders in the decision-making processes. Their votes will add up, but without great influence upon the direction of the march of the Community.

SOME PRELIMINARY EVIDENCE FROM THE ITALIAN CASE

To be fully validated, this general analytic scheme would require a systematic empirical research of the behaviour of national elites and of its consequences. As a first step in this direction, I will introduce here some exploratory evidence from one case, that of Italy. A number of elements make it an interesting one. Italy was one of the founding members of the EC; it is a large country but one that is normally considered as not very influential in European matters; at the same time it has displayed a strong (and up to the 1990s growing) support for European integration (Fig. 3). Moreover, there is a chronological coincidence between a period of strong deepening of the European integration, when important transfers of sovereignty have occurred (the adoption of the Maastricht Treaty, the preparation period for the establishment of the EMU and its implementation), and a crucial phase for the Italian political system when a long-term domestic equilibrium has been deeply shaken and a significant "elite revolution" has taken place (Cotta & Verzichelli, 1996).

For all these reasons, Italy seems a promising case for studying the strategies adopted by domestic elites to understand what factors explain them, and also to explore the effects of these strategies upon the domestic political game.

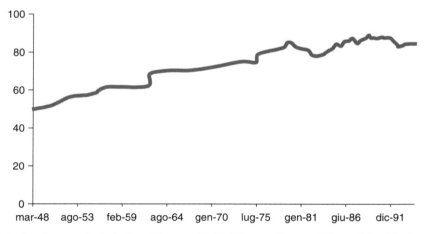

Fig. 3.   Support in Italy for Efforts to Unify Western Europe (Three-Point Moving Average) (data and figure kindly provided by Pierangelo Isernia).

The preliminary empirical evidence for what concerns the choice of strategies during the period of the great European transformation of the 1990s seems fairly clear: acquiescence has clearly prevailed over exit and voice even if the costs of this strategy for domestic political elites appear to have been substantial. It is currently acknowledged that the process of monetary integration in Europe has been led by Germany and France (Dyson & Featherstone, 1999; Moravcsik, 1998), and that Italy has followed suit, paying more attention to avoiding the risk of being excluded from it (Dyson & Featherstone, 1999, pp. 486–495) rather than attempting to direct the course of this policy. Acceptance of European policies in the field of monetary integration has entailed for Italy a very serious fiscal adjustment between 1990 and 1997: the highest combined increase of taxation ($+4\%$) and decrease of public spending (-3.2%) in Europe (Padoa Schioppa Kostoris, 2000). If we add the two indicators together, we have a sort of "European loyalty index", on which Italy scores 7.2 points, the highest value for all the 11 Euro countries. This fiscal adjustment has entailed a serious slowdown of investments and it can be surmised also of economic growth (Italian growth rates have indeed been constantly below the European average during this period).

If we read this story from the point of view of domestic political elites, we have a situation where they have substantially lost ground in terms of quantitative and qualitative control over expendable resources. They have been forced to spend less (mainly by way of cuts to infrastructural investments and transfers to local authorities) and under greater constraints deriving from externally defined regulations. This has produced a decreased ability to win the support of electoral clienteles through the traditional distributive micro-policies (Cotta, 1996). At the same time, they have had to increase the tax burden falling upon a large part of the electorate, hardly a way to compensate for the other aspect.

Why have Italian elites chosen acquiescence (at least to a predominant extent) rather than pursuing exit or voice? If we consider that traditionally Italian politicians had relied strongly upon distributive policies for building and maintaining their bases of popular support, even if this had meant over time a staggering buildup of state debt (Cotta & Isernia, 1996), we might be surprised by the fact that apparently, they have accepted so easily the new European policy course even if it implied significant costs for them.

The "idealistic" explanation is that Italian political elites were strongly pro-European and were therefore prepared to face the sacrifices to uphold their faith. Evidence for this interpretation can be easily found in the recurrent pro-European declarations of parties, new cabinets and countless political leaders. Yet this explanation seems a rather weak one: a more careful analysis of pro-European statements suggests that in the previous years they were made in a rather perfunctory way and never had a crucial role in the political platforms of the governing parties (Conti & Verzichelli, 2005). The more realistic explanation is that they were not able to follow a different path. For a number of reasons any other strategy was precluded to them (and the pro-European utterances were more an embellishment of this than substance).

Why was exit unsustainable and voice not a realistic option? I suggest here that an *exit strategy* was clearly a non-starter because of the even heavier political costs it would have entailed. European integration had been used from its very beginning by governing elites as an important component of their political legitimation. The ability of centrist parties to ensure to the electorate the linkage of Italy to the "European train" (an image frequently used in the media language to define the position of the country vis-à-vis the Community) of stabler democracies/richer economies had been recurrently presented as a crucial component of their performance, as it is clearly shown by a systematic analysis of election manifestos and party declarations (Conti & Verzichelli, 2005).[10] The benefits and costs of specific European policies had been much less at the centre of political attention, as if the dominant question was more the fact of belonging to a larger and safer community than the policies this community produced (Cotta, 1992). From the 1970s onwards, the leading opposition party (the Communist Party) had also increasingly used the European element to gain acceptance into the political system. First, by developing the concept of Euro-communism, then, once this strategy had proven unsuccessful,[11] by going to great lengths to win admission into the European Socialist Party, and by presenting the European Community as the positive embracing community at the moment when the Soviet Community had to be refused and the Atlantic one, even if accepted, could not be proposed to its followers as the main symbol of political good.

These internal elite positions were matched by a broad support for Europe in the public opinion (Ammendola & Isernia, 2005). This support at the mass level had increased over time and had proven extremely stable. To determine in which way elite and mass attitudes towards European attitudes have been related to one another is a relevant research question that cannot be addressed at length here. It seems sufficient to suggest that, if political elites may have been at first ahead of the masses in supporting the European enterprise, later their success in convincing public opinion of the advantages of integration had produced a situation where it would have been rather difficult for elected politicians not to conform to the predominant Europhilia of the population.

Table 1.   Italian Mass Attitudes on Europe and National Identity: Some
Preliminary Findings.

(a) National Pride	
Very/rather proud of being Italian	92%
Proud of Italy	
For its institutions	16%
For its world influence	30%
Economic successes	46%
Army	52%
Scientific/technological results	81%
Sport	82%
Art and nature	93%
(b) *Different Measures of Support for Europe*	
Very/somewhat favourable to European unification	89%
Europe good thing for Italy	83%
Very/somewhat sorry if EU dissolved	70%
More advantages than disadvantages	63%
(c) *Eurobarometer Idealistic Support*	+39%
(Net support minus net benefit: it shows those that support Europe in spite of lack of benefits)	
(d) *Confidence in National and European Government*	
Your personal interests are better protected	
By EU institutions	47%
By Italian government	24%
e) *Favour Euro against Lira*	79%

Data from CIRCaP mass survey (1999) – questions a, d, e – and Eurobarometer (1998).

Such predominantly pro-European feelings of Italian population have persisted until recently (as is shown by Eurobarometers and by the national surveys conducted in 1999 and 2001 by CIRCaP of Siena which provide a more detailed picture about them) (Table 1). Any government adopting an exit strategy at a time when Europe was moving a crucial step ahead would have easily run into the risk of being accused in front of public opinion by its opponents of betraying the consolidated assumption that Italy's well being is best assured by being fully part of an integrated Europe.

In contrast, pursuing a *voice* strategy would have meant for Italian political elites to fight, during the Maastricht Treaty negotiations, for less stringent criteria for the participation in the EMU or, after the Treaty was approved, for a more lax interpretation of the criteria or for a delay in its implementation. There are some signs that attempts were made in this direction (Bini-Smaghi, Padoa-Schioppa, & Papadia, 1994, p. 23; Dyson & Featherstone, 1999, p. 511; Ferrera & Gualmini, 2004; Cavatorto, 2005), but they mostly failed or were not pursued with determination beyond a very preliminary stage (Moravcsik, 1998).[12] The reason is that the whole Euro affair was dominated (once the UK had decided on "opting out", i.e. for an exit strategy) by a very strong alliance of the two strongest *voice* positions in this field (France and Germany). The weakness of the Italian negotiating position had much to do with the macroeconomic and budgetary record of Italy, which originated directly from the way Italian political elites had conducted themselves in the domestic competition during the previous 10–15 years (using high levels of deficit spending to finance distributive policies, piling up a huge public debt and frequently making recourse to competitive devaluations of the lira) (Cotta & Isernia, 1996). Moreover, it is not even clear whether a voice strategy pushing for less stringent conditions would have been supported by a large sector of domestic public opinion. In fact during these years the fiscal profligacy of governing elites had been increasingly under attack at home by opinion leaders and technocrats who asked explicitly for more stringent external constraints with the purpose of imposing "virtue" on domestic politicians.

Italian political elites were thus squeezed between a strong Franco-German voice strategy that was difficult to challenge and massive internal support for Europe. Acquiescence (with limited adjustments) was thus the most probable outcome.

A point that should be discussed more thoroughly is whether in fact, as it is sometimes suggested, Italian elites pursued deliberately a strategy of acquiescence in the European arena in order to be *forced to do* what they in any case would have *preferred to do* (i.e. policies of financial austerity), but were not able to because of internal opposition. There are undoubtedly some elements of truth in this interpretation, provided that a distinction is made between different elite groups. It is well known that some non-elective components of the Italian elites (technocrats, economic experts and even some representatives of the central bureaucracy) shared this kind of reasoning and sometimes did not refrain from proclaiming it explicitly. European constraints were for them the only way to discipline the domestic political game. This interpretation, however, seems much less plausible for the greatest part of the elective elites. To affirm that they were in reality averse to the typical policies they had systematically pursued in the past and that they deliberately wanted to undermine them, would require strong positive evidence. We have on the contrary significant evidence that domestic elites had recurrently tried to "protect" themselves from Europe even when accepting its policies. The long Italian record of delays in the application of European directives can be interpreted as an instrument for reducing the negative effects (for domestic elites) of Community policies that they had not been fully able to influence according to their political preferences (Giuliani, 1992). Why, otherwise, such strong champions of Europeanism should have dragged their feet in implementing policy goals they shared? Some specific evidence that Italian political elites were not so keen to change past domestic practices can be found also in the way adaptation to the Maastricht criteria was pursued when it was time to implement the treaty. Rather than touching seriously at current expenditure (social expenditure and costs for public employment, etc.), governing elites preferred to cut investments and to increase taxation in part automatically, owing to the effects of inflation, and partly by shifting – via the so-called "Tax for Europe" – some of the responsibility on the strong shoulders of the European Community. Large-scale privatisation of state-owned assets was another instrument.[13] Italian politicians knew that they had no realistic alternative to accepting European policies, at the same time they were not so willing to cut the branches on which Italian electoral politics had been sitting for long. Their behaviour, more than being characterised as one of pursuing through "European means" what they could not achieve with the instruments offered by domestic politics, was that of adapting to something that was largely outside their control and had to be reckoned with.

It is true that in this way Italy "was saved by Europe" (Ferrera & Gualmini, 2004), and that some of the most serious vices of domestic policy-making, in particular the predominance of distributive and spending coalitions, were partially corrected owing to the constraints imported from outside. It is less clear, however, that this was the main goal pursued by elected politicians.

INTERNAL CONSEQUENCES OF ACQUIESCENCE

After this preliminary exploration of the European course followed by Italian political elites it is time to discuss what may have been its internal consequences. Acquiescence to European developments has had the obvious advantage of preserving continuity with the traditional pro-European position of the country and of saving domestic political elites from a conflict with the long term pro-European attitudes of the population (and of great part of the opinion makers). Adopting during the negotiation of the Maastricht Treaty an exit strategy, as the one chosen by Britain with the opt out clause, would have been extremely difficult to justify in view of that tradition and of the predominant orientations of public opinion. Moreover, later, when it came to the implementation of EMU it is easy to imagine what could have been reactions in the media and in mass public opinion if Italy had been left outside (by its own choice or by that of the other European partners). In particular, given the new political landscape that had developed following the crisis of the traditional governing parties and of the political elites expressed by them (Cotta & Verzichelli, 1996), there was a rather clear perception among the politicians, then at the helm of government, that an exclusion of Italy from the Euro would have strengthened the secessionist positions of the Lega, the new strong party of Northern Italy. This party would have been able to exploit such an event portraying it as a serious failure of Italian central government and a consequence of the inefficiency of the Italian state burdened by the weight of the South.[14] We should also remember that the Italian government, during the period leading to the Euro decision of 1998, was supported by a coalition of parties that would not easily have weathered a serious challenge to its legitimacy. Its margins of victory in the popular vote had been small and it was particularly weak in some of the richest and most advanced regions of the country (North-west and North-east); the opposition was still angrily protesting for having been deprived of its place in government "through a parliamentary coup" in 1994;[15] and the largest party of the coalition was the Left Democrats (DS), the main successors of the Communist Party, then in office for the first time and a party for which, as we mentioned before, the adoption of a pro-European policy stance had been a crucial element of its legitimacy.

Nevertheless, it is worth remembering that the steps taken to win admission into the EMU, in addition to the other recent developments of European integration (in particular the whole process of completion of the single market), have rather clearly reduced the ability of domestic elites to control some important instruments of political action. The possibilities of using competitive devaluations are gone; budgetary policies are now under strong European oversight; the public sector has had to be shrunken very significantly; state aids to industrial firms and to disadvantaged regions have been seriously curtailed and must now follow more stringent European rules. This suggests that some well-established means, which the Italian politicians had used extensively in the past for winning popular consensus and the support of important interest groups have been lost or were at least seriously weakened.

At the same time, Italian domestic elites have not significantly increased their influence in the European arena. We have thus a situation where the domestic position of political elites appears to be significantly altered: a serious reduction in their freedom of internal action with no comparable gains in terms of external influence. This seems a fertile ground for changes. Political elites losing crucial resources should either adapt to the new situation by transforming themselves to gain new political instruments or else face the challenge of new elites and possibly give way to them.

Do we find evidence that something of this kind has happened during these years? A positive answer does not seem unwarranted. It is easy in fact to point to the temporal coincidence between the critical phase of the adaptation of domestic policies to Europe, owing to the completing of the European single market, the signing and ratification of the Maastricht Treaty and the beginnings of the preparations to its implementation and the dramatic crisis the Italian governing elites, continuously in power since 1948, have had to face. Challenged from different sides (new parties such as the Lega, reform movements such as the one promoting the referenda for changing the electoral laws, plus the prosecuting branch of the judiciary strongly supported by public opinion and the mass media) the old elites expressed by Christian Democracy, Socialist Party and the other small "lay" parties (Republicans, Social-Democrats, Liberals) were rapidly disrupted and displaced (Cotta & Isernia, 1996; Cotta & Verzichelli, 1996; Bufacchi & Burgess, 1998). After that a complicated process of rebuilding and restructuring of domestic elites began to unfold.

This is surely not to say that during this period the adaptation to Europe was the only crucial factor in the demise of the old elites. Yet its relevance within a wider syndrome of factors cannot be easily dismissed. If we accept a *Tocquevillian-Paretian* explanation of the crisis of Italian elites, and suggest that the success of the multiple external challenges was due to the fact that these elites had been seriously weakened, not so much by these challengers, but by the loss of some of the crucial resources for mobilising electoral support they had controlled in the past, and it was this which opened the road for the new challengers (Cotta, 1996; Cotta & Verzichelli, 1996), then the relevance of the European connection becomes plausible. Undoubtedly, the serious decline of internal resources available for sustaining the traditional distributive policies on which Italian elites had largely counted in the past was to a great extent a result of their own doing. In the 1980s the "large public deficits-growing public debt-rising interests rates" spiral had started eating away the resources available for distributive purpose (Verzichelli, 1996). With the end of the 1980s and the beginning of the 1990s, the European developments had put an extra pressure on the correction of budgetary policies and thus necessarily on the reduction of expenditures.

At the same time, they were putting monetary policies and other internal policies under growing control. On the one hand, domestic elites were falling under stronger constraints; on the other, the difficulties of the internal adjustment to European requirements severely exposed in front of the media and thus of public opinion their inadequacy in keeping pace with European transformations. The potential risks deriving from this that Italy could be excluded from the future developments of European integration were becoming widely felt.

In the following years the vacuum left by the crisis of the old elites opened a delicate phase of reconstruction and consolidation of new elites and this happened to coincide precisely with the implementation period of the EMU, that is to say when the stringent standards set by the EU had to be met by Italy. The centre-left alliance of the *Ulivo*, combining in an unprecedented way former communists and splinters of the old Christian democracy, had to pass the European test (which required adopting austerity and free market measures) while it attempted to consolidate itself. Passing the European test with honour was not enough to achieve its consolidation. In fact Prodi, the Prime Minister under whom the lira made it into the euro, was quickly dismissed and subsequently sent into "political exile" in Brussels![16] And before the next elections three different centre-left cabinets followed. The difficulties the government alliance faced in making the centre and left work together had to a significant extent to do also with the austere policies pursued to achieve the European goal.[17]

One might ask at this point whether, given the strong pro-European feelings of Italian public opinion, the European loyalty of governing elites has increased popular support for the national government thus compensating for the costs of implementing the European decisions. That does not seem to have been the case. Our data indicate that popular support for national institutions remains low and people have more confidence in European institutions than in the national government as an instrument for protecting their rights (Table 1). It seems then that the advantages of integration were ascribed to the European Community, and the costs to the domestic elites! These data suggest a rather problematic situation for national political elites increasingly squeezed between popular support for supra-national institutions and the costs of integration they have to impose on the citizens.

Is this situation going to change, and how? Will Italian mass attitudes vis-à-vis Europe begin to transform? Can we expect that Italians, instead of directing towards domestic elites their dissatisfaction with austere domestic policies induced by European constraints, thus perpetuating a strong pro-European attitude and high levels of dissatisfaction towards the domestic government, will begin to express a greater Euro-scepticism?

Given the strong tradition of support for Europe and the difficulty in perceiving which among the internal policies is dictated by Brussels, unless the political debate begins to focus on this, a spontaneous change in mass attitudes is probably not in the cards. It is easier to hypothesise some re-adjustments on the side of elites which are directly affected by the new situation and have a better perception of the nature of the multi-level political game. We should therefore expect that either the elites in power (squeezed between costs of Europeanisation and public support for Europe) will try to strengthen their voice at the European level to obtain less costly European policies or that proposals for partial exit/opt out (so far unheard of in the Italian political establishment) will be put forward by less conventional political forces. In fact some signs of change going in these directions came from the past Berlusconi government, under which both strategies of voice and exit began to receive a greater consideration than before. More than once the prime minister or the finance minister openly expressed willingness to put up a strong fight in Brussels for the modification of the Stability Pact; in the end, however, this remained more a rhetorical position for internal consumption than a serious policy initiative at European level. The "voice" was heard more at home than abroad. As for exit, there was indeed a greater readiness to opt out of some European initiatives, as in the field of common military procurements or against certain steps in the direction of judiciary coordination. Probably, the strongest act indicating a disaffection vis-à-vis Europe was the decision to side with the US rather than with France and Germany on Iraq. Formally, we cannot term this choice an exit option since the EU had not taken an official position on that matter. It signalled however the readiness of the centre-right governing elite not to consider European cohesion as its primary goal. Finally, politicians of the centre-right have started to play with idea of putting the blame on Europe (and especially on the euro) to justify their domestic failures.

CONCLUDING REMARKS

This limited presentation of the Italian case is obviously not enough to provide the exhaustive empirical evidence that would be required for fully validating the theoretical framework developed in the previous pages. It has however offered some useful hints to suggest that this is a relevant direction of research to be pursued. The discussion of other cases, where political elites seem to have adopted, in a more resolute way, the strategies of voice and exit, would add important elements for a better understanding of the factors explaining these choices and for assessing their consequences. If one were to develop this analysis, France and Germany would be particularly suitable cases for exploring problems and implications of a voice strategy; the United Kingdom for those of a (partial) exit strategy. In the previous pages I have in fact briefly mentioned instances where the political elites of these countries have adopted these strategies, indicating also some of the problems related to them. Obviously, none of the cases can be fully reduced to one specific strategy only. We have seen, also from the Italian one, that the predominant option (in that case acquiescence) did not completely exclude elements of the other two. Other cases would probably reproduce some mix of strategies, yet we must probably expect that during a defined period of time a country and its political elite will predominantly be characterised by one of the three options.

What seems sufficiently clear is that, to understand what will happen on the European scene and on the national scenes of member states, we must pay more attention to the special position of domestic political elites who are increasingly challenged by the double role they play, being at the same time involved in the domestic game (where their political fate is in the end decided) and in the European one. The combination of opportunities and constraints deriving from this double environment is what increasingly stimulates their choice of strategies. Through the analysis of these we will gain a better understanding of the links between the two main polities coexisting in Europe, the nation state and the supra-national union.

NOTES

1. The breakdown of democracy in Weimar Germany is perhaps one of the most extreme cases.

2. On one side the destruction of the Austrian empire and partially of the German and Russian empires, on the other the birth of Austria, Czechoslovakia, Estonia, Hungary, Lithuania, Latvia, Poland, Ukraine and Yugoslavia. Some of the new states disappeared again either during the inter-war period (Armenia, Azerbaijan, Georgia and Ukraine) or after the Second World War (such as the Baltic States) or their boundaries were dramatically altered (Germany and Poland).

3. France and the United Kingdom had to wait for the Suez crisis to come to terms with their reduced international role.

4. For colonial powers decolonisation problems have maintained significant importance, but they did not entail any more competition with other European

countries; one could say that they have become "internal" matters that concern the question of citizenship, political rights.

5. This was a factor that for a long time has made the Communist Party unacceptable for governing roles in Italy.

6. For a discussion of some of these data gathered by the United States Information Agency (USIA) see Ammendola and Isernia (2005).

7. By this expansion certain countries profit more from some policies (France, for instance, from the Common Agricultural Policy) and other countries from other policies (Spain and Portugal from cohesion policy).

8. It is easy to notice how international failures (Johnson, Carter) or successes (Nixon, Reagan) have weighted for the popularity of American leaders.

9. For a preliminary attempt to use these concepts to analyse elite strategies in Europe see Cotta (1997). These notions have been used for the European context also by Weiler (1999).

10. There is no space here to discuss in greater depth the reasons and functions of pro-European attitudes in Italy and why nationalism was overshadowed by such a strong pro-Europeanism. This was not an obvious result at the beginning of the new Italian democracy. Nationalist positions were far from weak both in the Left and in the Right as it was shown for instance by the attacks to De Gasperi over the peace treaty coming from both sides of the political spectrum. It is interesting to notice that the leader of the PCI, Togliatti, sought with some of his writings to gain credits for this party as a "national force" by presenting it, in spite of its international linkage with the Soviet Union, as the true heir of the national tradition of the old Liberal Party.

11. In the East the negative Brežnev's reaction left little space for such developments and in the West the limited success of the PCE (Spanish Communist Party) reduced the possibility of creating a significant "family" of reformist Communist parties.

12. Ferrera and Gualmini (2004) offer on this point a more favourable evaluation of the results obtained by Italian negotiators than Dyson and Featherstone (1999), and point to the ability of the Italian negotiating team for the Maastricht Treaty to obtain some conditions that would have later made Italian participation to the EMU easier. The Italian predominant preoccupation not to be excluded from any European agreement is clear, however, also from their analysis.

13. It is probably not a case that privatisation of state industries became acceptable once domestic elites had lost a large measure of political control over them as a result of the more stringent rules of the internal European market following the adoption and implementation of the Single European Act (SEA).

14. This may seem a bit strange in view of the current positions of the Lega which now generally follows a line of Euro-scepticism or at least of Euro-criticism. Yet one should not forget how quickly this party has corrected over the years its positions in many fields when this suited its tactical needs.

15. It must be remembered that the Berlusconi I cabinet, formed after a clear electoral victory of the coalition set up by the media tycoon (and this was the first time that in Italy elections had been clearly fought as a competition between two alternative coalitions) (Bartolini & D'Alimonte, 1994), was brought down by a parliamentary vote following the decision of the Lega to leave the coalition (Katz and Ignazi, 1996).

16. The governing coalition was, to say the least, a difficult one: the strongest party was the post-communist DS, which for reasons of electoral competition had had to accept (but without great pleasure) a prime ministerial candidate expressed by the smaller and fragmented parties of the centre as better able to win the centre voters against Berlusconi (as it happened). Moreover, the coalition needed the support of the extreme left Communist Refoundation to have a parliamentary majority, and this party did not like the economic and budgetary policies required by Maastricht.

17. The leaders of the DS in particular had to face a growing internal opposition from the left wing of the party and from the leftist trade union (CGIL) that put them in a difficult position.

ACKNOWLEDGEMENTS

A first extended draft of this paper was written at the Minda de Günzburg Center for European Studies of Harvard University during the fall of 2000. I am grateful for the hospitality I could enjoy there and for the intellectual stimuli provided by the rich and diverse group of scholars in residence at the Center. I also want to acknowledge the friendly collaboration of Pierangelo Isernia and Luca Verzichelli of the Centre for the Study of Political Change of the University of Siena and the many lively discussions with them on our common research project on "The impact of European integration on the Italian political system". An Italian version of this article appeared in Cotta, Isernia and Verzichelli 2005.

REFERENCES

Ammendola, T., & Isernia, P. (2005). L'Europa vista dagli italiani: i primi vent'anni. In: M. Cotta, P. Isernia & L. Verzichelli (Eds), *L'Italia in Europa. Elite, opinione pubblica e decisioni* (pp. 117–169). Bologna: Il Mulino.

Bartolini, S., & D'Alimonte, R. (Eds) (1994). *Maggioritario ma non troppo*. Bologna: Il Mulino.

Bini-Smaghi, L., Padoa-Schioppa, T., & Papadia, F. (1994). The transition to EMU in the Maastricht Treaty. *Essays in international finance*. Princeton: Princeton University Press, No. 194.

Bufacchi, V., & Burgess, S. (1998). *Italy since 1989: Events and interpretations*. London: Macmillan.

Cavatorto, S. (2005). Attuare Maastricht e la politica delle "rigidità flessibili". In: M. Cotta, P. Isernia & L. Verzichelli (Eds), *L'Italia in Europa. Elite, opinione pubblica e decisioni* (pp. 333–368). Bologna: Il Mulino.

Conti, N., & Verzichelli, L. (2005). La dimensione europea del discorso politico in Italia: un'analisi diacronica delle preferenze partitiche (1950–2001). In: M. Cotta, P. Isernia & L. Verzichelli (Eds), *L'Italia in Europa. Elite, opinione pubblica e decisioni* (pp. 61–115). Bologna: Il Mulino.

Cotta, M. (1992). European integration and the Italian political system. In: F. Francioni (Ed.), *Italy and EC membership evaluated* (pp. 204–215). London: Pinter.

Cotta, M. (1996). La crisi del governo di partito all'italiana. In: M. Cotta & P. Isernia (Eds), *Il gigante dai piedi di argilla. Il governo di partito e la sua crisi nell'Italia degli anni novanta* (pp. 11–52). Bologna: Il Mulino.

Cotta, M. (1997). The political dynamics of European change. In: H. Peeters & M. Tonveronachi (Eds), *Europe in transition* (pp. 16–29). Tilburg: Tilburg University Press.

Cotta, M. (2000). Defining party and government. In: J. Blondel & M. Cotta (Eds), *The nature of party government. A comparative European perspective* (pp. 56–95). Houndmills: Palgrave.

Cotta, M., & Isernia, P. (Eds) (1996). *Il gigante dai piedi d'argilla. Il governo di partito e la sua crisi nell'Italia degli anni novanta*. Bologna: Il Mulino.

Cotta, M., Isernia, P., & Verzichelli, L. (Eds) (2005). *L'Italia in Europa. Elite, opinione pubblica e decisioni*. Bologna: Il Mulino.

Cotta, M., & Verzichelli, L. (1996). La classe politica: cronaca di una morte annunciata. In: M. Cotta & P. Isernia (Eds), *Il gigante dai piedi di argilla. Il governo di partito e la sua crisi nell'Italia degli anni novanta* (pp. 373–408). Bologna: Il Mulino.

Downs, A. (1957). *An economic theory of democracy*. New York: Harper & Row.

Dyson, K., & Featherstone, K. (1999). *The road to Maastricht*. Oxford: Oxford University Press.

Ferrera, M., & Gualmini, E. (2004). *Rescued by Europe. Social and labour market reforms from Maastricht to Berlusconi*. Amsterdam: Amsterdam University Press.

Field, G. L., & Higley, J. (1980). *Elitism*. London: Routledge & Kegan Paul.

Flora, P., & Heidenheimer, A. J. (Eds) (1981). *The development of welfare states in Europe and America*. New Brunswick, NJ: Transaction Books.

Giuliani, M. (1992). Il processo decisionale italiano e le politiche comunitarie. *Polis, 6*, 307–342.

Higley, J., & Gunther, R. (Eds) (1992). *Elites and democratic consolidation in Latin America and Southern Europe*. Cambridge: Cambridge University Press.

Hirschmann, A. O. (1970). *Exit, voice and loyalty: Responses to decline in firms, organizations and states*. Cambridge: Harvard University Press.

Katz, R., & Ignazi, P. (Eds) (1996). *The year of the tycoon*. Boulder: Westview Press.

Linz, J. J. (1978). The breakdown of democratic regimes: crisis, breakdown and reequilibration. In: J. J. Linz & A. Stepan (Eds), *The breakdown of democratic regimes*, vol.1. Baltimore: The Johns Hopkins University Press.

Lundestad, G. (1998). *"Empire" by integration. The United States and European integration, 1945–1997*. Oxford: Oxford University Press.

Moravcsik, A. (1998). *The choice for Europe*. Ithaca: Cornell University Press.

Padoa Schioppa Kostoris, F. (2000). *Budgetary policies and the administrative reform in contemporary Italy*. Documento di Lavoro n. 11/00. ISAE, Rome.

Pierson, P. (1996). The path to European Union: An historical institutionalist account. *Comparative Political Studies, 29*, 123–164.

Putnam, R. D. (1988). Diplomacy and domestic politics. The logic of two-level games. *International Organization, 42*, 427–460.

Sartori, G. (1987). *The theory of democracy revisited*. Chatham: Chatham House.

Schumpeter, J. A. (1942). *Capitalism, socialism and democracy*. New York: Harper.

Verzichelli, L. (1996). Le politiche di bilancio: il debito pubblico da risorsa a vincolo. In: M. Cotta & P. Isernia (Eds), *Il gigante dai piedi di argilla. Il governo di partito e la sua crisi nell'Italia degli anni novanta* (pp. 189–239). Bologna: Il Mulino.

Waltz, K. (1979). *Theory of international politics*. New York: Random House.

Weiler, J. (1999). *The constitution of Europe*. Cambridge: Cambridge University Press.

POLITICAL ELITES AND CONSPICUOUS MODESTY: NORWAY, SWEDEN, FINLAND IN COMPARATIVE PERSPECTIVE

Jean-Pascal Daloz

The research upon which this article is based was carried out during academic stays in several Nordic universities. It is part of a larger comparative study undertaken a few years ago on elite ostentation – that is the deliberate display of wealth, substance or superiority – and legitimation (Daloz, 2003). The main themes addressed are essentially symbolic and cultural, which, admittedly, have not been the ones favored by elite specialists. In this respect, I have to confess that, while I have gained much from the standard literature available on the subject, I have been compelled to fashion my own lens, through which, so to speak, I could examine elitist issues from an original angle.

At a *sociological level*, my aim is to offer a critical look at the classics of social theory dealing with the elite display of hierarchy. Here, the enlightening work of a lot of remarkable sociological thinkers deserves to be considered. One ought to discuss Spencer, Sombart, Weber, Simmel, emulationist interpretations of status (from the theory of imitation formulated by Tarde to American functionalists) but also 'trickle down' perspectives, or others who approach the question in terms of 'conspicuous and

Comparative Studies of Social and Political Elites
Comparative Social Research, Volume 23, 171–210
Copyright © 2007 by Elsevier Ltd.
ISSN: 0195-6310/doi:10.1016/S0195-6310(06)23008-4

vicarious consumption' (Veblen), 'social distinction' (Bourdieu, 1979), up to contemporary analysts of the post-modern condition. One could mention as well many Marxist authors, or Elias, Baudrillard, Goffman. Theories elaborated by these scholars are all worthy of note and intellectually stimulating. However their main defect is that, often basing their analysis on one particular case during a given period, they have claimed to provide sociological laws. For instance, since its publication in English, cultural sociologists have debated vigorously the applicability to the United States of Bourdieu's reading grid (e.g. Lamont & Fournier, 1992; Holt, 1997). On the basis of a sound acquaintance with both ethnographic and historical literature dealing – directly or indirectly – with upper-class individuals or groups, my concern has been to argue about the cultural transferability of the various above mentioned models. The intention is to show how considerable differences from one society to another – as well as, sometimes, across historical periods within the same society – challenge universalistic views.

From a *political science perspective*, my goal is to provide empirical research to reveal how political elite representation (understood as combining cultural perceptions, embodiment and presentation of self[1]) is experienced rather differently from one context to another. More precisely, I favor an interpretative approach of politics (Chabal & Daloz, 2006), the ambition of which is to produce 'thick descriptions' (Geertz, 1973, 1983) of the symbolic relations prevailing between representatives and those represented. Clearly, the question of the legitimacy of *political* power cannot simply be reduced to that of *social* legitimacy. In a way, this is what validates political science as a discipline independent of sociology. Consequently, the issue of political actors' eminence and ostentation is raised in rather different terms. This is especially obvious when the representative dimension of modern democracies is considered: i.e. taking into account professional politicians' relative dependence on the population they are supposed to represent. We are of course confronted here with the question of the very definition of the political realm, the degree of differentiation between the political and social spheres and the extent of the institutionalization of specialized political roles.

In political science (e.g. Edelman, 1964) or political anthropology (e.g. Balandier, 1980), resorting to external signs of power is most often analyzed in negative terms by those authors who are inclined to deconstruct such manifestations. One conventional approach to the symbolic and theatrical dimensions of power is to point out the links between eminence, respectability and domination. Actually researchers have been overly concerned with denouncing political uses of the symbolic. Yet, it is comparatively most rewarding to study the extent to which different people tolerate symbolic distance between the representatives and the represented. Understanding how, and why it matters, entails looking beyond the so-called 'objective' social factors extant and entering the world of local meanings. In many settings, the political elite need not apologize for its eminence, which is easily accepted and merely generates deference or indifference, admiration or envy (Veyne, 1976).

Clearly, one of the most interesting research areas is that which studies the impact that the advent of democracy and universal suffrage have had on the image of the representative. We know that the increase in buying power brought about by economic development created the modern 'consumer', who acquired the right to be treated with respect by businesses competing for customers. We know too that the narrowing of the gap between social classes (at least in 'advanced Western countries') has led to less unequal living conditions. Could it also be the case that the acquisition of the full rights of citizenship, including the vote that confers upon ordinary people the control of the government's fate, reduces the 'prestige' (Goode, 1978) of political actors? Perhaps. Nevertheless, it cannot simply be assumed that deference toward politicians is lessened by the obligation they have of treating every citizen equally (Shils, 1969). There are huge cultural variations, even among apparently similar democratic countries.

In this respect, I am particularly fascinated by the Nordic ones which represent extreme cases of what I am inclined to call 'conspicuous modesty'. According to the logic of egalitarian-minded societies, where people are not expected to display social differences, political actors prove to be most anxious about their self-image. There, being noticed approvingly goes through a style of presentation tending toward a great simplicity. Accordingly, politicians cultivate an image of modesty, which is hardly found elsewhere. The effects of *Jantelagen/loven* (Auchet, 2004) – meaning the informal rule that discourages feelings of superiority – can be felt among all members of the elite,[2] but they are even more powerful when it comes to politicians who cannot be seen to ignore its application.

In this article, I will report findings from my research in Norway, Sweden and Finland.[3] My purpose is twofold. First and foremost, to emphasize Nordic singularity in contrast to other settings. Second, and to a lesser extent, to highlight potential differences between the three countries considered. This research was mainly conducted by means of interviews with different categories of political actors (MPs, retired ministers, Parliament officials, board members of political parties, etc.)[4] but also with top journalists.

As a result of my comparative studies, I have reached the conclusion that elite ostentation is mainly expressed in five ways: the appropriation of the finest goods, ceremonial pomp, refined manners, the display of a certain kind of entourage and possibly physical appearance. My empirical research is therefore related to these five facets, each of which will be considered in turn. Of course, in the Nordic case, the whole approach is inverted, as I am led to explore the deliberate *avoidance* of ostentation.

PRESTIGE GOODS

All sorts of distinctions can be made concerning prestige goods: for instance, between the most durable like precious stones passed down from generation to generation and the ephemeral ones, or between those which seem to exert a universal fascination, like gold and others valued only in some places. The question of borrowings and possible syncretism is also most appealing for the comparatist and countless illustrations could be given here. In many cases, prestigious goods must be studied by taking both their symbolic and practical value into consideration. What I mean is that a 'Veblenesque' approach only paying attention to them as status symbols tends to under-estimate their functional dimension. For example, limousines or jets must certainly be analyzed in terms of attributes of power and status enhance-ment. However, one cannot deny that they also have concrete functions of 'comfortableness' and rapidity for ubiquitous elites bound to do extensive traveling. Normally, in modern democracies, top political actors inherit or acquire all kinds of prestigious public assets, but these must be returned at the end of their mandate. Even presents officially given to them are sup-posed to be surrendered to a public museum. The famous affair of Emperor Bokassa's diamonds offered to Valéry Giscard d'Estaing no doubt discred-ited the French President and contributed to his defeat in the 1981 elections.

Nevertheless, there are still significant differences among contemporary democratic states. Nordic ones prove to be rather intolerant in this respect. Not only do the press and the public constantly scrutinize the use of public goods temporarily made available to officials – which comparatively speak-ing are rather limited and ordinary – but they also appear uncompromising as far as the display of private prestigious goods is concerned. Swedish or Norwegian political elites are extremely conscious of the positive or negative impact their symbolic attitude may have on their image. As regard public goods, one may evoke, for instance, the figure of Tage Erlander rendering even his pen after having served as Prime Minister for so many years. As for private goods, the former chair of the Norwegian Conservative party showed me a diamond ring offered by her husband – a successful business-man – and admitted that she felt she was not able to wear it openly when she was a politician. Likewise, she may now drive a BMW car but would not have dared doing so before.[5]

In my comparative research, I am more particularly looking at the dress appearance of politicians, their use of cars, the external and internal aspects of official or private residences and eventually culinary dimensions. This section will focus on these aspects.

Adornment/Dress Appearance

Beyond other obvious ones (like the protection of the body and the man-ifestation of a regional or community identity), the role of clothes as a badge of social rank is well known and considerable literature is available on the topic. Both historians and sociologists point out that a nice outfit is prob-ably the least onerous distinctive sign one can obtain. For instance, owning a house was (and is often still) unaffordable for most working-class people. But wearing a suit or an elegant dress and momentarily putting a good show outside has been an accessible ambition for many. Nevertheless, people all dressed up may appear more or less at ease, which allows one to spot possible impostures. Anthropology teaches us about the extreme variety of clothing all over the world. Sartorial distinction may be related to the quality of material, the number of pieces, aesthetical decoration, the labor involved in its making, etc. If the superiority of some clothing is sometimes very conventional – e.g. when some colors are monopolized by the elite according to sumptuary laws – it often expresses a high status position in a concrete way. To illustrate: the large sleeves of the Chinese mandarins or the full dresses of upper-class ladies indirectly proved that they did not have to perform any manual work. The world of dressing is generally highly com-petitive but strategies remain culture specific. In some cases, it is more dis-tinguished to keep to a traditional dress code (with limited but significant variation possibilities), whereas in others, too much conformity might dam-age one's reputation.

In my comparative work on political elite representation, I have often realized how important clothing is. Generally, in present-day democracies, most politicians have to reconcile two conflicting requirements. One being similarity (representatives needing to remain proximate enough to those for whom they speak) and the other being relative eminence (to demonstrate the value of their role as spokesperson or government official). In between extreme cases (like Gandhi purposely wearing sandals and some ministers tailcoats or top hats on some occasions) the usual compromise is the suit. This aims at demonstrating relative solemnity without excessive pretence. Having said that, it is interesting to study clothing strategies in relation to concrete situations (electoral meeting, official ceremony or informal party gathering in the summer, etc.). Direct observation and interviews with political actors give us an idea about the way they envisage their dress appearance.

As regard Nordic countries, interesting evolutions may be emphasized. For a long time, being decently dressed seemed to go without saying. Birgitta Dahl – former Speaker of the Swedish Parliament – considers that it has been a sign of 'respectfulness' for political functions and institutions. Just as workers in the 19th century used to wash and change before attending association meetings in the evening, it is expected – even from radical politicians – to wear a proper outfit in the *Riksdag*: so as to give the image of a respectable person.[6] In Sweden, in the 1950s, it was still essential for a male political actor to wear a three-piece suit, a white shirt, a tie and a hat. An important factor that should be taken into consideration here is that until the end of the 1960s, most political meetings were held indoors. "Even when it took place in a movie theatre or a village hall, one felt obliged to be nicely attired when addressing the audience from a podium".[7] However, especially since 1968, it has, for instance, become common to speak in public gardens, sometimes even perched on a beer case with many on-lookers around. In this kind of setting, being too formally dressed may prove to be embarrassing and could counter an aimed feeling of proximity. In other words, the situation commands proper attire. Yet, it would be irrelevant to give a determinist picture here. If a lot of the politicians I interviewed stress upon the fact that they have "to feel comfortable with their clothes", there are obvious contradictions between the various roles they have to play and their personal image. Some young MPs underline that you should not make too many concessions and remain "as genuine as you can",[8] or "wear clothes that fit your age".[9] On the other hand, many a politician attach great importance to observing proprieties. For instance, a Finnish MP who urgently needed to fetch a file at her office in the Parliament over a weekend told me that she suddenly felt ashamed when she realized she had jeans on and was actually seen in them.[10] Another one, a former Minister of Finance, declared that in Finnish politics "both fancy and too 'everyday life' styles should be cautiously avoided" but admits that she tends to dress more casually in her constituency than in the capital city.[11] In any case, it is more and more evident that "you can make a statement with your clothes"[12] and that an individual look is crucial in a 'personalization of politics' context. This may also be related to communication strategies and definitely to the ever-growing influence of the media. We shall revert to that.

As their counterparts from other democratic settings, Nordic politicians are confronted with contradictory requirements potentially affecting their trustworthiness. To be well-dressed may be perceived as revealing serious-ness "like the reassuring figure of a banker always tidily dressed".[13] On the other hand, looking too elegant may create an impression of elitist distance. In that respect, Scandinavian countries prove to be rather intolerant. My view, and it can be no more than impressionistic, is that Sweden is more 'formal' than Norway (itself probably a bit more so than Denmark). Yet in Sweden, both male and female top Social Democrats (like Pierre Schori or Margot Wallström among others) have been criticized for dressing up too smartly. On the contrary, the Finnish President, Tarja Halonen, was re-proached for her "insufficiently presidential" look at the beginning of her mandate. In that country, the famous Independence Day evening reception – which is broadcasted on television – has been a special occasion where top elites are expected to be stylishly dressed. Media enjoy making comments about the originality, tastefulness and at times shocking nature of (especially female) politicians' appearance. Some political actors like Heidi Hautala, leader of the Greens regret having to spend so much money for a dress that they will never put on again.[14] The President had to state recently that what matters on this occasion is to celebrate the birth of the country and not to make it a lavish fashion show. But others do believe it crucial to make a good impression on that day. It is now much less common than before to wear fur coats for obvious ecological reasons. Nevertheless, MP Astrid Thors does not hesitate to wear one on the 6th of December reception because mink breeding is not an insignificant economical activity in her constituency. Political representation can also be studied bearing in mind these kinds of meaningful details.

It is most interesting to consider presentation of the self in relation to the political parties' respective sensitivity. Hoping to project a different image, both Greens and Leftists often wish to show that they are just like the ordinary people they claim to represent, and certainly not "like Conserv-atives in grey suits".[15] Yet, they may be torn between the desire to express their different politics sartorially and the realization that they might have to sacrifice their unusual image in order to be taken seriously. For instance, when the Greens first entered the Swedish parliament they debated on whether the men should wear suits and the women skirts. An interesting compromise was found by a male MP, Birger Schlaug, who decided to wear woolen cardigan: giving him a kind of jacket-like respectability but still asserting his distinctive identity. Nordic parliaments are full of anecdotes apropos unconventional attitudes of this kind. In Finland, Klaus Bremer of the Swedish People's party was rebuked for coming to the *Eduskunta* in shorts on a hot summer afternoon, whereas his Green colleague, Pertti 'Veltto' Virtanen, a former rock musician, would generally keep his beret on his head. Too much eccentricity may go against conventional dress codes, and compromise has to be reached as regard these symbolic issues. For example, within the Norwegian Parliament, six young new MPs from the Socialist party purposely chose to wear very 'relaxed' clothing. "We all have a radical background as street activists, we definitely don't want to look like others".[16] There is no official dress code in the *Storting*, just unofficial rules for the matter. But when confronted with this attitude, the Speaker of the Parliament threatened to have one enacted if the leftists did not abide by the usual conventional habits. Finally, an agreement was reached upon which no tie but jacket was required for men when sitting in plenary sessions. Jeans and sport shoes are not accepted either, but there was no objection raised on participating in a commission with a t-shirt in the summer or a sweater in winter. The only exception was the opening session in the presence of the king, when all men have to wear a dark suit and a tie. "On that day, everybody must look nice and tidy, I do not want to offend anybody and be disrespectful towards the institution: not meaning the royal institution – I am a republican – but the Parliament".[17]

Interestingly enough, it appears almost impossible to impose any dress code to women. Hans Brattestå, the Secretary General of the Norwegian Parliament who is in charge of protocol, admits that although he asks his assistants to strictly control any male violation of the agreed rules, to reprimand female MPs on their clothing would be considered as sexist. He had to acknowledge that they were actually the ones who sometimes introduced a laid-back attitude within the Parliament.[18] For instance, black jeans or short skirts are accepted. In the *Eduskunta*, rules are also informal but depend very much on the current Speaker's views. At the moment, women are not allowed to have bare shoulders nor mini-skirts. Recently, a young Green MP, Rosa Meriläinen who used to wear very short skirts[19] in plenary sessions, was asked to dress more decently. Female members from her party asked her to concentrate more on parliamentary work and less on her looks.[20]

But to make oneself known as a politician increasingly means to imposing one's personal image. Some older politicians would deplore what is often presented as an 'Americanization' of Nordic political life and they regret the times when ideological debate was very much favored and politicians knew how to serve ideas while relatively keeping themselves in the background. By contrast, younger ones do not hesitate on stating that previous generations hardly realize how much the political scene has changed. For instance, rising Conservative figures like Ine Marie Eriksen in Norway or Tove Lifvendahl in Sweden attach great importance to individual political communication. "Today we are in competition not only with other politicians but also with show business stars or sports celebrities; you have to be noticed if you want your ideas to attract attention", says Ms Eriksen. While she would wear rather neutral colors simply to make a comment, she deliberately opts for vivid ones when participating in a debate. She is also very conscious about the fact that in collective photos representing party leaders, it is important to show various looks which complete each other.[21] 'Nonverbal communication' also matters a great deal to Tove Lifvendahl. She became well known in Sweden for wearing t-shirts displaying the slogan 'Capitalist' she owns about 20 of those. She admits that she would sometimes change three times a day for different audiences: for instance, jeans when she goes to a gymnasium, jacket and skirt at the office and evening dress for a reception. The Swedish Conservatives are presently striving to attract young people and have even hired a teenager to advise the party on youngsters' habits and expectations. In this case, the strategy is obviously collective and indeed Public Relation specialists have been resorted to.[22] Admittedly, this is still rather unusual north of the 55th parallel. In both Norway and Finland, political communication is not as developed as in many other democracies. Politicians sometimes rely on party collaborators who happen to have some experience in the field, but in a rather informal and friendly way. 'Information secretaries' are available in some parties but they mainly concentrate on press release drafting. Yet, it can be heard in Stockholm that if the Liberal party was so successful during the 2003 elections, this was partly due to Lars Leijonberg's new look – enhanced by the famous fashion designer Camilla Thulin.[23] To give another illustration, Norwegian journalist Solveig Ruud says that she used to get phone calls from political party headquarters when she was working for the television: requesting details about the color of the studio walls or that of the presenter's suit.[24]

The tabloid press or women's magazines (like *Kvinner og Klær* – Women and Clothes – in Norway) commonly dedicate pages to the best-known politicians' look, asking 'experts' to make comments about them. In some extreme cases, the media do not hesitate to ask some politicians to appear in a humorous and slightly scandalous posture. For instance, in Norway, a photograph depicts Torild Skogsholm 'entubed' and apparently naked (the tires being an allusion to her position of Minister of Transportation). Similar illustrations could be given as regard Finnish political figures. Of course, commentators shocked by such developments are justified when moaning over what has become of Nordic politics; whereas others would tend to think that it is pleasant to see politicians not taking themselves too seriously. Beyond these normative viewpoints, I think this trend opens attractive avenues for future research on political elite representation.

Residence

Not only is the house by far the most important status object, but it also serves as a container and showcase for most of the other goods. Indeed, beyond their fundamental function as a shelter, dwelling places have often been one of the major vectors of ostentation, though it is important to point out extreme cultural variability in this respect (Rapoport, 1982). In numerous 'traditional societies', habitations are used to express collective identities much more than distinction and it is only after long and complex evolutions, that they finally became status symbols (see for instance Duncan, 1981). When studying elitist dimensions, one is led to take numerous aspects into account: location, 'aloofness', architecture, castles or palaces magnifying their owners, parks, elite competition within residential areas, antechambers, reception rooms, furniture, decoration, etc.

In my comparative studies on political actors, I am inclined to dissociate three levels of investigation: private homes, official residences and offices. The study of private homes, which may play an important symbolic role in some situations – for instance, George W. Bush's ranch in Crawford – is often most revealing of the ways in which political representation is experienced. For Nigeria, I showed that if the elite generally endeavor to build most impressive houses, the latter are often located in their community of origin, even when it is a miserable village or an overcrowded suburb. In this context, we are dealing less with residential distinction than with logics of symbolic ascendancy depending on proximity with potential supporters (Daloz, 2002a). Official residences also constitute a fascinating topic. To give just one illustration, when studying the Elysée Palace in Paris, it is most revealing to consider whether Presidents actually live there (Gaullist tradition) or just govern from there; whether they want to give a personal touch to the place or on the contrary intend to express a symbolic continuity with their predecessor. As for offices, they are of course potentially much more accessible to social scientists and they may be very meaningful as far as politicians' presentation of self is concerned.

In Nordic countries, elites generally speaking seldom build showy mansions. As Annette Kullenberg points out, the wealthiest people in this part of Europe hardly flaunt themselves; they would rather tend to use their money to protect their privacy by living apart (on an island for instance[25]). There certainly are a few notorious exceptions – like tycoon Kjell Inge Røkke in Norway or Björn Wahlroos (CEO of the Sampo Bank) in Finland – as well as some prestigious residential areas such as *Kulosaari (Brandö)* or *Westend* near Helsinki. As for top politicians, they rarely possess very impressive houses and when they do, it becomes a controversial issue immediately. Bo Lundgren, the former leader of the Conservative party was criticized for having bought a nice house in a posh Stockholm area. Prime Minister Göran Persson's recent acquisition of a farm with some land in the famous *Södermanland* (south of the capital city, where a lot of successful industrialists have settled) is endlessly commented upon by journalists who did not hesitate to speak of a 'small castle'. Consequently, political actors have to be careful about the conspicuous image their residence or neighborhood might convey. For instance, Kaci Kullmann Five, then Minister of Foreign Trade in Norway, had been blamed for having a swimming pool in her garden. I was told by a journalist that she later accepted to grant a TV interview at her place provided the above-mentioned status symbol would not appear in the background.[26]

But as a Finnish MP commented, "it all depends how you present things". What should be avoided is to give the impression that you are conspicuously wealthy and successful, since the average people expect you to dedicate yourself first and foremost to the service of your country. On the other hand, "if you use the image of your residence in a clever way: explaining nicely how you have designed, arranged it, the reactions may be quite positive".[27] This is, for instance, the case with current Finnish Prime Minister Matti Vanhasen's private house in the vicinity of Helsinki. It is notoriously quite huge, but many people are well aware that it was to a large extent built with his own hands. This is very well perceived, especially in the eyes of his (rural) party supporters. In a similar way, some politicians have willingly accepted that journalists visit them in their summer 'cabin', which gives a nice impression of ordinary Nordic life in the countryside but also eventually brings to mind one's childhood, or one's grandparents.

Official residences are rather rare in Nordic countries apart from royal palaces or the ones meant for the Finnish President.[28] Even prime ministers usually stay in their own private house – though some places are available

for banquets and other ceremonies. Nevertheless, it is now seriously envis-
aged that Premiers should stay in State buildings for security reasons. This is
going to be the case in Oslo. Many ministers are known to live in rather
ordinary flats. MPs are usually entitled to free accommodation when they
are not from the capital city. For instance, in Norway, 142 apartments of
different sizes are meant for those who come from at least 40 km away from
the *Storting*. They are furnished but electronic equipment (television,
kitchen device) have to be bought. In Sweden and Finland, MPs get an
allowance for accommodation, though in Stockholm some small flats were
acquired by the State – a decision which symptomatically raised some con-
troversy. Of course, as one would expect in this type of cultural environment, possible misuse of official residences is kept under close scrutiny.
Scandals related to accommodation are quite rare. In 2002–2003, a senior
Labor politician, Trond Giske, was accused by the press of unduly having
an official flat at his disposal in Oslo whereas he already owned another one
(which he was actually renting!).[29]

As for offices, with a few exceptions (like some within the Ministry of
Finance in Stockholm), they are not very impressive and in any case should
never look extravagant. On the other hand, designer furniture in the Nordic
style can often be seen and we do know this can be quite expensive. As
indicated earlier, in the type of research I opt for, it is particularly relevant
to observe how political actors decorate this special place – where they
receive visitors – in such a manner as to give indications about themselves.
However, in parliaments, for instance, the standardization of the rooms
allows MPs a rather limited amount of leeway. They can only give a personal touch by means of objects or pictures. But even then, it seems that
many representatives feel more or less compelled to select some referring
either to their political activities or constituency. For instance, a Norwegian
Socialist MP displays a photo of his party's youth league, a flag from the
Landless People's Movement he was given in Brazil and a poster of his
hometown soccer team.[30] It would certainly be instructive to systematically
study MPs offices but, so said in passing, most conversations I had in the
three countries were held either in the cafeteria or a Parliament meeting
room – which is not insignificant and rather different from the experience
one may have with their counterparts from other parts of the world. In both
Norway and Sweden, it is possible to borrow works of art from National
museums but problems sometimes occur when they are to be returned for
temporary exhibitions. In Oslo, a considerable budget is also made available
to buy modern art.[31] New acquisitions are momentarily displayed in the
central corridors and MPs are allowed to choose one piece each. Some

people regret that purchases are sometimes made abroad instead of systematically supporting local artists. The questionable taste of some pieces
can also be much debated. This is the case, for instance, of a collage of five
photos of Richard Nixon, especially one where he was definitely not at his
best. The Secretary General of the Parliament has grounds for dreading the
reaction of American visitors when confronted with such an image likely to
look a bit derisive.[32]

Research on symbolic aspects of politics tends to concentrate excessively
on the issue of elite domination over the rest of the population, thus ne-
glecting the fact that self-assertion is quite often primarily a matter of competition among the elite themselves. In this respect, possible symbolic
struggles to obtain the most impressive offices are worth studying. The
distribution is usually dependent upon electoral results and seniority considerations. Carl I Hagen from the populist Progress party was really proud
to obtain the office formerly held by the leader of the Conservative party in
Norway. For want of space in Oslo, Stockholm as recently Helsinki, an-
nexes have been built out of the historic building housing the Parliament.
However, opinions differ as to whether it is more prestigious to stay in the
new buildings which are generally more spacious or the old ones. Moreover,
as it was to be expected with these borderline cases, some young radical MPs
would go as far as saying that they do not feel at ease in the Parliament
premises anyway because the latter are too imposing: creating an awkward
feeling of distance vis-à-vis ordinary citizens. Here we are faced with an odd
debate between those who have no objection with official buildings being
impressive because of the institutions and the values they represent, and
those who see them in terms of 'symbolic violence'. It is true that the
Eduskunta, for instance, built a few years after independence as a symbol of
statehood, may appear massive and somewhat intimidating. On the other
hand, less than 10 years ago it was still without security gates and metal
detectors.

At the ministerial level, one of the most interesting research areas is that
of how newly appointed Ministers settle in. In Norway, it has occurred that
some would be dissatisfied with their predecessor's arrangements. "The
office was terrible, not worthy of a place meant to receive official foreign
visitors. The curtains were ugly; I had them changed immediately. At the
beginning I had to bring some of my own painting reproductions. There was
hardly any money available to make improvements to the room. I also
wanted to give it a note of femininity".[33] In Sweden, when a Minister moves
in, he is entitled to change the furniture. Social Democrat Leif Pagrotsky
(currently holding the Education, Research and Culture portfolio) decided

to move all the furnishings around when he became Minister of Industry and bought avant-garde ones. Since the former ones were not at all old or worn, this could only become a contentious issue.

To end this section with an eloquent remark, the social scientist used to other environments can only but be struck by the relative accessibility to politicians' offices, even at the highest level. I was told both in Norway and Sweden that at the beginning of the 1970s, one could virtually reach a Minister's office without being checked. Since the assassinations of Olof Palme and Anna Lindh, and also since 9/11, controls have no doubt intensified. But in a comparative perspective the prevailing impression is still one of amazing approachability.

Vehicles

Like horse-drawn carriages in the past (e.g. Stone, 1967), it is well known that in many countries cars have been a primary object of competitive display. In the United States, they could still be perceived as an outstanding symbol of power under Woodrow Wilson, of success in the 1920s and of just a middle-class status 30 years later. However, if it has now become a fairly common machine in industrialized societies, this is far from being the case in Third World countries. Furthermore, there is of course car and car. As with other prestige goods taken into account here, the relation between the elite and prestigious vehicles would deserve a more extensive treatment, but will have to be summarized. As regard politicians, I mainly study personal and official cars and, when appropriate, other vehicles (like planes, helicopters, boats, etc.) but, as we shall see, taxis may also be a relevant topic. In terms of image, there is definitely a world of difference between a Dutch or a Swedish minister going to his office by bike or public transportation and a politician systematically using an impressive limousine with a driver. In France, where it is estimated that there would be at least 400,000 service cars, it is fascinating to study how political actors know full well how to operate on several registers according to circumstances: at times majestically entering official court-yards, seated at the back of their cars, at other times driving themselves, sometimes also deliberately parking a few blocks away in order to be seen arriving on foot.[34] In his book on the French President's rituals, D. Fleurdorge (2001) showed how Jacques Chirac tried to create a new impression, sitting in the front of a rather ordinary car, with no escort, opening the door and carrying his satchel himself during some of his official visits in the French provinces. However, during the 'cohabitation period', he would remain on the rear-seat of a much bigger vehicle and wait for the Prefect or his aide-de-camp to come and open the door for him. The factors I usually take into consideration are the makes[35] and types or models,[36] their age, their more or less imposing appearance.[37] Of course, I also study whether political elites tend to take the back or front seat or even drive their own vehicle, and whether they are preceded by an escort or not.

Unlike in a place such as Nigeria where they play an important role as regard elite image shaping (Daloz, 1990), private automobiles are far from being crucial in Nordic countries. There, it is rather common to have a Volvo or a Saab: spacious cars that could be considered as status symbols in some other European countries. Apart from a few upstarts from the new technology sector – like the Finnish Rytsölä brothers who used to parade in flashy Lamborghinis – even the wealthiest members of the elite hardly bother to acquire ostentatious vehicles. And when they do, this would immediately attract not only attention but also controversies. As can easily be foreseen, this is all the more true for political elites. Tage Erlander did not even have a driving license and Swedes remember that his wife used to drive him around. In Sweden, Green politicians purposely maintain very old cars to show how disdainful they are of this means of transportation – the paradox being that the latter are much more polluting than new models. Political parties in the three countries hardly possess any cars and politicians have to use their own, rent some or ask fellow members to transport them when campaigning. Members of the government usually sit at the back but they see no objection in inviting a journalist to join them for a quick interview on their way to the airport, which again shows an indisputable lack of formalism.

In comparison with other countries, official cars and drivers also prove to be quite exceptional.[38] In Norway, only the Prime Minister, the Minister of Defense and that of Foreign Affairs have a car at their disposal on a permanent basis. The other ministers must share a pool of vehicles made available after having booked for them. In Sweden and Finland, Ministers as well as some other top officials are entitled to a car, mainly for security reasons. Yet, ironic comments were made after Prime Minister Göran Persson acquired a large BMW – allegedly to stretch out his legs due to his back problem – or when Finnish President Tarja Halonen recently received a very powerful Mercedes Benz. As usual, the press would play a watchdog role, eager to expose any possible abuse. For instance, the Finnish media asked why the Ministry of Defense discreetly bought an expensive limousine for General Gustav Hägglund, Chairman of the EU Military Committee in Brussels. They constantly check whether service cars could be used for private activities. Of course, drivers may always mention 'official purposes' but, to take an example, some newspapers enquired about Paavo Lipponen's (former Prime Minister and presently Speaker of the Parliament) use of a vehicle from the *Eduskunta* to transport his family on a semi-official/semi-private trip during summer 2004.[39] In Sweden, a merciless newspaper disclosed a picture of a regional Governor's official car parked in a place reserved for disabled people.[40] In Norway, there was a serious debate in order to decide whether the Prime Minister's vehicle should be allowed to use bus lanes in order to avoid traffic and save time in the morning. Some commentators did not hesitate to say that he should queue like every citizen but it was finally to be accepted in the name of security. Likewise, 20 years ago, there was a debate as to whether MPs should have a free car park near the Parliament. At that time, the Conservative Prime Minister actually refused! But this was to be implemented later. Needless to say, from a comparative cultural perspective, these types of hesitations would be meaningless in many parts of the world.

Extreme checks with regard to the use of taxis also prove to be most significant. In Sweden, even the Minister of Justice, Per Unckel (presently Secretary General of the Nordic Council of Ministers) was reproached for taking a taxi every morning. Others, like Yvonne Ruwaida (a Green MP), ran into trouble when they tried to be reimbursed without being able to produce all the required receipts. In Helsinki, the MPs receive a 'taxi card' but information about the way they use this means of transportation is made public and media closely scrutinize this, going as far as awarding depreciatory titles of 'taxi king' and 'taxi queen'. The pressure is so intense that some politicians reach a point where they think twice about taking taxis on a regular basis, although they certainly deem it necessary. They are under the impression that newspapers actually dictate their behavior.[41]

In the three countries, most MPs are entitled to free seats in trains or planes: either enjoying a permanent travel card or having their journeys refunded. In Norway, it is hoped nobody is taking undue advantage of the system, knowing that it would be difficult to make systematic controls. But social pressure is so high that 'scandals' are quite exceptional. In Sweden, some problems arose because several politicians were not able to keep a tight check on their accounts. At a higher level, the question as to whether prime ministers should use scheduled air services or special jets has been debated. At the time when Carl Bildt was negotiating Sweden's EU membership, he asked for more planes. But this proved to be quite controversial. In Norway, the head of government does not permanently have a plane at his disposal. Officials generally use regular air lines (in business class) or special charter planes when the need arises. Significantly, on the occasion of the 2004 royal wedding in Spain, the Norwegian Crown Prince and his wife were among the very few VIP guests who did not use a private jet. However, for security reasons, it seems preferable to avoid traveling with other passengers. When governmental planes (or helicopters) are used, journalists closely scrutinize whether trips are really official or not. At times, the situation happens to be rather ambiguous. For instance, Prime Minister Göran Persson went on an official visit to Madrid but then used the same plane to go to Malaga for what looked like a private stay. Interrogations were raised but the fuss made about it finally faded away. To give another illustration, Jan-Erik Enestam (Finnish Minister of the Environment) was accused of using an army helicopter for an electoral meeting when he was Minister of Defense. What is at stake here is the question of the borderline between public and private business or between governmental and electoral activities: rather touchy subjects in this part of Europe!

Culinary Aspects

When taking into consideration its vital aspect, it is certainly difficult to treat food as a 'prestige good' exactly like others. Nevertheless, what people eat and how they eat may play an important role as regard ostentation. The specialist could mention a lot of fascinating perspectives that can be found in archeological (e.g. van der Veen, 2003), historical (e.g. Strong, 2002), anthropological (e.g. Dietler & Hayden, 2001) or sociological literature among others (e.g. Wiessner & Schiefenhövel, 1996). Once again, to go even slightly into detail would oblige one to devote quite a number of pages on the topic. One may study what is served and, for instance, consider the classic distinction (Braudel, 1979) – sometimes questioned (Flandrin, 1999) – between the traditional quantitative distinction (ability to satisfy the appetite of many guests, to provide them with more food than other members of the elite) and a more modern emphasis on quality (gastronomic, aesthetical, original, exotic). Culinary aspects may easily be related to the other facets presented above or hereafter: residence (which should permit to entertain guests decently), distinguished manners (table manners, etiquette, expertise about wine and dish, conversation, etc.), domestic service (waiters, cook, master of ceremonies), pomp (presentation of food, rituals, shows offered to the guests), adornment (dressing up for a reception, possibly servants in livery), and entourage ('going out' with somebody, ornamental reification of women). Service in the double meaning of the way courses are served ('à la française', 'à la russe') and of the set of dishes (cutlery, plates, glasses and other accessories which every member of the elite should possess and know how to use) might also be taken into account.

From my political science perspective, what proves to be most interesting is the way sharing a meal possibly allows for both a representation of distinction (high table, placement, who is served first? can eat first? etc.) and a representation of likeness (sharing a meal as affirmation of solidarity: everyone being actor and spectator). Banquets may play a crucial socio-cultural role and in fact be a microcosm of a given society. I explore the compatibility of the two symbolisms: allowing at the same time to reaffirm a socio-political order and a sense of communion – which is essential as far as political representation is concerned (Daloz, 1999).

Without going as far as pretending that Gabriel Axel's famous picture *Babettes Gæstebud* (1988) – showing a puritan community suspicious about good food – is representative of the Scandinavian relation with grand eating, we have to admit that, in Nordic countries, cookery does not have the obsessional prominence it often has further South or East. Local specialists actually recognize that, for a long time, meals have been rather unsophisticated, and local gourmets that top restaurants were hardly available even in capital cities. This is fortunately much less the case nowadays.

As far as political elites are concerned, food also constitutes a good indicator of the low level of tolerance whenever any extravagance is suspected. In the case of Sweden, one thinks of Mats Hults, the former Mayor of Stockholm who had to resign because he was accused of spending too much money with his collaborators in restaurants for so-called seminars. A pleasant development is that he is presently in charge of the employers' organization hotel business/catering section![42] In a country where transparency is such a prized principle, it is quite possible for any citizen to have access to politicians' dinner bills. Once again, media exposures can go incredibly far. Not only was Göran Persson pointed at for having celebrated his 2002 election victory in *Gondolan* – an exclusive restaurant in Stockholm – but *Aftonbladet* newspaper took no hesitation in publishing an article about the fact that he recently bought expensive mint sweets in NK – a famous department store of the Swedish Capital city! In Norway, Victor Norman, Minister of Employment, was also accused of not having respected the NOK 800 limit (wines included!) enacted by his own ministry for food bills and eventually had to resign. It should be specified that as a former Professor of Economics he became used to eating with businessmen ignorant of the existence of such restrictions.

In Finland, journalists would also try to find out how much top politicians would spend on their meals. During the Kekkonen era, the Finnish President did not have to 'show off' at all since he was so obviously *the* leader. By contrast, followers from his 'inner circle' – like Karjalainen who at a time used to see himself as the number two of the regime and a potential successor – could be rather ostentatious. They had to prove their importance one way or the other. And one of the ways in which to do this was precisely to organize dinners. The restaurant on the top of the Vaakuna hotel – built for the 1952 Olympic Games – was, for instance, a place where elites would meet. Under the influence of the powerful Russian neighbor, it was still common to feast for hours in those days.

However, if in Norway and Sweden sumptuous banquets are sometimes held – notably in the royal palace – for some specific occasions, the striking Finnish institution is, of course, the sauna. The idea according to which major political decisions have been made in such places is far from being untrue. Though 21st century elites might meet more often on a golf course, there is no doubt that saunas still play a central role. Accredited journalists like going regularly to the Parliament sauna so as to gather information in an informal setting. Reciprocally, the major press groups organize sauna parties in their building with top political actors. It has been more particularly a male habit – very much tied with heavy drinking. Nowadays, interestingly, President Tarja Halonen is also making use of informal gathering: inviting prominent female figures into her own sauna.[43]

It is always fascinating for a political scientist specialized in elite studies to be at the Parliament cafeteria – whether in Oslo, Stockholm or Helsinki – watching top political figures queuing like others before getting their food. From a foreign perspective, this may look quite strange and, for instance, a Russian senior official once asked "but where is the VIP room?" when invited for lunch at the *Storting*.[44] This raises a very instructive question: how should you behave with elite from other countries not sharing your cultural codes? We shall return to this at the end of the article.

ENTOURAGE

In what concerns the entourage, I am interested in vicarious ostentation through the display of spouses, possibly mistresses, servants, etc. Here it is important to make a distinction between the people around a political figure who increase his or her prestige because of their own distinction or because they offload him/her of certain tasks. In the first case, I study glamorous (particularly female) company, whose display is critical to the assertion of social status in some cultural contexts. In Nigeria, for instance, the conspicuous affirmation of 'predatory' sexuality enhances the political profile of politicians, who frequently seek to assert their authority by seducing their opponents' female companions (Daloz, 2002b). In France too, for a long time, demonstration of 'virility' has been more often than not a political asset for the legitimation of power. Beyond this aspect, I consider society life, flaunting other elites likely to enhance one's own image, art patronage, etc. As for the second point, it is worth noting that, in high political spheres, servants (maids, cooks, ushers, body guards, etc.) still play an important role, possibly contributing to increase the rulers' standing.

Of course, north of the 55th parallel, the picture is entirely different. Politicians may indeed instrumentalize their entourage but in a very opposite way: aiming at emphasizing their commonplaceness. Going back to an issue mentioned above in respect to the behavior of Nigerian politicians – that is, the display of sexual life – the situation is quite the reverse. In Finland, Riitta Uosukainen, former Speaker of the Parliament, wrote very openly about her personal life in a book, which attracted wide attention all over the world – notably a famous passage about a water bed. This gained her sympathy, especially from women of the same age who found that she was courageous to make such revelations and identified themselves with her. In Sweden, the case of Gudrun Schyman, who was until recently the leader of the Left (ex-Communist) party, is also instructive in this regard. She has spoken publicly about her private life, saying that she was not just a politician but also a human being – 'mother', 'lover', etc. Her confessions about a singularly messy life seem to have done her standing no harm, particularly among party members. During one of the last election debates, when party leaders were asked to summarize their program, she began by saying: "I am Gudrun Schyman; I am an alcoholic ..." and went on to speak of her chaotic personal life. In other words, she sought support by stressing her private weaknesses, obviously widely shared in society. Although this may well be an extreme occurrence, it serves to illustrate the point that in Sweden representative legitimacy derives largely from a demonstration of a type of ordinariness that is appealing to the voters concerned.

The interest currently taken in the private lives of politicians is most revealing of new trends in the political game in the north of Europe. Admittedly, because of the Lutheran Church's influence on society, there has always been little scope for dissociating personal attitude from political role. Unlike what happens within catholic cultural environments, the behavior expected from someone holding official functions needs, as it were, has to be confirmed with impeccable private credentials. Yet, media coverage of intimate matters – and the way some politicians exploit it for political purposes – is without precedent. For instance, it is revealing to learn that a gossip magazine like *Se og Hør* now has an accredited correspondent in the Norwegian Parliament. This said, it is difficult to make generalizations as regard Nordic politicians' consent to expose their private life. It seems to be a rather individual decision. In the three countries I have met some who are quite reluctant to give any information on their spouses and even less on their children. For instance, young Norwegian MP Ine Marie Eriksen told me that she would never speak of her boyfriend to the media or have any picture with him published. "Once you have tolerated journalists' intrusion into your private affairs, it proves to be most difficult to stop".[45] Her Finnish colleague, Rosa Meriläinen, shares her view: considering that she has the right "to get drunk on Saturday without the rest of the country knowing about it".[46] On the other hand, when public figures keep their private life absolutely secret, it can be used against them. For instance, Paula Lehtomäki, the brilliant 30-year-old Minister of Foreign Trade, Cooperation and Development in Finland, was heavily criticized for having got married without announcing it and later for refusing to say who her husband actually is.

Those who willingly use their entourage to 'sell themselves' seldom do it in a conspicuous way, although one might mention a few exceptions which prove the rule. Beyond the case of some famous businessmen, like Vesa Keskinen (owner of a famous village shop in Finland) who seems to flaunt a new girlfriend every week, politicians using their female companion to enhance their image are indeed rare. One thinks of liberal politician and marketing consultant Olaf Thommessen in Norway, who married famous Swedish top model Vendela Kirsebom. In Finland, after having kept her in the background, Esko Aho started to appear more frequently with his beautiful wife toward the end of the 2000 presidential campaign, realizing that his popularity was growing because of her. However, in most cases, political actors would rather refer to their family with the intention of showing that they are a good husband or wife, father or mother. For instance, ex-Prime Minister Paavo Lipponen was shown preparing breakfast for his children and his Norwegian counterpart, Jens Stoltenberg, taking his own to school. Actually, media like to ask politicians how they "cope with the family"? Esko Aho was in trouble when his wife mentioned that his participation in household matters was mainly limited to a phone call once in a while. In Nordic countries, many Swedish or Finnish citizens would remember famous pictures showing top political figures taking care of domestic chores, like, respectively, Prime Minister Thorbjörn Fälldin washing his socks in his tiny rented flat or Bjarne Kallis (ex-leader of the Christian Democrats) ironing his shirt. From the Conservative to the leftist side, if many MPs certainly want to protect their most intimate life, they also consider that you may give private details about yourself, your companions or your parents when it is indirectly relevant politically speaking. For instance, Tove Lifvendahl would accept it to a certain extent: she has agreed to pose with her adoptive mother and to make some revelations, but demanded to check the contents of the article before it was published.

Of course private matters can play a certain role in the political debate and positively or negatively affect the image of politicians. During the 2000 presidential campaign in Finland, Tarja Halonen was reproached for having been a single mother, cohabiting with a man who was not her daughter's father. There were even rumors about lesbianism! Generally, Nordic countries are rather tolerant as far as morals are concerned and sex scandals are almost inexistent. Yet a divorce, for instance, can be an issue and have political consequences. Political figures divorcing is quite common nowadays. The question here is clearly whether the politician is going to appear as a villain or a victim, especially when the couple projects a model image – as was the case with Prime Minister Matti Vanhasen who suddenly announced his separation in April 2005, while he was the prospective candidate of his party for the forthcoming presidential elections in Finland.

On the question of servants, having a full-time maid would hardly be acceptable for most politicians in this part of Europe. Indeed, rulers receiving many guests may be assisted by employees. But administrations tend to resort to catering enterprises and there are much less servants than used to be the case. In Norway, "even having an au pair girl may be perceived as something negative and should be avoided; it looks much more democratic to take one's children to the kindergarten".[47] As for political assistants, one should not be ostentatious either. In Finland, each MP receives some money enabling him/her to pay one person. Some prefer being helped in the *Eduskunta* and others in their constituency. It is also possible to have somebody in both places but this means that each would only get half a salary. In Sweden, a lot of young people assist politicians, for instance, in making surveys. They usually come from the Youth section of their party. In Norway, some money is also intended for hiring secretaries who work jointly for several MPs. Nowadays, due to the development of personal computers, many politicians do a lot of things by themselves. Of course, some political parties also have specialized political advisors. More particularly, in Finland, preliminary contacts may be made exclusively through the assistant who is the same person welcoming you at the entrance of the building. This gives an impression of relative distance. But most of the time, Nordic politicians would avoid having one think that they are being served.

REFINED MANNERS

When I meet political elites for interviews, I always pay attention to the way I am introduced to them. There is quite a difference between a prominent person making the effort to come out of his/her office in order to welcome you (or even downstairs as it happened with former Swedish Minister of Culture, Bengt Göransson[48]) and others having you introduced very formally by their secretary and not even getting up from their chair (as I have sometimes experienced outside Scandinavia). Manners refer to the behavior of a person toward others, aiming at producing desired effects. The ways people speak, behave, stand, are distinguished when they express social superiority. In contrast with the *external* signs mentioned in the above sections, manners are *inner* ones. This is very important for the comparative study of elites. While in some cultures, these incorporated signs prove to be most crucial – witness the importance attached to a distinguished accent in England – in others, social status is mainly expressed through the display of expensive status symbols affordable by anybody wealthy enough. Ostentation may be a question of having or being.

Manners need to be understood in terms of a general tension between modest civility and display. As regard elitist manners, they are irreducible to one single logic. For instance, they may involve a great show of arrogance, extravagance and a demonstration that you are powerful enough to ostensibly free yourself from restrictive norms. Historically, one would think of ancient aristocratic behavior before court life or evoke Napoleon who was notoriously, and purposely, rude. But elitist distinction would more often go through a perfect self-command and an understanding of prevailing codes of courteousness. Paradoxically, by controlling yourself you control others, as N. Elias (1974 [1936]) has shown. Here, the study of gesture is of utmost importance. When I watch political actors, I am always interested in the way some would maintain their composure in any circumstances, whereas others would have very gesticulative attitudes. In the first case, superiority is expressed through a demonstration of great ease, calculated and always appropriate gesture. The second one has more to do with vivid theatricality. Both can be efficient and ostentatious. Of course, while there is no doubt that constructing and maintaining a public body has been one of the means

by which the elite uphold their superiority, comparative analysis has to
take the cultural variability of human gesture into account (Bremmer &
Roodenburg, 1991). Language is the other major theme to be considered.
We know that many theoretical perspectives can be found in related literature. As for my own studies, they mainly focus on the sophistication of
political actors' speech. To which extent does it sound elitist or affected by
the constraints of political representation – often drawing political actors to
place themselves at the same level as their audience? Like gestures, it should
be recalled here that language is nothing natural, but highly conventional
and tied to a specific culture.

In the three countries under consideration, great 'stirs' are quite rare.
When watching parliamentary debates, one definitely knows that we are
very far away from London, Seoul or even Paris. At worst, angry MPs
would go as far as clenching their fists in Stockholm.[49] In Helsinki, raising
one's voice on the benches of the *Eduskunta* would be unthinkable and
orators would usually read their speeches, almost passing as lecturers. Those
who have experienced other tribunes (like the European Parliament) admit
that there is "much less self-expression in Finnish politics, perhaps at the
cost of dynamism".[50] In Oslo, shouting is almost inexistent as well, but
television debates can get hot.[51] Undoubtedly, self-controlled gesture has
nothing to do here with ostentation but should be interpreted as a cultural
feature as well as a sign of respect for political opponents and democracy. It
is however acknowledged by young MPs, like Tove Lifvendahl in Sweden,
that they are most conscious about the way in which they move their body.
Her Norwegian colleague Ine Marie Eriksen attaches great value to staying
very natural but she reckons that facial expression counts a lot. "You
cannot make your way in politics if you look glum or lacking enthusiasm".
Peter Wolodarski, a journalist who has been participating in media training
organized for Swedish politicians from the Liberal party, told me that the
exercise is mainly "intended on improving the capacity to respond efficiently
to questions, but gesture is corrected when need be".[52] Many political actors
I spoke to mentioned that they learned how to control their posture when
they were on television – either through experience or after advice given.

A glimpse into language issues certainly does not invalidate the general
impression of 'conspicuous modesty' we have had so far.[53] To be fair, it
must be conceded that for the past decades some brilliant politicians, well
aware of their intellectual superiority, did not think twice about showing it.
In Sweden, this was the case of both Olof Palme and Carl Bildt. Furthermore, eloquence might possibly be the one political attribute that escapes
rigorous censorship, since the capacity of a politician to be articulate is

much admired. Nevertheless, the Swedes well remember the 1976 debate between Olof Palme, the Social Democrat with an aristocratic background, and Thorbjörn Fälldin, from the Centre (ex-Agrarian) party, whose electoral posters showed him on a tractor in front of his farm. The former, who was clever and extremely self-assured, clearly prevailed in the debate over his tongue-tied and hesitant opponent. Yet, Palme went on to lose the elections partly because voters had found him too arrogant, too assertive and therefore insufficiently 'Swedish'. According to the politicians I interviewed, speaking in such a 'Swedish way' would involve avoiding any demonstration of superiority, though not insinuating that you underestimate your audience either. The capacity to confront your opponents' views in a 'relaxed way' is also most valued. In this respect, Göran Persson's capacity to combine sound (non-technocratic) reasoning, informal and rather consensual speech, is often considered positively.

Having said this, two important factors certainly have to be taken into account. First, the ideological one. Conservatives do not exactly speak like Socialists or Populists (who often know how to use shock formula efficiently). Representatives may betray their class origin, their high or relatively low level of education. In Norway, Kaci Kullmann Five was often criticized for her refined language, her smart district accent and felt rather bad about it, saying there was nothing she could do because she was "educated that way".[54] Audun Lysbakken from the Socialist party agrees that leftist politicians may have unorthodox expressions, although he would reckon that he speaks in a different way at the Parliament, on television or during meetings. In both cases, the political actors seem to be conscious of the existence of a standard, legitimate way of speaking, beyond their respective ideological and class background. Yet, on the Conservative side, there seems to be a more didactic style: "I do not hesitate to use a high-level language, even if this induces defining some words";[55] whereas more radical politicians seem to play the card of extreme ordinariness: "Unlike so many others, driven by the obsession to save face anyway, I do not mind confessing that I ignore something. What matters most is to look 'honest and direct'".[56]

Second, in continuity with what has been said above, political discourse naturally depends very much on the situation. In the three countries, if politicians all emphasize how fundamental it is to express oneself in a simple and distinct way, they also take the kind of audience they are addressing into account. Within specialized committees or when giving a speech at a university, one may be rather sophisticated and technical, whereas when you speak on the radio to a large and heterogeneous audience, you have to adopt a rather plain style – which may prove to be problematic at times, bringing upon risks of simplification and misinterpretation. Other dimensions could be mentioned here: for instance, the use of dialects in Norway; that of Finnish or Swedish in Finland; that of foreign languages when political actors address immigrant communities or assemblies abroad.

Finally, an unexpected issue, which came across during field research and would require more investigations, is that of 'authorized' speech. In Finland, under the Kekkonen era, some top members of his inner circle took the liberty to make statements in the name of the President although their speech had not been previously endorsed. This was an ostentatious but risky way of demonstrating their importance. By contrast, due to the very collective approach of decision-making, most Nordic politicians would rather speak cautiously in the name of their party or institution – which again confirms typical self-effacement attitudes.

CEREMONIAL POMP

Pomp refers to sumptuous display within official ceremonies. The study of pageantry is obviously central in a comparative analysis of political elites laying a stress on ostentation. For centuries, rulers all over the world have been trying to offer a spectacle of unparalleled magnificence meant to demonstrate their power and foster their image. A number of topics are to be considered here. I will mention only a few. The question of rituals exploiting both solemnity and codified reiteration is worth taking into consideration since they constitute a crucial way of exhibiting elite supremacy. When analyzing political rituals in contemporary societies, I am mainly interested in the combination of two conflicting requirements: to be in accordance with traditional, institutionalized patterns legitimizing the governors, and subtle variations aiming at slightly differentiating the manifestation from similar previous ones (in order to imprint it on memories). Proxemic research, that is the semiotic approach of space, is also extremely important when one studies concrete and symbolic distance, the emphatic political use of height, light, sound, etc. Unlike what could be expected, there are no ubiquitous formulae for that matter, nor are there universal perceptions either. Both anthropologists and historians have shown how conceptions as regard the symbolic 'construction' of rulers are conventionalized. For example, ostentation may rest on complex strategies based on aloofness or extreme visibility. The same goes for temporality. If in Northern Europe or North America, punctuality is highly prized, to arrive on time in Sub-Saharan

Africa is to display inferiority. It should be added that elite leisure activities entailing a ceremonious representation (at the opera, at the race-course, etc.) may also prove worthy of study.

Much of my research tends to support the proposition that pomp is hardly resorted to in Nordic countries, including in the Scandinavian royal courts. However, a distinction should be made between theatricalization aiming at symbolizing statehood and the one enhancing individuals' image. On some occasions and in a certain sense, Nordic politics can be quite formal, especially in Sweden and Finland. The Nobel Prize banquet in Stockholm or the Independence Day reception in Helsinki look very ceremonious from an outsider's perspective. However, what is at stake here is the country's greatness which sometimes needs to be manifested. If this is definitely not Buckingham Palace, do not tails, bow-ties, medals, the female dress show and also obvious repressions of spontaneity somehow keep up a tsarist or aristocratic flavor?

On the other hand, when we consider political actors individually, in their everyday activities, they generally look extremely informal from a comparative perspective and, as was emphasized above, incredibly accessible. Democracy has changed many things and has enabled people with a working-class background to have political careers. Often socialized in very small towns or within trade unions, they were often to bring their tradition of proximity with the average citizens to the very top: imposing a style of simplicity to the whole political class, including its more conservative elements. During interviews, I heard anecdotes from Nordic politicians appalled at the showy behavior of their French counterparts (a well-known Minister of Culture, party leaders from the Communist party, etc.) by contrast with their own low profile. Even the solemn entrance of the National Assembly Speaker is quite amazing from a Finnish MP's point of view.

In Nordic countries, there is often unease with public figures giving themselves in spectacle. What proves to be rejected – especially by the older generation – is the present trend whereby political elites and media conspire to stage public 'performances'. The theater of representation is acceptable only when it is meant to convey the role to which political actors are expected to conform: a publicly salient position entailing a certain type of demeanor, with limited leeway. In other words, men and women in charge of politics should content themselves with humbly serving the great values and ideas of their respective repertoire and not become individuals pretending to be too much at the fore. To take a recent example, Norwegian Prime Minister Kjell Magne Bondevik was accused of being too fond of honors. His behavior has really set people talking about a 'change of attitude'. If he formerly was seen as a dedicated leader with a passion for politics, since his come-back – following a nervous breakdown, which by the way had gained him even more sympathy from the public, and a subsequent resignation – he would now be too eager to parade with top figures like Bill Clinton and Ariel Sharon or even attend the society wedding of Stein-Erik Hagen (one of the wealthiest self-made men in Norway) and Mille-Marie Treschow (heiress to a large family fortune). To top it all, he was controversially awarded a decoration from the king in September 2004. This would have passed unnoticed in many countries, but what seems to have shocked many Norwegians is that it went against the tradition whereby you might possibly be entitled to such a reward in return for your services after your career has ended, definitely not when you are still in power. An elder from the Labor party commented '*Bondevik er en jåle*' (pretentious, like a lord) which made the headlines of a newspaper. Of course, all this may be interpreted in terms of politicking (for instance, inviting the Israeli Prime Minister to one's home town perhaps looks scandalous from a leftist point of view, but probably much less so in the eyes of a Christian Democratic party supporter). Yet I would think that it also reveals deeply rooted perceptions.

The same goes for prestigious leisure occupations. Admittedly, gone are the days when just taking holidays out of the country was badly thought of. Generally speaking, traveling abroad is no longer considered as a privilege and Nordic politicians easily spend a weekend in a foreign capital or a fortnight's holiday in the Canary Islands – as so many of their fellow citizens would. Yet, staying in a five-star hotel in Mauritius, like President Chirac does, would certainly raise objections. Symptomatically, among the mini-scandals ('mini' of course from an outsider's perspective) which have affected Nordic politicians in the past few years, much of this has to do with private or official journeys abroad. For instance, Tuula Haatainen, the Finnish Minister of Education was accused of staying at overly exorbitant hotels during a visit to the United States. Likewise, in the famous Murtala Local Government affair in Sweden – where some public money was used to pay for private spending – accusations mainly concerned journeys abroad.

A recent survey of 53 Swedish MPs, with added participant observation (Barrling-Hermansson, 2004), proves that they positively want to project an image of 'banality' and 'ordinariness' – in other words, to appear to be 'like every other Swede'. The study was based on the MPs' self-portrait: it asked them to choose the image they would like to give of themselves. Obviously, their replies may have fitted their own PR strategy but they are, nevertheless, useful in that they allow assessment of the criteria they adjudged to be most relevant in this respect. The majority of respondents wanted to be depicted in some ordinary everyday activity: house cleaning, gardening, looking after the children, taking a walk, etc. Most instructive were the responses of those who changed their minds: one realized that a picture in an expensive restaurant would be inappropriate and proposed instead to be photographed hunting in the woods; another revised her earlier idea of a golf course and suggested a summer family photograph in the garden (Daloz & Barrling-Hermansson, 2004). It should be added that the responses did not differ according to party affiliation.

PHYSICAL APPEARANCE

This final rubric did not occur to me from the outset. I realized that political elites are also led to ostensibly take care about their physical appearance. Following the example of other celebrities cautious to constantly present an image in accordance with their official portraits, they have to conform to expectations – all the more so when they are under the spotlight. Some authors consider that make-up, hairdressing and other techniques meant to beautify oneself can be related to adornment. I am reluctant to accept this combination because the body is a 'given', and therefore latitude for intervention is much more limited. Except in the case of a few people pretty much blessed by nature, what is involved here is improvement or at least keeping oneself fit. It is appropriate to make a distinction between operations involving beauty surgeons (Silvio Berlusconi's face-lift, etc.) and the everyday use of cosmetics. Historically, spending hours at the dressing table in order to be suitable for the day's social engagements used to be an elitist activity (e.g. Gunn, 1973). It may be related to Veblen's (1899) model in terms of 'conspicuous leisure': taking care of one's body involves having time at one's disposal but also assistance from skilled people – servants in the past and beauticians nowadays. There is no question that the diffusion of cosmetics, perfumes, etc. during the 20th century has reduced the ostentatious aspects of such practices. Nonetheless, sociologists have good grounds to say that embodied traits are often a good indicator of social position.

Here, I will not venture into the big question of the canons of beauty which are of course eminently varied according to periods and cultures, even though it can be a very interesting subject from a comparative political perspective. Let us just think about stoutness which happens to be a comforting sign in some places: connoting success and capacity to help (like in the case of Nigeria 'big men') or affability (Helmut Kohl), in contrast to slenderness: increasingly connoting dynamism in the West.

What is most remarkable, as far as Nordic countries are concerned, is how much ordinary looks can be prized. Admittedly, handsome politicians like Premier Minister Jens Stoltenberg in Norway or Thomas Bodström (the Swedish Minister of Justice) know full well how to take advantage of their great charm. It is also true that, in Finland, there are some people to deplore the fact that Tarja Halonen accepted to be photographed with her bathing cap at the swimming pool – which may not appear very 'presidential'. Yet, it seems that her lasting popularity is precisely due to the fact that she indeed incarnates an average citizen.[57] Conversely, for more than 20 years, Norwegian Conservative leader Kaci Kullmann Five was plagued with recurrent comments about the barrette she would constantly wear on the right side of her head. She has been trying to explain that it is the most convenient way to do her hair, but it was interpreted in some newspapers as giving her a typical 'Bærum' look (the 'posh' Oslo area where she comes from and which she used to represent in Parliament). A hairdresser working for the television even proposed to change her style entirely: cutting and dying her hair! But she categorically refused.[58] What is most revealingly is that her successor at the top of the Conservative party, Erna Solberg, a rather corpulent lady, seems to be considered as 'closer' to the people: precisely because of her average appearance.[59]

Of course, Nordic female politicians personally have to look after and pay for their beauty care. They may, however, enjoy the free services of a make-up specialist before a television program. In Sweden, for example, if this would take just 1 min for men (a little bit of face powder), ladies are asked for what they would like and the process may take from 5 to 20 min.[60] In Finland, rather much against a long tradition, male politicians are also more and more prone to adopt a soft, polished look. Here, would it not be relevant to update classical analysis on the king's/queen's 'two bodies' (Kantorowicz, 1957; Axton, 1977) and adapt it to contemporary politics?

CONCLUSION

This article set out to explore how in Norway, Sweden and Finland the legitimacy of representation demands avoidance of ostentation by political elites. I found that, whatever the facets taken into consideration, the general trend is one of conspicuous modesty. Unlike what can be observed in some other places (like sub-Saharan Africa) where ostentatious flamboyance is key – since it is the material proof of the ability to nourish clientelistic networks, or more ambiguous cases like France and Japan, where political actors must play on two distinct, and not easily compatible, registers by simultaneously proving and transcending proximity, the lowest personal profile is expected in Nordic countries. American style self-promotion ('I am a winner'; 'See how successful I was in my professional career'; 'I am your best choice') would be counter-productive in such a context. It is instead the evidence of one's ordinariness and one's humble devotion to the public, which will carry conviction and strengthen the claim to act as 'representative'.

In this article, which deliberately concentrated on empirical, thick description rather than theoretical analysis, I did not directly confront the question of the possible explanations that can be given as regard such extreme perceptions and behavior. In some of my earlier works, I propose some nuanced interpretations which I will not repeat in detail here. Let me just say that some scholars stress a *mentality* (Daun, 1996, 1989) fashioned out of the perennial need for solidarity within a harsh Scandinavian environment in which low population density and a widely dispersed habitat favored self-control, equality and the avoidance of conflict. This *passion for equality* (Graubard, 1986) is far from being the same as egalitarianism since the Nordic societies privilege individuality, even if they stress the importance of the collective. It is different both from the American notion of equality of opportunities and from the French emphasis on civic equality. It is, rather, a matter of *similitude* – the importance of avoiding distinction from one's peers. Archeologists and historians as well as political scientists (see several contributions in Sørensen & Stråth, 1997) have contributed to this debate on cultural roots: referring to the Viking period, the virtual absence of feudalism and of course the influence of Lutheranism, with its moral code of austerity.

For their part, the Social Democratic politicians I interviewed in Sweden and Norway,[61] especially those from the older generations, argue that the origins of such attitudes are not to be found in ancient history. They believe that the primacy of anti-ostentatious behavior stems from the efforts of their predecessors who, at the end of the 19th century, were responsible for the creation of influential popular movements. This kind of interpretation can be considered together with theses whereby the idea of equality originates from a strong enlightenment movement in a predominantly rural setting.[62] Since the members of these movements often came from humble backgrounds themselves and had been socialized in the trade union tradition, they brought to the fore a concern for modesty and proximity. It would be this heritage that made them immune to ministerial pomp when in office and, it is argued their attitude would then have filtered through to the whole body politic.

I want to suggest that these two explanations – respectively, culturalist and ideological – are not mutually exclusive. There is little doubt that the Social Democrats were responsible for the emergence of the type of political legitimation that still prevails today across the political spectrum. At the same time, their success was due in no small measure to the fact that the model they helped fashion was in harmony with the prevailing socio-cultural norms. In other words, they succeeded in evolving a specific attitude to political representation precisely because that brand of political behavior fitted the environment within which modern politics developed.

Ostentation, as this article has tried to convey through various examples, is unacceptable and indeed unthinkable in this part of Europe. This makes the reference to my analytical grid – all too briefly presented – rather unusual here. However, from a comparative perspective, being confronted with this extreme rejection of any ostentation proves to be most fascinating.

There are slight differences between the three countries under consideration. Actually, a foreign scholar – usually considered as a 'neutral' outsider – is often provided with stereotyped cross-perceptions conveying a sense of competition, if not of minor hostility, between the three national identities. For instance, it is rather frequent to hear Norwegians content with being deemed 'even more modest' and 'less formal' than people from the two other countries. On their side, Swedes tend to show a sense of moral superiority, especially toward the Finns. They would deplore that the latter "have not entirely broken off with the ostentation tradition of the czarist period". The Finns themselves commonly regret that the Swedes do not fully take into consideration the great hardships they have suffered and that some political evolutions were entirely due to dire circumstances.

Although stereotypes are crude simplifications of complex realities they may contain an element of truth, and researchers are expected to compare these prevailing stereotypes against realities that can be objectively observed. As regard Finland, it is true that the situation has been ambivalent. Illustrations emphasizing both conspicuous modesty (in the Scandinavian way) and relative ostentation could be multiplied. Strikingly enough, it has been frequent for Presidents to depict their background as being 'a bit lower' than in reality (for instance, Kekkonen claimed that he was born in a house that did not even have a fireplace[63]). On the other hand, not only do we know that the former Constitution and *de facto* powers gave him the authority to appoint people in so many sectors but he sometimes made decisions in a fairly ostentatious way (for example, calling his aide-de-camp and unexpectedly promoting somebody right in the middle of a dinner). He used to dress in a smart way for official occasions but could take on the appearance of a woodcutter when in the countryside. Both registers make perfect sense. However, I would argue that Finland, which has had a mixed culture characterized by both democratic pluralism and a strong leader cult, is becoming closer to its Scandinavian partners, now that the tensions with its mighty neighbor have subsided. We know that the powers of the Finnish President have been reduced and that the system was 'parliamentarized' in 2000.

As I have pointed out above, when it comes to intra-Nordic comparisons, my view can be no more that impressionistic. However, I would like to submit the following ideas. First, if we look at things in a long-term perspective, the absence of feudalism (Denmark would be quite another story) and the shaping of a deeply rooted – mainly rural – mentality, discouraging feelings of superiority, are factors of similarity. Admittedly, Sweden became a great power in the 17th century and this may have led to status-consciousness and court pageantry aiming at emulating and impressing other European powers (e.g. Ellenius, 1988). Yet, a renowned specialist of comparative modern history (Burke, 1997) tells us that, even in this case, what can be detected is an alternative style, marked by a relative tradition of simplicity. If the nobility remains visible enough in Sweden (actually its present reproduction strategies would deserve a close study), we have to admit that there has been a general decrease in ceremoniousness at the royal court (e.g. Rundquist, 1995).

Second, in terms of political regimes and systems, it is obvious that the process of 'Finlandisation' has increased the cultural gap, which possibly already existed between Finland and its Scandinavian neighbors. On the other hand, if we look at the situation from the angle of both democratic parliamentarianism and welfarism, the discrepancy remains limited. The Cold War did not lead to authoritarian rule in Finland, just to 'semi-presidentialism' (which was also a consequence of the civil war). Above all, popular movements have played a rather similar formative role in the three countries. In all cases, we also find a strong belief in education and meritocracy, intended to reduce the distance between the social classes. This is definitely crucial for shaping mentalities and political style.

A third element which should be considered here from a comparative perspective is the national history of the three countries in relation to self-affirmation. Both Norway and Finland have quite obviously suffered from a somewhat 'peripheric image' vis-à-vis dominant respective neighbors. The solemnity of their Independence Day appears to be most important in the two countries, culturally speaking. The Finns also had to create a prestigious power image at the center so as to impress the Soviets. It is also quite understandable that the Norwegians celebrated the centenary of their independence with some glamour in 2005. But, again, it should be emphasized that pomp is meant to extol the country, the nation, the institutions and not really its leaders, as would be the case in some other parts of the world. Furthermore, it is also noteworthy that some Norwegians declared that it was perhaps "a bit too much". By contrast, an 'old country' like Sweden, allegedly one of the very first nation-states in Europe, does not have to put so much stress on glorification. To give an illustration related to tragic events: contrast the relative simplicity of Olof Palme's funeral with the very imposing one of Urho Kekkonen.

In any case, my results clearly indicate that *nowadays* in Oslo, Stockholm and Helsinki, elites 'who can handle things' are certainly well appreciated but they should abstain from 'showing off'. In that respect, studying confrontations with external models of perceptions and behavior proves to be most interesting. The question arises whether – for official visits abroad, when receiving a foreign guest, etc. – Nordic political elites should stick to their own code or submit themselves to other customs? Both attitudes may prove embarrassing. One may be criticized for not behaving in a Nordic way.[64] But on the other hand, one should avoid putting one's country in an awkward position. MP Rosa Meriläinen – who, as we saw, was once criticized for wearing 'indecent' clothes within the Finnish Parliament – felt she had to dress well when she was asked to welcome a Turkish delegation. "They already were to be surprised being received by a woman under thirty; I did not want to shock them deeply".[65] The same goes with her young colleague from the Socialist party in Norway, Audun Lysbakken, who would wear a suit when he is part of an official delegation going abroad.[66] In a way, abiding by other people's norms – even when they contradict your own views – may be analyzed as a supreme sign of modesty.

Finally, one should ask whether such modest conduct is likely to persist or not. During the field research, I came to realize how deeply rooted they are in the three countries. Nevertheless, I think a generational factor should be taken into consideration. Not only are young politicians often more educated, but I am under the impression that they aim at raising and maintaining a higher profile than many of their predecessors. The electoral system allowing voters to indicate preferences among political lists increasingly urges each politician to differentiate himself or herself in order to be perceived as an individual, and not just a party representative.[67]

Competition leads you to become 'a character' says Rosa Meriläinen. Hence the crucial role now given to personal websites, blogs, weekly diaries, etc. Ine Marie Eriksen, the above-mentioned Norwegian Conservative MP, goes as far as describing herself as a kind of 'salesperson' trying to persuade people that her product is the very best one. "Of course it is indeed important to have convictions and solid ideological knowledge. But it also matters to be able to communicate your ideas and this means understanding the logics of the new media society".[68] Unknown candidates and junior politicians seem more and more convinced that they have to draw attention to themselves. Being noticed may imply 'becoming an entertainer to some extent', especially at a time when disaffection with politics is feared. This certainly does not entail being ostentatious, but at least conceiving political activities in a more self-centered way than used to be the case.

NOTES

1. On this unusual approach about political representation, see *Elites et représentations politiques* (Daloz, 2002a) or my Chapter 10 in Chabal and Daloz (2006).
2. Admittedly, this rule appears less effective in respect of today's nouveaux riches but even here, it is important to point out that few will ignore it. Displays of ostentation are possible mainly outside their native country, for example when they are on holiday in the Mediterranean or the Swiss Alps (interview with Carl Johan Westholm, President of the Swedish Federation of Private Enterprises, Uppsala, May 18, 2001).
3. Some similar field research will be carried out in Denmark soon.
4. The aim obviously being not to generate statistical data but thick description, working on perfectly identical categories was not considered an indispensable methodological objective.
5. Interview with Kaci Kullmann Five Oslo, September 22, 2004.
6. Interview with Birgitta Dahl at the *Riksdag*, Stockholm, on May 14, 2001.
7. Interview with Anders Björck, Governor of the Uppsala region (formerly Chairman of the Council of Europe, Minister of Defense and First Deputy Speaker at the *Riksdag*), Uppsala, March 16, 2004.
8. Interview with Rosa Meriläinen (Green party), Finnish Parliament, Helsinki, April 6, 2005.
9. Interview with Ine Marie Eriksen (Conservative party), Norwegian Parliament, Oslo, October 1, 2004.
10. Interview with Astrid Thors (Swedish People's party), Finnish Parliament, Helsinki, April 7, 2005.
11. Interview with Arja Alho (Social Democratic party), Finnish Parliament, Helsinki, April 6, 2005.
12. Ine Marie Eriksen, (interview already mentioned).
13. Interview with Anders Björck, already mentioned.

14. Interview with Heidi Hautala, Finnish Parliament, Helsinki, April 8, 2005.
15. Interview with Rosa Meriläinen, already mentioned. Actually, Conservatives are also encouraged not to look too smart. Kaci Kullmann Five mentioned a debate with Social Democratic leader Gro Harlem Brundtland where the latter was wearing a solid gold necklace. "As a Conservative, I would not have dared wear such jewelry because it could have given rise to malicious comments" (interview already mentioned).
16. Interview with Audun Lysbakken, Oslo, October 12, 2004.
17. Idem.
18. Interview with Hans Brattestå at the Norwegian Parliament, Oslo, September 24, 2004.
19. She is a very controversial person who also has been attracting attention from the press subsequent to confessions that she used to smoke marijuana or because she would sometimes display very provocative badges.
20. Interview with the leader of the Green party, Heidi Hautala, above mentioned.
21. Interview with Ine Marie Eriksen, already mentioned.
22. Interview with Tove Lifvendahl, Stockholm, March 12, 2004.
23. Interview with Lennart Nordfors (consultant, former Deputy General Secretary of the Liberal party), Stockholm, March 19, 2004.
24. Interview with Solveig Ruud (*Aftenposten*), Oslo, September 27, 2004.
25. Interview with this journalist, author of two books on the Swedish elite (Kullenberg, 1974 and 1997), Stockholm, June 5, 2001.
26. Interview with Solveig Ruud, already mentioned. On the other hand, Carl I Hagen (populist leader in Norway) did not mind granting an interview by his swimming pool in Spain.
27. Interview with Astrid Thors, above mentioned.
28. Some top officials also enjoy official accommodation, like Region Governors in Sweden who may live in beautiful castles. This is why this type of position is particularly sought after and generally proposed as a kind of reward at the end of a career.
29. Interview with editor Halvor Hegtun *Aftenposten*, Oslo, September 21, 2004.
30. Interview with Audun Lysbakken, already mentioned.
31. From a comparative cultural perspective, it is always fascinating to see how contemporary art is fashionable in Nordic states. I am under the impression that those countries, often self-depicted as 'small and at the periphery', try to compensate this feeling by showing that they are in the artistic forefront.
32. Interview with Hans Brattestå, already mentioned.
33. Interview with Kaci Kullmann Five who was appointed minister at the end of the 1980's. NB exceptionally, the conversation was in French. I have translated the word 'dégueulasse' (which is quite strong) by 'terrible'.
34. Source: personal field research in France.
35. For instance, in France, Valéry Giscard d'Estaing adopted Peugeot cars to differentiate himself from his Gaullist predecessors – who fancied Citroëns – whereas François Mitterrand preferred Renaults: symbol of a nationalized company.
36. For example, both Arab and African elites are quite obsessed with differences between various Mercedes Benz models. In many countries, it is most significant to have a 500 model and not a 280.

37. Here one may think of tinted windows, flags, but also of the size of the car. For instance, the leader of the former German Democratic Republic, had insisted on getting his vehicle lengthened.

38. Actually, it seems that a lot of VIPs prefer driving themselves. For instance, this is the case of the Norwegian crown Prince or some top businessmen.

39. Interview with journalist Jarkko Vesikansa (*Suomen Kuvalehti*), Helsinki, April 8, 2005.

40. Interview with editor Peter Wolodarski (*Dagens Nyheter*), Stockholm, March 15, 2004. Speaking of photographs, several MPs told me that they now dread new mobile telephones including mini-cameras.

41. Interview with former Minister Arja Alho, already mentioned.

42. Interview with political editor Anders Linder, *Svenska Dagbladet*, Stockholm, March 23, 2004.

43. Interview with Pekka Ervasti, Managing Editor, *Suomen Kuvalethi*, Helsinki, April 7, 2005.

44. Interview with Secretary General H. Brattestå, already mentioned.

45. Interview already mentioned.

46. Interview with Rosa Meriläinen, above mentioned. However, due to the fact that she has formed a rather visible couple with her partner, Simo Frangen a TV celebrity, this has not been very easy.

47. Interview with Kaci Kullmann Five, already mentioned.

48. During my interview with him, in Stockholm on May 3, 2001.

49. Interview with Mats Eriksson journalist working for a news agency and based at the *Riksdag*, Stockholm, March 17, 2004.

50. Interview with Heidi Hautala, already mentioned. As a leader of the Greens in Strasbourg, she quickly realized how her style differed from those of her colleagues Joschka Fischer or Daniel Cohn-Bendit.

51. Interview with Aslak Bonde independent journalist, Norwegian Parliament, Oslo, September, 24, 2004.

52. Interview already mentioned.

53. Of course, studies by scholars mastering the various languages involved here lead to more sophisticated results. See for instance several contributions on the Nordic political campaign discourse in Gomard and Krogstad (2001).

54. Interview with her, already mentioned.

55. Interview with Tove Lifvendahl, already mentioned.

56. Rosa Meriläinen from the Finnish Green party. Interview mentioned above.

57. On the same line, she was seen buying a refrigerator in a department store and asking for 'bonus points'. If this situation was judged as utterly ridiculous by some, it appears that it has contributed to her 'one of us' image. Interview with journalist Timo Antilla, *Ilta Sanomat*, Helsinki, April 7, 2005.

58. Interviews with Kaci Kullmann Five and Solveig Ruud, already mentioned.

59. I heard such comments on several occasions. A more systematic enquiry would be needed here to confirm such perceptions.

60. Tove Lifvendahl, interview mentioned above.

61. Of course, the Finnish situation, where the Social Democratic party never enjoyed a hegemonic position, is rather different.

62. Again refer to some contributions in Sørensen and Stråth (1997).

63. Actually one was built when he was 3 years old. It was to be obliterated from an official photo presented at the occasion of his first presidential campaign in the 1950s.
64. So said in passing, this type of accusation may also be addressed to politicians who were posted abroad for a while and had allegedly a 'strange' attitude after their return. For instance, Jan O. Karlsson, the Swedish Minister in charge of the immigrants who had terrible relations with journalists and had to resign, was blamed for behaving like somebody 'from Brussels'.
65. Interview with her already mentioned.
66. Interview mentioned above.
67. On the dynamics of the electoral systems in the countries considered here, see Grofman and Lijphart (2002).
68. Interview already mentioned.

ACKNOWLEDGMENTS

Thanks to the universities of Oslo, Uppsala, Södertörn, Tampere and Helsinki for kindly providing academic hospitality. I also received some grants from the French CNRS and the Norwegian NFR, which were much-appreciated contributions. I express my gratitude to all the colleagues who contributed to making this research possible, with very special thanks for concrete help and fruitful discussions to Emil Uddhammar, Sverker Gustafsson, Katarina Barrling-Hermansson, Jörgen Hermansson, Li Bennich-Björkman from Uppsala; Åke Daun, Stockholm; Inga Brandell, Södertörn; Fredrik Engelstad, Trygve Gulbrandsen, Anne Krogstad, Aagoth Storvik, ISF Oslo; Harald Baldersheim, Knut Heidar, Øyvind Østerud, University of Oslo; Ilkka Ruostetsaari, Tapani Turkka, Olavi Borg, Tampere; Kyösti Pekonen, Jurri Mykkänen, Seppo Hentilä, Henrik Stelnius and Kimmo Rentola, Helsinki.

REFERENCES

Auchet, M. (2004). La 'loi de Jante' et l'imaginaire social scandinave. *Nordiques*, 4(April).
Axton, M. (1977). *The queen's two bodies*. London: Royal Historical Society Studies in History.
Balandier, G. (1980). *Le pouvoir sur scènes*. Paris: Balland.
Barrling-Hermansson, K. (2004). *Partikulturer: kollektiva självbilder och normer i Sveriges riksdag*. Uppsala: Acta Universitatis Upsaliensis.
Bourdieu, P. (1979). *La distinction: critique sociale du jugement*. Paris: Minuit.
Braudel, F. (1979). *Civilisation matérielle, économie et capitalisme, XVè–XVIIIè siècles*. Paris: Armand Colin.

Bremmer, J., & Roodenburg, H. (1991). *A cultural history of gesture*. Ithaca: Cornell University Press.

Burke, P. (1997). State-making, king-making and image-making from renaissance to baroque: Scandinavia in a European context. *Scandinavian Journal of History*, *22*, 1–8.

Chabal, P., & Daloz, J.-P. (2006). *Culture troubles: Politics and the interpretation of meaning*. London & Chicago: Hurst Publishers & The University of Chicago Press.

Daloz, J.-P. (1990). Voitures et prestige au Nigeria. *Politique Africaine*, *38*(June).

Daloz, J.-P. (1999). Pouvoir politique et ostentation: aspects culinaires. *Revue Internationale de Politique Comparée*, *6/2*(Summer).

Daloz, J.-P. (2002a). *Elites et représentations politiques: la culture de l'échange inégal au Nigeria*. Bordeaux: Presses Universitaires de Bordeaux.

Daloz, J.-P. (2002b). L'étalage de la vie sexuelle en tant que facteur de légitimation politique. In: P. Baudry, C. Sorbets & A. Vitalis (Eds), *La vie privée à l'heure des médias*. Bordeaux: Presses Universitaires de Bordeaux.

Daloz, J.-P. (2003). Ostentation in comparative perspective: Culture and elite legitimation. *Comparative Social Research*, *21*.

Daloz, J.-P., & Barrling-Hermansson, K. (2004). Représentation politique et modestie ostensible en Europe du Nord. *Nordiques*, *4*(April).

Daun, Å. (1996). *Swedish mentality*. University Park: The Pennsylvania State University Press (Swedish version, *Svensk Mentalitet*. Stockholm: Rabén Prisma, 1989).

Dietler, M., & Hayden, B. (Eds) (2001). *Feasts: Archeological and ethnographic perspectives on food, politics, and power*. Washington: Smithsonian Institution.

Duncan, J. S. (Ed.) (1981). *Housing and identity: Cross cultural perspectives*. London: Croom Helm.

Edelman, M. (1964). *The symbolic uses of politics*. Urbana: University of Illinois Press.

Elias, N. (1974 [1936]). *La société de cour*. Paris: Calmann-Lévy.

Ellenius, A. (1988). Visual culture in seventeenth-century Sweden: Images of power and knowledge. In: Collective, *The age of new Sweden*, Stockholm: Livrustkammaren.

Flandrin, J.-L. (1999). La distinction par le goût. In: R. Chartier (Ed.), *Histoire de la vie privée*, Vol. 4. Paris: Le Seuil.

Fleurdorge, D. (2001). *Les rituels du Président de la République*. Paris: PUF.

Geertz, C. (1973). *The interpretation of cultures*. New York: Basic Books.

Geertz, C. (1983). *Local knowledge. Further essays in interpretative anthropology*. New York: Basic Books.

Gomard, K., & Krogstad, A. (Eds) (2001). *Instead of the ideal debate: Doing politics and doing gender in Nordic political campaign discourse*. Aarhus: Aarhus University Press.

Goode, W. J. (1978). *The celebration of heroes. Prestige as a social control system*. Berkeley: University of California Press.

Graubard, S. R. (Ed.) (1986). *Norden: The passion for equality*. Oslo: Norwegian University Press.

Grofman, B., & Lijphart, A. (Eds) (2002). *The evolution of electoral and party systems in the Nordic countries*. New York: Agathon Press.

Gunn, F. (1973). *The artificial face: A history of cosmetics*. Newton Abbot: David & Charles.

Holt, D. B. (1997). Distinction in America? Recovering Bourdieu's theory of tastes from its critics. *Poetics*, *25*.

Kantorowicz, E. (1957). *The king's two bodies: A study in medieval theology*. Princeton: Princeton University Press.

Kullenberg, A. (1974). *Överklassen i Sverige*. Stockholm: Tiden.

Kullenberg, A. (1997). *Urp! sa överklassen: Eliten i Sverige*. Stockholm: Tiden.

Lamont, M., & Fournier, M. (Eds) (1992). *Cultivating differences: Symbolic boundaries and the making of inequality*. Chicago: The University of Chicago Press.

Rapoport, A. (1982). *The meaning of the built environment*. Beverly Hills: Sage.

Rundquist, A. (1995). Pompe en noir et blanc: Présentation officielle des dames à la cour de Suède. *Actes de la Recherche en Sciences Sociales, 110*(December), 65–76.

Shils, E. (1969). Reflections on deference. In: A. A. Rogow (Ed.), *Politics, personality and social science in the twentieth century: Essays in honour of Harold D. Lasswell*. Chicago: The University of Chicago Press.

Sørensen, Ø., & Stråth, B. (Eds) (1997). *The cultural construction of Norden*. Oslo: Scandinavian University Press.

Stone, L. (1967). *The crisis of the aristocracy 1558–1641*. New York: Oxford University Press.

Strong, R. C. (2002). *Feast: A history of grand eating*. London: Jonathan Cape.

Veblen, T. (1899). *The theory of the leisure class: An economic study of institutions*. New York: Macmillan.

Veen, M. van der (Ed.). (2003). When is food a luxury? *World Archeology, 34/3*(special issue).

Veyne, P. (1976). *Le pain et le cirque: Sociologie historique d'un pluralisme politique*. Paris: Seuil.

Wiessner, P., & Schiefenhövel, W. (Eds) (1996). *Food and the status quest: An interdisciplinary perspective*. Providence: Berghahn Books.

SEDUCTIVE HEROES AND ORDINARY HUMAN BEINGS: CHARISMATIC POLITICAL LEADERSHIP IN FRANCE AND NORWAY

Anne Krogstad and Aagoth Storvik

A nation is in itself an invisible entity and in that sense it will always be *imagined* (Anderson, 1983, p. 14). In line with this view, Walzer (1967, p. 194) maintains that a state or a nation must always be personalized before it can be seen, symbolized before it can be loved, imagined before it can be conceived. In this respect, national leaders are in a special position. They not only represent the interests of the people, but also sum up the national community, what the nation *is*, at the same time as they lead. But how do they do this? To answer this question we will compare French and Norwegian politics.

A striking observation is that French politicians appear as more glamorous and seductive than their Norwegian colleagues. Astonishing characterization of French politicians support this impression. The press reports about the dynamic and passionate Jacques Chirac, the "femme fatale" Edith Cresson, the "decisive seducer" Nicolas Sarkozy, the beautiful and charming Ségolène Royal and about "Mr. Testosterone" Dominique de Villepin. Admittedly, Norway also has a prime minister who often is characterized as

Comparative Studies of Social and Political Elites
Comparative Social Research, Volume 23, 211–245
Copyright © 2007 by Elsevier Ltd.
ISSN: 0195-6310/doi:10.1016/S0195-6310(06)23009-6

handsome and charming, but the lack of such characteristics are more profound than the opposite.

In this article we study a special form of political leadership, the Charismatic Leadership. We have two main questions. The first is whether political charisma is expressed and commented upon differently in France and Norway and the other is whether there are differences in the ways men and women perform charismatic leadership, and whether they are perceived differently.

The aim of the article is threefold: First, to show the existence of a specific type of charisma, the *ordinary human charisma*. Through a type of role distance, it is possible for a politician to become vibrant and alive, but yet not different from ordinary people. This particular type of anti-authoritarian charisma is touched upon by Max Weber in his writings on charisma, although not very extensively. The second purpose is to show that certain forms of charisma are more common in one national context than in another. Different forms of charisma accentuate different sets of national and cultural repertoires of evaluations (Swidler, 1986; Lamont & Thévenot, 2000). The third purpose is to show how certain forms of charisma are gendered. This means that they are not equally accessible for men and women.

CHARISMA AND LEADERSHIP

We take as our point of departure Weber's well-known taxonomy of forms of authority (Weber, 1947; 1968). Traditional authority, which first of all characterizes pre-modern societies, is based on inherited privileges and positions. Legal authority, which is often termed rational and bureaucratic, is based on position and competence. In addition, it is impersonal. By contrast, charismatic authority is personal, not positional. It has one main feature, authority legitimated by the appeal of leaders who claim allegiance because of the force of their extraordinary personalities. Weber saw this kind of authority as liberation from the alienation, which the bureaucratic "iron cage" represented. The essence of charisma is a sort of life and vitality, which is the opposite of the formality of bureaucracy and the roles and conventions of traditional society (Weber, 1968, p. 24). Consequently, charisma implies a sort of renewal. According to one of Weber's most heavily quoted passages, charisma is based on "the devotion to the exceptional sanctity, heroism or exemplary character of an individual person, and of the normative patterns or order revealed or ordained by him" (Weber, 1968, p. 46). The charismatic leader has, in other words, exceptional qualities and is accordingly "set apart from ordinary men and treated as endowed with supernatural, superhuman, or at least specifically exceptional powers or qualities" (Weber, 1968, p. 48).

The three forms of authority that Weber speaks of are ideal types that do not exist in their original forms. Both in France and Norway political power is formally based on legal authority. Both countries are democracies with democratically elected political leaders. But even in political systems based on legal position, charisma is viewed as crucial, especially in top positions (Weber, 1994, p. 166). A political leader who only follows regulations and order in a typical bureaucratic manner is, in fact, described as "useless" (Weber, 1994, p. 160). True political leadership is and ought to be something different from legal-bureaucratic leadership.

There are, however, certain differences in the challenges to political leadership position in small countries in contrast to world powers. Weber argues that any numerically "large" nation is confronted by tasks of a quite different order from those devolving on other nations "such as the Swiss, the Danes, the Dutch or the *Norwegians*" (Weber, 1994, p.75, our italics). By this he means that people who are "small" in numbers and in terms of power "have different obligations and therefore other cultural possibilities" (Weber, 1994, p. 75).

In addition to size, which will have consequences for the politicians' tasks and roles in the respective countries, form of society will affect charisma. Weber saw charismatic authority as both a pre-modern and modern form of leadership, but he feared that charisma would wane with the onrush of modernity (Bryman, 1992). Graham Little (1985, 1988), however, argues that charismatic political leadership is most common in highly modern countries. Especially, he argues, it is found among well-educated people who live like modern intellectual "aristocrats". Ann Swidler (1979) regards this the same way. She claims that a charismatic leadership might be easiest to accomplish among upper middle class people, with their intellectual open-mindedness and their scepticism toward rules and traditions. Both Little and Swidler, however, acknowledge that this is a different form of charismatic leadership than the type described by Weber. The essence of charismatic leadership, the appeal a leader has, is still basic, but this appeal may be based on a relation of *equality* rather than on the total allegiance to a superior leader that Weber had in mind. Little describes this new type of charisma as characterized by play, creativity, humour and an exploring attitude. By this, he introduces elements of freedom and unpredictability to charisma, qualities that are often found in "personalities" or "eccentrics". Although the relation between leader and follower can be quite *symmetrical*, something which is relevant to our study, this kind of charisma is marked by a sort of intellectual superiority, which means that both leaders and followers can put themselves above all traditions and customs (Little, 1985, p. 134). This form of charisma is, in some respects, contrary to ordinariness, and it therefore stands in opposition to the charisma of the ordinary human being, which we will try to elaborate on in this paper.

Swidler refers to Erving Goffman's (1959, 1961) notions of "presentation of self" and "role distance" in order to describe how her certain type of charisma is attained. According to Swidler, not every type of role distance will be perceived as charismatic – it must necessarily express certain values cherished by the followers. In order to study these, Swidler introduced the term "cultural repertoires" (Swidler, 1986), a term Lamont and Thévenot (2000) later have adopted for comparative research and termed "national cultural repertoires of evaluation". These repertoires of evaluation consist of sets of tools in the form of frames of interpretation and strategies of legitimization that are employed within specific national contexts (Lamont & Thévenot, 2000). We will bring this perspective with us in studying the respective national and cultural repertoires of evaluation in France and Norway.

What we have identified as a human form of charisma, which departs from the more common understanding of charisma as supernatural, almost divine, is inspired by the writings of Weber. In *Economy and Society* he claims that a charismatic principle, which originally was directed toward the legitimization of authority "may be subject to interpretation or development in an *anti-authoritarian* direction" (Weber, 1968, p. 61, our italics). Even in *asceticism* there may be charismatic authority. This often has a basis in what he terms a charisma of "suffering", which may sometimes result in radical change (Weber, 1968, p. 53).

If charismatic authority, as Weber maintains, lies in the appeal a leader has as heroic or anti-authoritative, our assumption is that France will gravitate toward the *heroic* and Norway will gravitate toward the *anti-authoritative*: more specifically what we have termed an *ordinary human charisma*. It is as an ordinary man or woman, a politician gains appeal and status as a political hero in the Norwegian society.

There are not only differences in the orientation and meaning of charisma that have struck us as conspicuous in the comparison between France and Norway; the concept "cultural repertoires" also has made us sensitive to the different domains to which one can link charisma in relevant and legitimate ways. We have already mentioned heroism and "ordinariness/humaneness".

Another domain that is sometimes associated with charisma is *eroticism*. As mentioned in the introduction, descriptions of French politicians are permeated by sexually laden words.

While personal appeal, which Weber claims is so central to charisma, is coupled to eroticism/sexuality in French politics, sexual references in the description of Norwegian politicians are almost non-existent. And if they are employed, they are much more indirect. Here the expression "the power of character", which Tjeder (2003) has suggested as a characteristic of Nordic mentality, deepens the telling expression Daloz (2003) has employed to describe the appearance of Norwegian politicians as "conspicuous modesty".

How, then, does gender influence political leadership in these two widely different contexts, one a political cocktail consisting of passion, seduction and drama, and the other assumingly uncharismatic, unromantic and desexualized? It is evident that the charismatic leader Weber had in mind was a man, something he does not mention but takes for granted. In this respect it becomes pertinent to ask what happens when the political leader is a woman. In addition, we claim that charisma not only is about appeal – the ability to arouse enthusiasm – it may also have a sexual-seductive dimension. It has been pointed out that beneath the gender neutrality which characterizes the typical rational-legal authority there is a masculine subtext (Kanter, 1977).[1] Charismatic heroic authority has even more profound masculine connotations. In her book *Compassionate Authority* Kathleen Jones (1992) maintained that our traditional understanding of authority is associated with the male, while the understandings we have of the female tend to be uncoupled with the understanding of authority. We will, however, argue *against* a portrayal of relations of authority as categorically gendered. With Skjeie (1993, p. 225) we claim that in principle charismatic authority is open to both men and women. But we also claim that men and women employ the main element of charisma, appeal, in different ways linked to different cultural and political repertoires. For instance, we will try to show that the ascetic and ordinary human charisma is better suited for women than the heroic form of charisma.

In order to operationalize the main question in this study – whether (gendered) charisma is expressed and commented upon differently in France and Norway – we have formulated the following research questions:

- How common is charismatic characteristics in French and Norwegian politics?
- Is charisma evaluated positively or negatively by the surroundings?
- Which politicians are said to be charismatic in the two countries?

– Which reasons are given for such characterization in the two countries?
– Do the same dimensions contribute to male and female politicians' charisma?

The analysis is based on a review of newspapers, magazines and political biographies in search for cases of charisma according to the evaluations of journalists and biographers. These empirical cases of charisma will be related to the theory of Weber, Little and Swidler. Through this comparison we will try to expand and draw new implications for the theory of charisma. In addition we will try to explain differences in charismatic leadership in the two countries by using the concept of national cultural repertoires. In our study the content of these repertoires will be tied to different traditions of leadership and political representation. Through historic and institutional processes repertoires are formed – also gendered repertoires – which can explain why certain patterns of actions or interpretations are more frequent in one nation than in another. However, these repertoires do not determine action. They merely determine which interpretations and patterns of actions the actor can choose from (Swidler, 1986).

DATA AND METHODS

We have chosen to compare Norway and France for different reasons. The two countries are both similar and different in interesting ways. Both are modern western countries, with highly developed welfare states and with a rather large public sector. The party formations, with the left-right divide, share certain fundamental commonalities (Baldersheim & Daloz, 2003). But there are also striking differences. The elitism and the strong hierarchy of the French society are clearly different from the more egalitarian Norwegian society. In addition, gender relations are perceived differently in the two societies.

Since the two countries in many ways is such an unlikely pair for comparison, the approach chosen in this study may be termed *contextual* and *reflexive* rather than comparative in the strict sense of the word (Baldersheim & Daloz, 2003). Initially, the aim is to gain an understanding of preconditions and options for political charisma. The method is inspired by an approach that anchors the reception in what, broadly seen, seems to "make sense", in what seems legitimized within the two contexts (Chabal & Daloz, 2006). However, cases which challenge peoples' views on political leadership will be of interest, not least because they occasionally reveal where the borders between legitimate and illegitimate political leadership is drawn. Let us underline that we discuss the role models of representation, myths and ideas play in national cultural contexts (Saguy, 2000). In other words, the study is concerned with how different actors argue, portray themselves and portray the world, and not necessarily how the world "is" – something that does not make it less interesting to study.

If one is interested in studying national cultural repertoires, the main representatives of political parties, the political leaders, appear to be an excellent choice. In opposition to other leaders they have been chosen by the people and therefore they must have some appeal in large segments of a country's population. The empirical study includes top politicians, i.e. presidents (in France), prime ministers (in both France and Norway), candidates for the two mentioned positions and central ministers/party leaders. Since the presidents and prime ministers are those that to the highest degree sum up the nation, we have given them the most attention. These leaders are selected from 1945 and until now. This gives us an idea of what present day politicians have to relate to. The broader material, which also includes ministers and party leaders, is selected from 1980 to 2006 and is meant to give a more extensive picture of political leadership in general in this period.

Our data have several sources. First, we base our article on observations and interviews in former studies on politicians in Norway and in the Nordic countries. Here we draw on Krogstad's studies from the early 1990s and until now. These include observations of how politicians present themselves in the public (Krogstad, 1999, 2000; Gomard & Krogstad, 2001). Second, we base the study on 38 interviews with Norwegian party leaders, deputy party leaders, general secretaries and leaders of program committees in the eight largest parties (Aardal, Krogstad, & Narud, 2004; Krogstad, 2004). Third, we base this article on Krogstad's fieldwork among French politicians in 1988 and follow-up observation during the 1990s (Krogstad, 1999).

Since – according to Weber – charisma also lies in "the eye of the beholder", in peoples' recognition of a leader's charismatic authority, we have supplemented the above mentioned data with personal characterization and pictures of political leaders in a large body of texts. This is our main empirical source. For the period 1945–2000 we base the analysis on political biographies produced by social scientists and more popular writers. For the period 2000–2006 we have collected material (newspapers, magazines, journals) produced in a systematic library search. This includes personal characterization of politicians in both countries. Through reading these texts we try to identify who is described as charismatic, and why. Are there explicit or implicit reasons given in the texts for characterizing a politician as charismatic? Which adjectives in the texts are used to characterize the charismatic politician?[2] The identified repertoires of charisma are then compared to the pre-existing theoretical works on the topic.

FRANCE: HEROIC CHARISMATIC LEADERSHIP

According to historians specializing in European monarchies, nowhere else in Europe were the gaps between the top and the bottom of society as visible as in *Ancien régime* France. In spite of France being the origin of the bourgeois revolution, the country is still known for – and affected by – Louis XIV's Versailles (Chabal & Daloz, 2006). According to Daloz (2003, p. 54), the advent of the 5th Republic in 1958, and the subsequent presidentialization of the political system did not put an end to the aspects of elitism and ostentation in French politics.

While Norwegian politics has been characterized by a divide between reason and feelings and by a strong belief in persuasion by the use of arguments, French politics with its historic lines to famous salons, court intrigue and revolution, is more into conspiracies, dramas, aestheticism and eroticism. According to Hufton (2000), issues of privilege and signs of social differentiation have been a constant obsession. Reason and feelings seem to melt together. Emotional persuasion is openly recognized as an important part of political life, and in this context charisma – the ability to arouse enthusiasm – is central. Politics is not only seen as a rational discussion between citizens, but as an emotionally based relation between the elite and the mass.

The "grandeur" of French political leaders is not surprising in view of France, in contrast to Norway, being imbued with the heritage of a Great Power tradition. Also in the realm of culture and ideas, France has been an exporter of political inventions and cultural models (Baldersheim & Daloz, 2003). These simple facts will have clear consequences for the performance of French leadership.

France has had many great leaders, but in the post-war period President Charles de Gaulle (president from 1958 to 1969) was the greatest. He was predominantly seen as charismatic and an inspiration for later French politicians, all of whom claim a part of his mantle. De Gaulle himself had many reflections on leadership, especially military leadership, and was familiar with many of the classic works in this field, including Machiavelli (Chalaby, 2002). His own philosophy of leadership went in direction of charismatic leadership, and he also developed views on how it was possible for a leader to make such an image. Drake and Gaffney (1996, p. 19) point out that many who have studied French politics have misunderstood what Gaullism really is. Gaullism is not a political ideology, but a theory of leadership. According to the two authors, de Gaulle did not have a political ideology. His ideology was the greatness of the country.

In order to make people listen, de Gaulle maintained that two conditions were important: authority and charisma. One could obtain *authority* through self-control and inner strength. A political leader should not be similar to the people. On the contrary he should be different from them. De Gaulle was never viewed as ordinary, as one of the masses; rather he was viewed as quite pompous. Earlier this was generally regarded positively by French voters, but has later been seen as a more dubious trait (Drake & Gaffney, 1996). According to de Gaulle *charisma* demanded that the leader was somewhat withdrawn so that an impression of mystique, or surprise, was created. It was also important that the leader portrayed himself and performed acts that could symbolize his grandness. De Gaulle himself appeared as a man with grand ideas, mostly concerning the central role of France in the world. This view also dominated his political speeches. In his press conferences he used two thirds of the time to talk foreign politics and one third of the time to domestic politics (Chalaby, 2002, p. 158). To him foreign politics was closely linked to internal political affairs. His 10 most employed words were, in this order: "France", "the country", "the Republic", "the state", "the world", "the people", "the nation", "prosperity", "peace" and "future" (Chalaby, 2002, p. 154).

De Gaulle put much consideration into making emotional impacts on the people, to catch their fantasies. As he once said: "One does not move crowds without elementary feelings, violent images and brutal invocations" (Chalaby, 2002, p. 169). De Gaulle conceived the people as a mass characterized by irrational feelings and fantasies. This certainly put restrictions on the use of common sense and logical argumentations to persuade them. De Gaulle was not being particularly known for using either of them. On the contrary, he had faith in the Machiavellian tradition where the leader tries to dominate the formation of opinion through the use of emotion and flattery.

De Gaulle mixed a heroic mythical and romantic leadership ideal with democracy and French republican ideals. According to Hayward (1991) he was, in fact, the first French president who was able to unite personal leadership with a stable democratic government. Later on, all French top politicians have had to relate themselves to de Gaulle's leadership (Gaffney, 1988). By ritual and symbols Pompidou, Giscard d'Estaing, Mitterand and Chirac, all employed the heroic charisma that de Gaulle added to the position.

George Pompidou had all the constitutional tools and symbols his predecessor had, and in his speeches and press conferences he underlined his authority. However, contrary to de Gaulle, he did not refer to himself in the third person. On several occasions he rather tried to portray himself as an ordinary Frenchman: "As President of the Republic, I would constantly remind myself that I am only one Frenchman among many, and therefore that I am able to understand them and their problems" (Safran, 1985, p. 154). These efforts at identification with the people failed, and he was soon to be regarded as an indecisive, weak and uncharismatic leader figure.

In spite of his somewhat pompous leadership style, de Gaulle had been able to establish a close relation with the French people. In speeches he addressed people directly and downplayed party politics. President Valéry Giscard d'Estaing, who admittedly was less pompous and more downplayed, was not able to attain the same intimacy. With his good looks, elegant appearance and aristocratic background, he gave the presidency a natural glamour, what we may term *effortless superiority*. However, his elitism nevertheless created a social barrier.

During the 1980s and 1990s it became clear that French politicians on the one hand had to be visionary, superior and presidential, and on the other hand, had to be ordinary and close to the people (Drake & Gaffney, 1996, p. 23), a rather tall order. In 1981 the socialist, François Mitterand, was elected as president on a program that openly rejected the Gaullist style, a program of change and democratization. He had been a strong opponent to the Fifth Republic's institutions, especially the presidential office itself, which he characterized as a permanent *coup d'état*. However, only few months after taking up office, he started to behave in ways that resembled his predecessor, de Gaulle. He was called monarch, patriarch (uncle/father) and sphinx: the combination of power and mystique created the basis for his charisma. When he was asked whom he addressed, the individual or the mass, he answered that he always tried to reach the individual among the thousands or millions: "If I can manage to do that, I speak to them all" (*Aftenposten,* 27 May 1989).

Jacques Séguéla, founder and creative director of one of the largest advertisement bureaus in France, was the person who created Mitterand's personal appeal during the presidential elections of 1981 and 1988. In 1981 Séguéla made use of Mitterand's age and experience, and selected the forceful, but also pacifying slogan "La force tranquille". Also in the 1988 election Mitterand was portrayed as a calm, brave, patriotic, but also cool and mystical man, with inner strength. Further on he was portrayed in the serene role as a defender of a country threatened with an uncertain future.

He was not at all an old man who had lost his "juices", something that his opponents tried to hint, but according to the advertisements, a mature patriarch who could gather old and young, right and left, and who, similar to ideal family fathers, stood for a friendly, but decisive guidance characterized by tolerance, flexibility and consensus (Krogstad, 1999).

While French newspapers still ask whether Mitterand was the last great president in France (*Le Point*, 5 January 2006; *Le Monde*, 3 January 2006), his successor to the presidency, Jacques Chirac, nevertheless made "grandeur", "bravery", "passion" and "will" into his trademark. His declared aim, which could have been taken from de Gaulle's mouth, was to make France the leading and most dynamic country in Europe: "La France en tête". In Chirac's case both personal and bodily characteristics seemed to add to his charisma, with power, sensuality and elegance as the main elements. Early in his presidential period, Chirac had a confrontational, almost aggressive style. However his media strategist, Thierry Saussez, leader of *Images et Strategies*, contributed to a change in the image of Chirac, from a cold and calculating one to a softer, and also vaguely sexy and sensitive image. In his elegant suits from Guy Laroche, Chirac was portrayed as a modern statesman. Toward the end of his presidency, however, Chirac was increasingly portrayed as old and politically weak (*Marianne*, 14 January 2006). He nevertheless still mastered gallantry. This was certainly demonstrated when he met the newly appointed German chancellor Angela Merkel for the first time. In an aristocratic manner he kissed her hand.

Chirac was often accused of elitism. In the first round of the presidential election in 2002, when he received only three percent more votes than Jean-Marie Le Pen of *Front National*, his main solution was to declare a struggle against the elite culture in the French political system. The appointment of Jean-Pierre Raffarin as prime minister – a man one assumed was "ordinary" – did not have the anticipated effect. Neither did Prime Minister Dominique de Villepin, who Chirac appointed in 2005.

As with Chirac, Villepin's charismatic potential seems to lie in the combination of greatness, passion and elegance. Villepin was educated at École Nationale d'Administration, the super-elite finishing school for technocrats which has furnished most of France's presidents and prime ministers since the 1970s. He has been a career diplomat, written several books about poetry and culture – and a book about Napoleon. His speeches are flowery and loaded with feelings, almost turgid. With his lofty, grand plans, there is much of the French grandeur to Villepin, and he has been characterized as "a bulimic politician" (*L'Express*, 19 January 2006). Critics describe him as a patrician aristocrat – his full name is Dominique Marie Francois René

Galouzeau de Villepin. He is also a proponent of anti-Americanism, and in this respect he pursues the heritage from de Gaulle. Villepin was clearly opposed to the US and British invasion of Iraq. In this way he demonstrated the well-known French exceptionalism in the foreign policy. With his effortless superiority, he represents a recognizable heroic charismatic political type in French politics. However, it is sometimes argued that his effortless superiority is staged, as when he once posed in a swimming suit after having a bath. A French newspaper declared this the most spectacular and most prepared ascent from the sea since that of Ursula Andress in the James Bond movie *Doctor No.* (*Le Point*, 5 January 2006). Villepin is also described as one who lacks "human touch".[3] In this respect he is even described as an "autist" (*Liberation*, 13 March 2006).

Jean-Marie Le Pen, the long time leader of the Front National, has been a comeback figure in French presidential elections. Le Pen stands out. He portrays himself as an "anti politician", as one "who always speaks the truth". He has made it his trade mark to be "uneducated". "If you mention Schopenhauer, he will think of a German brand of beer" his ex-wife claims (Globe, 1988, no. 27), who admittedly is not very friendly minded. Le Pen is sometimes characterized as "brutal", "primitive", "shameless" and "a France without its civilized hypocrisy". This also adds to his charisma: It gives him a distinctive stamp compared to the politically cultivated elite cliques. Images of original male strength and sexuality seem to be contained in this form of charisma. Le Pen has criticized his male enemies of being feminine, soft and even homosexual (Levy, 1989,p. 108). Through a symbolism of exaggeration he employs the feminine as a border marking between him self and other men. His own masculinity is put forth as dominating and the masculinity of his enemies as bleak in comparison. The dichotomy heterosexuality/homosexuality is thereby made central in the hierarchy of masculinity. By feminization of, and almost humiliation of male political opponents, he himself symbolizes a stronger masculinity, something in addition to other men (Krogstad, 1999).

The last French politician to be mentioned in this section is Nicolas Sarkozy. Sarkozy is often referred to as a "seducer" (*Paris Match*, 5 March 2006; *Marianne*, 17 March 2006). However, he is mostly known to be an ambitious and decisive politician. In 2005 a journalist asked whether in the morning, while shaving, he sometimes thought about becoming president. "Not only when I am shaving," was the answer (*The Atlantic Monthly*, September 2005).

The immodest Sarkozy demonstrates a form of authority which is far from the matter-of-fact authority of Villepin. Sarkozy is rather an example of *superiority with effort*, a charisma fought for. In this respect both Le Pen and Sarkozy represent something relatively new in French post-war politics. Admittedly Sarkozy has a bourgeois, even an aristocratic background. But he also has an immigration background: his father was a Hungarian aristocrat, his mother was a Greek. And Sarkozy does not hide the fact that he has fought hard in order to enter top politics. As he himself says: "Nothing was ever given to me; I fought for everything I have" (*The Atlantic Monthly*, September 2005). He is described as "having a twitchy, all-elbows manner and no one would call him warm or easygoing" (op. cit.). His brutality, it is said, is covered in milk and honey (*Le Nouvel Imbécile*, March 2006). Sarkozy trusts few, he does not enter into stable political alliances, but fights alone against everybody. Even in his leisure time he is a "lone rider" as he cycles mile after mile, alone on his bike, every week.

Compared to most other presidents and presidential candidates in France, Sarkozy nevertheless seems to be close to the people (*Le Nouvel Observateur*, 30 June 2005), but in a different way than Le Pen. He wants to be where the people are, and he tries to do something with the problems that people face in their daily life. This has led him on tours around France, being pictured at places where there are problems and crisis, something that was also the strategy of de Gaulle. This closeness to the people combined with an explicit strategy of finding practical solutions to political problems instead of retreating to ideological formulations, adds to his charisma.

This examination of some central French politicians, whether they are termed aloof or close to the people, educated or uneducated, insiders or outsiders, lead with or without effort, demonstrates that legitimized political leadership in France is linked to a heroic charismatic ideal. Both the portrayal by the politicians themselves and the characterization of them point to this. The craving for charismatic leaders can also be read from negative evaluations of politicians. As mentioned, the elder Mitterand was referred to as one who had lost his "juices" by his opponents. Dry and boring politicians are not regarded favourably. Lionel Jospin, who was previously mentioned as a candidate for the 2007 presidential election, was rejected by some as boring and uncharismatic, "as cheerful as a tube of glue" according to the newspaper *Liberation*.

What is it then, that determines the French charisma? Common to all the cases we have discussed, is that the leader portrays himself as a figure of authority, even though some try to assume a more "ordinary man" image, which points to the dilemma of being both above and part of the people. The asymmetric relation between the leader and the people is in line with the description Weber gave of the heroic charismatic leader as aloof and superior. Furthermore, many of the leaders seem to refer to – and are associated with – well-known cultural stereotypes of masculinity and sexuality (Connell, 1987).

NORWAY: ORDINARY HUMAN CHARISMATIC LEADERSHIP

Contrary to France, which is one of the largest states of Western Europe, Norway is among the smallest (4.5 million inhabitants), without ambitions of power. For 400 years Norway was occupied and ruled by foreign nations (Denmark and Sweden), and the ethos of Norwegian politicians are marked by the long-time fight for independence and national sovereignty. This laid the basis for Norwegian politics concentrating on questions within the border of the nation state.

If Norway has visions of international stardom, it is perhaps in the moral and peace making disciplines, as the term "kindness regime" indicates (Røkenes & Sirnes, 2005). Several studies show that Norwegians like to think about themselves as relatively equality orientated (Gullestad, 2001; Lien, Lidén, & Vike, 2001). Equality, or sameness, is a basic motive that sums up the Norwegian political ideal and that contains great rhetorical power. Not least in the political field, where politicians are dependant on the support of the voters, it is important not to be too filled with oneself, to appear modest and low key – at the same time as one is leading.

With reference to works from anthropology, political science and history (Klausen, 1984; Sørensen & Stråth, 1997; Slagstad, 1998), Henningsen and Vike (1999) argue that Norway and the Nordic countries are strongly characterized by a special type of power, what they term "ordinary peoples' power". This kind of peoples' power almost reaches an elitist position, they claim. Since Norway never had any nobility in the strict sense of the term, this "elitism of the people" is related historically to enlightened people that had the *agrarian society* as a dominating model and the *farmer* as an elevated and enlightened cultural hero (Larsen, 1984). This has created an agrarian bias in the Norwegian political ethos, with a down-to-earth orientation and pragmatism. This ethos, Henningsen and Vike (1999) claim, has contributed to undifferentiated political arenas and weak conditions for the expressive dimension, for rhetoric, playfulness – and charisma.

Henningsen and Vike are not willing, however, to see this tendency to anchor political leadership in the people as an expression of an undeveloped and provincial cultural disposition compared to countries with a cultural and social elite hegemony. Rather, they want to explain the solid, fantasy-lacking and anti-elitist political ethos as a result of a different Norwegian – and partly Nordic – modernisation process. In this process the idea of similarity, of being equal, is seen not only as a characteristic of the life world of the *local* community, it also permeates national political life. The argument the two authors put forth is that the political elite in Norway is possibly unique in the sense that it is formed by extremely successful grass roots mobilization, not least among the religious lay movements. *More* people have taken part in the creation of the political public in Norway than in most other Western democracies, including France. This is reflected in a political style where contact with grass roots, integrity and predictability play a central role. The equality orientation is not the same as the abstract ideal of the continental Enlightenment (Slagstad, Korsgaard, & Løvlie, 2003, p. 15). It is an ideal which is ascribed a local and substantial meaning in connection to the practical orientation of everyday life (Henningsen & Vike, 1999).

How is this rural political ethos expressed? First of all by scepticism toward urban styles, classic education, elegant rhetoric and elaborate gestures. A modest, low-key appearance and a tendency to honour others, not oneself, are central elements. For example, the American political scientist Harry Eckstein had the following impression of the typical Norwegian parliamentarian in the 1960s:

> The manner in which authority, especially high authority, is generally wielded in Norway contrasts sharply with the manner in which it is exercised in highly inegalitarian countries [...]. The great thing even among parliamentarians, for example, is to appear to be a regular fellow: practical and commonsensical, well-versed in dull facts, rather inelegant, unimpressed, indeed embarrassed by success. One displays certain rustic graces such as quiet attentiveness, amiability, a lack of cantankerousness, disrespect and disdain; but one also displays a certain rustic clumsiness: a monotonous delivery, a bare style, a lack of "manners" (although, not of courtesy). (Eckstein, 1966, p. 156)

This fascinating collection of low-key adjectives gives a nice summing up of where Norwegian present day politicians come from. To get further away from Weber's heroic charisma would be hard. Jean-Pascal Daloz (2003), who has compared the use of ostentation as signs of political power in several countries in the world, argues that Norway and the Nordic countries are extreme cases. His studies show that Norwegian politicians even today cling to portrayals of themselves as ordinary men and women. This is underlined by ministers taking the metro to their work, queuing up as everyone else in the canteen and having their personal telephone numbers appear in the directory. According to Daloz, these attitudes are all the more

remarkable ones as they seem to apply across party lines. "Never emphasizing one's power or wealth seems to be an implicit code: not only in the
left-wing parties, but also among the most conservative ones" (Daloz, 2003,
p. 49). The tradition for this under-communication of power is probably
stronger in the left-wing parties. However, Daloz is right in pointing out that
the notion of elite itself is not used or accepted in any party. Norwegian
politicians would rather view themselves as political representatives, occasionally leaders.

This impression is confirmed in interviews with leaders, deputy leaders,
general secretaries and leaders of program committees in the eight largest
parties in Norway (Krogstad, 2004). In these interviews the politicians stress
a close association with the people, often coupled to moral and values. On
an open question about how they, as Norwegian politicians, can create trust
and credibility, variations of the following expressions were used. "Integrity", "closeness to people", "must not distance ourselves from the people",
"be concerned with what the people is concerned with", "not stand above
the people", "be one of the people", "must be able to say things in ways the
people understands", "must be able to convey what every day problems
are" and "must identify with most people". One of the politicians maintains
that "a pompous rhetoric works badly here – the rhetoric should rather be
modest and careful". Another politician claims that "it is important to
portray oneself as non-spectacular". Other characteristics mentioned are
honesty, sobriety, decency, reliability, recognizability, generosity and engagement. Also humour and high spirits are said to be good qualities.

In these anti-rhetorical and anti-spectacular ideals linked to being an
ordinary human being, there is a dilemma, as many researchers have pointed
out (Nylund, 2001; Daloz, 2003). Politicians in any society have a special
task. They are both representatives of their respective voters and they are
leaders. They are both part of and above the "we-community", whether it is
the party or the people. In Norway this double task has a special form since
it is carried out in a cultural landscape where egalitarian ideals are especially
strong. Equality in itself, and also rhetorical references to equality, represents an argumentative resource in the building of charismatic authority.
Independently of statistically proven equality or not, equality, and also its
opposite, difference, are used as arguments by people who compete over
resources (Lien et al., 2001). A description of Norwegian politicians as uncharismatic will therefore be too unrefined. It will be a question of what to
look for, of what gives legitimacy.

As in the case of France, we will start looking for charisma in the politicians after 1945. The previously mentioned low key style characterized

most of the social democratic prime ministers after World War Two: de Gaulle's parallel in Norway, Einar Gerhardsen (ditch digger and longtime prime minister from 1945 to 1965), Trygve Bratteli (originally employed in construction), Odvar Nordli (accountant). Similar to de Gaulle, Gerhardsen gained moral legitimacy through his participation in the Resistance during the Second World War. During his time as prime minister he insisted on living in a modest apartment in a working class district on Oslo's east side. Admittedly, he sometimes retorted to a flowery language and marked gestures. However, when reading his speeches today, one is struck by the "general commonplace", and this is what makes Gerhardsen into one of the greatest speakers in the post-war period (Johansen & Kjeldsen, 2005). He knew his public. He lived among ordinary people. His exemplary manners were characterized by both "character" (Tjeder, 2003) and "conspicuous modesty" (Daloz, 2007, this volume).

There are, of course, examples of other leadership styles in Norway. A former leader of Parliament, Carl Joachim Hambro (Conservative Party), had an urban-oriented, elaborated and engaging way of speaking. Also the labour movement had a charismatic type of politician, the enthusiastic speaker with ties to the lay movements. Martin Tranmæl, for example, had exceptional talents in agitation, organization and tactics which he combined with a sense of class and moral engagement. He demonstrated a strong sense of affinity to those he spoke to and worked for. Large audiences could be spellbound. According to former Prime Minister Trygve Bratteli (Labour Party), the important thing for Tranmæl was to get the message through to the everyday man, and in particular those who, like himself, had led a farmer's existence and were about to find their place in "a new and strange world".[4]

Although Gerhardsen and Tranmæl had different rhetoric and style, they were both regarded as charismatic leaders, however of the *ascetic* type. It was this ascetic leaning that linked them to people. They lived as ordinary people. Contrary to ordinary people, this modest way of living was chosen. In this respect, these politicians were both ordinary and extraordinary at the same time.

What then about the present day politicians – are they charismatic? Some of them are. However, their charisma is still very downplayed compared to French heroic charisma. Pomp, ambition, cultural and educational capital – in short, all kinds of demonstration of superiority – are deemed suspicious within Norwegian political culture. This is reflected in the parliament, *Stortinget*, which is one of the most egalitarian parliaments in the world (Heidar, 1997). As late as 2000 as much as 35 percent of the political elite had a working class background (Gulbrandsen et al., 2002). This relatively modest background probably has affected the ways to perform politics in Norway.

The politicians' hesitance when it comes to demonstrating authority is also permeating their language. In this respect, there are some interesting differences between the Nordic countries. In a comparative study Bauhr and Esaiasson (2001) revealed that to a much larger degree than Swedish and Danish politicians, Norwegian politicians demonstrate affinity with their voters in televised election debate programs. Swedish politicians, for instance, are much more oriented toward demonstrating responsibility and competence. Another aspect of election discourse is the use of symbolic appeals associated with the creation of identity. Such appeals may be seen as a shorthand method used by speakers to convey information in such a way as to create unity between themselves and the voters. Håkansson (2001) found that symbolic appeals are more common in Norwegian than in Danish and Swedish debates.

In other words, we find a low key, unity-oriented leadership style in Norwegian politicians: there are few, if any, examples of the heroic type of charismatic leadership. However, we find politicians with *charm*. While charisma indicates exceptional powers and qualities in a person, we think of charm as a milder and more unstable form of charisma.

What kind of charm do Norwegian politicians have today then? As mentioned, they are far from heroic-charismatic. The only Norwegian politician who might come close to this ideal, is perhaps the former leader of the Progress Party, Carl I. Hagen. In line with French tradition he is well dressed, gallant and an excellent rhetorician. His speeches are often characterized as seductive. But this characterization is not meant positively, it is rather used by his critiques to convey an image of cynicism. The other Norwegian "charmers" are not associated with a seducer image. Admittedly, Jens Stoltenberg is commonly viewed as both handsome and charming, but his charm is commonly regarded as "boyish" and "playful" rather than "sexy". His informal style does not, however, place him in an elevated position, but in a *symmetric* relation to his voters. As newly elected leader of the Labour Party in 2002, he was termed "a charmer with power avoidance" (*Dagbladet*, 27 December 2005).

The Norwegian charisma is neither heroic nor sensual. Politicians who are now characterized as charming combine informality and humour with honesty and sincerity. The ascetic charisma that characterized the previous generation of politicians is more or less gone and the seriousness and solemnity along with it. Now some of the most popular politicians are almost like *comrades,* which indicates a more symmetrical relation to the voters. But not all "buddy" politicians are regarded as charming, so what is it that creates the charm?

The X-factor seems to be about a moderate type of renewal. This renewal means that a politician overcomes some of the problems associated with former political traditions. Or the renewal expresses the values and orientation of a new generation of voters. The renewal can both be seen in the political roles of the politicians and in their political ideas. Further, renewal can be linked to gender, age, sexual orientation, background, etc., and it can be about performance and self-presentation. Renewal, for instance in connection to gender, can contribute to the charisma, but this is rarely enough in itself. It is through establishing a distance to conventional ways of performing leadership – we may call it role distancing, as does Goffmann (1961) – that the charm is established. However, even role distance toward tradition may not be enough. And not all forms of distancing are successful. The role distance must signal deviance, a break with tradition, which at the same time expresses values that are common to the people or groups of the people (Swidler, 1979, p. 78). This role distance makes the politician less stereotyped, more vivid, like a human being of flesh and blood. When a politician behaves differently to expectation, people may think that they get a glimpse of the person behind the role.[5] With Weber one could say that the person appears as extraordinarily human, though perhaps not as "supernatural". Swidler links this form of human charisma to relations characterized by equality.

If we regard some of the recent years' party leaders in Norway in this light, the red wine drinking party leader Valgerd Svarstad Haugland represented fresh and new breath in the Christian People's Party. Thanks to her, the party could suddenly embrace younger and more liberal voters. Similarly, it is clear that the "laughter-inclined", woman of the world, career diplomat Åslaug Haga, departed from the earlier generations of rural leaders of the Centre Party (formerly the Agrarian Party). This gave her a wider appeal among voters. Kristin Halvorsen departed from former leaders of the Socialist Left by being a young, modern woman who also used mini skirts. Labour and Integration Minister, Bjarne Håkon Hanssen, represented a down to earth style in a Labour Party that is increasingly accused of not being close enough to the people anymore. His slimming process, during which he was pictured in the papers on tread mills and with weight lift apparatuses, added to his popularity (*Verdens Gang,* 29 December 2005). In the Progress Party this kind of popularity might not have been an advantage for a politician. Its party leader, Siv Jensen, is certainly popular, but she has to be careful not to be termed "populist". What is needed then, is politicians who are seen as credible and responsible.

GENDER-BASED CHARISMA IN A HISTORIC CONTEXT

The link between gender and charisma until now has been discussed in an indirect way. In this section we will elaborate on what frames of action charismatic leadership offer men and women, especially concerning presentation of self. As usually is the case with gender, class is an underlying dimension.

The type of charismatic leadership which has been common among French politicians is not gender neutral. As Skjeie (1993) argues, is it not possible for charismatic leaders to be both personal and gender neutral, at least not as long as gender is seen as a vital part of one's personality, we would add. However, it is not evident that a focus on personality will favour men more than women, she claims. As mentioned, women in politics frequently represent something new and refreshing. And even though politicians always will seek support in tradition, in the male heroes from the past, charismatic authority in principle has an open form; it can be filled with new personal profiles, as long as they have a genuine character (Skjeie, 1993).

What is needed, then, is an analysis of how open this form is to women and men in different contexts. If one takes a quick look back to the 18th century, it becomes evident that women in the saloons under the former French regime had influence on political decisions which were made. Aristocratic women attained this influence, either as independent political or economic agents, or indirectly through their abilities to persuade and influence men in positions of power. Sensual charisma was part of the reason why some women had political power. In the name of democracy, the French Revolution put a stop to much of this exertion of power. Women lost their right of admission to public places where political decisions were made, and they were also denied the right to vote. The first country which gave all men the right to vote (1848), was one of the last countries to extend this right to women (1944). Thinkers of democracy like Montesquieu and Rousseau saw the combination of politics and eroticism as very unfortunate, as something which had to be avoided at any price in the New Republic.

Eroticism was seen as enemy number one for the new democracy. The revolution was a pietistic reaction against the aristocracy and their reckless lifestyle, hedonism and vanity. But the revolt was perhaps mostly targeted on the sins of the *female* aristocracy (Landes, 1988). Especially queen Marie-Antoinette became a symbol of the evil and shallowness of the aristocracy (Hunt, 1991).

Even if the French Revolution represented a revolt against the aristocratic lifestyle, some elements of this lifestyle were passed on, but in other forms. In an analysis of Sweden, Tjeder (2003) argues that the aristocratic lifestyle coexisted to some degree with the puritan orientation, characteristic of the bourgeois class in the 18th and 19th centuries. Hard work, piety and self-control were seen as the ideal form of life: unfolding from the *inner character*, rather than from the search for shallow pleasure.

As in Sweden, the power of inner character became an ideal in Norway. Contrary to Sweden, Norway did not have aristocracy, and developed differently historically, but the *revolt* against the aristocratic way of life still made its mark. Cultural influence from the French Revolution and the French democracy thinkers was felt, especially in the Norwegian constitution of 1814 (Slagstad, 2003). Aside from this French influence, thoughts from German Enlightenment were also imported in the 19th century, and made their mark on the Norwegian nation building process. The genuine Norwegian element, however, was borrowed from the old farmers' society. The farmer and the farmstead community became Norwegian emblems. Without any prior Versailles tradition, the "pure" and "natural" became dominant values, with little competition or modification. In other words, there were few examples of superiority, unless we include the superiority Danish, and later Swedish, kings exerted over Norway, and which created much opposition.

Female politicians' scope for political action and performance in Norway must be understood against this background. The old peasant society had fairly strong traditions for gender equality (Steinsland, 2005). In their historical analysis Melby, Pylkänen, Rosenbeck, and Wetterberg (2000), relate this to the strength of the agrarian society and a North European marriage pattern, which lead women to marry late. This rural Enlightenment period presented the fundament for a special political culture into which the lower classes were welcomed. The idea was educated and informed farmers and workers. Women were included in this education process. The marriage pattern granted them more rights than women experienced in other Western countries. Most women married by the age of 25 or 26. At this age they were grown up, quite independent and could demand more than younger women.

Also in later historical periods, Norwegian women gained more power than women in other parts of Europe, not least because of the radical marriage legislation. In 1913, Norwegian women were granted the right to vote. The feminist movement in Norway became early allied with politics and the Norwegian state apparatus. Already by 1987, Helga Hernes (1987) called the Norwegian state "female friendly" and named the alliance between the state and feminists "state feminism".

We believe that this historical background partly can explain why women's entry into politics in the 1970s and 1980s was different in Norway and France. In interviews with French and Norwegian female politicians Apfelbaum (1993) claims that French female politicians who attained their positions in the 1970s seldom regarded their success as a result of their own abilities. Instead they explained their upward mobility by circumstances in the surroundings, more specifically their appointments by a superior, often called the "prince". Such appointments of female politicians were often the target of much speculation. According to Apfelbaum (1993, p. 417), this shows French women's lack of entitlement. In the 1980s, this lack of entitlement seems to vanish among female politicians, but also in this period they refer to a certain *souffrance* in narratives of their own political lives.

The Norwegian female political leaders interviewed by Apfelbaum (1993) were not questioning their own legitimacy. Rather, they all celebrated the fact that they were both women and politicians. The political stage into which Norwegian women entered was clearly different from that of France. The most common form of authority which was demonstrated, was not the charismatic but the rational or legal form of authority, oriented toward positions and qualifications. Although this is not completely gender-neutral, it nevertheless seems to have given female politicians more manoeuvring space (Skjeie, 1993). One astonishing event was Prime Minister Gro Harlem Brundtland's appointment of the so-called "female government" in 1986. The press from all over the world reported the story of a government where 44 percent of the cabinet were women. Since then, the percentage of female ministers in Norway has remained at about this level.

While most women in the French political elite are recruited from outside politics, it is more common for Norwegian politicians, both women and men, to work their way up the ladder, from the local to the national level (Apfelbaum, 1993). In addition to this, Norwegian parties set quotas for female participation early on, which also led to an increase in the number of female politicians. According to Apfelbaum (1993), Norwegian female politicians take their own role more for granted than what their French colleagues do. It will, however, be interesting to study how the French parity law will affect the French political system regarding gender and leadership.

FRANCE: A DOUBLE STANDARD

At the beginning of her career, the one and only female prime minister in France, Edith Cresson, was perceived as attractive – yes, even sexy. Her mentor, Francois Mitterand, is supposed to have remarked at one occasion "Charming, isn't she?" (Ramsay, 2003). As we know now, Cresson was to become the most unpopular prime minister in France ever. Invoking associations with the French saloons and their ensembles, Cresson was seen as a reincarnation of Marie-Antoinette. According to Ramsay (2003) the political execution became just as brutal. Later, Cresson proclaimed that "French politics is a living hell, unless you are old and ugly". This statement could be rhetorically intended, of course. In any case, there was great interest and attention paid to her looks when she was appointed prime minister. One thing is a politician's self-presentation; it is another thing how she is perceived by the public. Speculations flourished as to how Cresson got her appointment in 1991. The President, Francois Mitterand, was attributed a role beyond the formal role French presidents have in appointing prime ministers.

The role eroticism plays in French politics must be understood as a result of the particular value it has within French society in general. The heterosexual relation is described as a *non-antagonistic* relation, an alliance between men and women. This alliance is a national emblem, deeply anchored in French mentality (Saguy, 2000). In language and literature one often sees a celebration of the differences between the two genders. The supposedly happy alliance between men and women is acknowledged by people from all political segments and is even elevated as a particular form of French feminism (Ezekiel, 2002). According to Apfelbaum, all French female politicians who she interviewed had a strong focus on heterosexual dynamics. The close relationship between men and women is described in terms of seduction, romantic play, longing and *amour gallant* (Apfelbaum, 1993, p. 423).

Cresson's "seductive" qualities did not make her charismatic. In other words, there is another standard for women than for men. However, one French female politician who is considered, at least by some, to be charismatic is Simone Veil (Ramsay, 2003). In 1974 she became the first female senior minister in France. But for Veil, it was not sensual qualities which made her charismatic; she was not portrayed as a seductress. Her position in French politics must be understood in the light of her background. Veil is Jewish and was in a German concentration camp during the war. In her case, it is probably her role as a former victim which gives her a moral status, and her charisma appears to be of an ascetic type.

While Cresson and Veil downplayed the role their gender had for their political career, Ségolène Royal, who is regarded as one of the most popular and charming politicians in France today, used another strategy (*Le Monde*, 31 January 2006; *Paris Match*, 15 March 2006). As the first in the country who had a baby while she was a minister, Royal paraded her motherhood in the media, giving interviews from the hospital bed shortly after giving her fourth birth. In this "superwoman" act Royal mixed fertility with competence, using the former to prove the latter (Perry, 2005). Royal revitalizes the question of Skjeie (1993), i.e. if not only paternity but also maternity can be a source for charismatic leadership. Royal has argued that women, and of course, indirectly herself, are more down-to-earth, caring and community-oriented than men (Ramsay, 2003, p. 146). Therefore women also make other political priorities than men. This kind of rhetoric describes women as essentially different from men. Womanhood is presented as a guarantee for moral qualities. The image which is created is that of a certain superhuman being in the moral sense. While Cresson used an egalitarian approach portraying herself as "as good as" men, Royal used a differentialist approach, portraying herself as "better than" men. According to Perry (2005), this marks a shift from seeing womanhood as a handicap to exploiting it as an asset. Both strategies seem to illustrate that French women are caught in a double bind. Both minimising and accentuating differences are fraught with danger in a political environment in which heroic charisma and gender stereotypes prevail.

Motherhood as a metaphor of leadership represents a new invention in the French political field. However, along with a paternalistic charisma it still accentuates an *asymmetrical* relation between leader and follower, that of a parent–child relationship. Seen in accordance with the strong emphasis on heterosexual relations in French society, this can be a high-risk strategy. Fear of a desexualized French society has been expressed, and the almighty mother is often seen as a threat (Ezekiel, 2002). In Apfelbaum's interviews with female politicians of the 1970s and 1980s, references to their families were rarely made in contrast to Norwegian female politicians who did this all the time. Instead, the French female leaders accentuated the dynamic relation between men and women.[6] Royal appears to acknowledge that an image as a dominant mother (*Le Nouvel Imbécile*, March 2006) can create problems for her in a country where the heterosexual pair relation is so central. She has tried to balance the perception somewhat by also referring to the more well known part of the French cultural repertoire. "The two most important things in life are to be a mother and a loving wife," she claims (*Femmeactuelle*, 27 February 2006). However, a loving wife is not primarily a seductive mistress, but instead perhaps someone who attends to her husband's "needs"? By this combined manoeuvre she probably tries to avoid being characterized as a dominant mother and as a new Marie-Antoinette, shallow and evil.[7]

NORWAY: GENDERED EXPRESSIONS OF ORDINARINESS

It is our impression that the relatively uncharismatic and non-erotic Norwegian climate was more admissive for women than the French charismatic-sensual climate. We shall see that the down-to-earth Norwegian political ethos has laid grounds for experimentation and diversity.

Few male Norwegian politicians have been perceived as charismatic or seductive. We think it is fair to say that the first generation of female political leaders adapted to this situation. Illustratively, they were sometimes called "men in skirts". This picture changed with the massive female presence after the 1980s. Female politicians have filled most kinds of ministerial posts. A former ceramist has served as minister of defence. A lesbian crime novelist has served as a minister of justice. A minister of oil and energy gave birth while in office and refused to state the name of the father, and was respected by most people for this (*Aftenposten*, 31 January 2000).

At the parliamentary election in 1993, three women were candidates for the position of prime minister. These were three extremely different women, each with their own distinct style of leadership. One of them, Gro Harlem Brundtland from the Labour Party, was perceived mainly as what Little (1988) calls a strong leader. The other, Kaci Kullman Five from the Conservative Party, was mainly considered to be very clever, but with little appeal to broader groups of people. The third, Anne Enger Lahnstein from the Centre Party, was more of what Little identifies as a group leader, very much in tune with ordinary people. With her down to earth style, Lahnstein was the one who came closest to the Norwegian form of charisma, the ordinary human charisma. She is also the "No-Queen" who, in the referendum of 1994, is said to have prevented Norway from joining the European Union. This exemplifies how Norwegian politicians can gain support by their protests against foreign interference.

While French charisma mostly seems to be attributed to men, this is different in Norway. As a matter of fact most of the politicians, which have been described as charming in Norway since 2000, appear to be women. But in Norway the charm is especially placed on what is conceived as a *human touch*. Not surprisingly, this kind of charisma seems to exclude women to a lesser degree than the more heroic charisma. The demonstration of being human nowadays seems to involve telling stories of private feelings or private life to the media. This kind of display is by no means safe. One can be easily accused of overdoing it, being too intimate and being an embarrassment to oneself and others. One example, however, which demonstrates the potential gain, is well illustrated by former Prime Minister Kjell Magne Bondevik. The prime minister experienced his highest popularity rates after he had revealed his mental depression, during which time his deputy prime minister (Lahnstein) had to step in.

One of the party leaders who is often regarded as charming is Kristin Halvorsen (*Dagbladet*, 13 September 2003; *Dagbladet*, 23 November 2005), although her popularity decreased somewhat after she became Minister of Finance. She also seems to be good at the balancing act between the personal and the public (*Aftenposten*, 1 September 2005). After a very intense election campaign, she admitted that there had been times when she just had wanted to put a paper bag over her head. Likewise, after a frustrating party congress, Halvorsen commented that she "looked like something the cat dragged in", and that afterwards she experienced hair loss as if she had recently given birth (Halvorsen, 2004, p. 88). On other occasions Halvorsen has expressed an interest in clothes, home decoration and fashion. These types of utterances illustrate that she is a human being of flesh and blood, just like ordinary people, or at least like ordinary women. The impression that she talks with and is accessible to ordinary people, is sustained through her personal blog and her frequent participation in Internet debates (Krogstad, 2006). She also shows openness and honesty by revealing how she uses humour and debate techniques as weapons in order to win television debates (Halvorsen, 2004, p. 88). Touching male opponents on their arm when they start to talk has been one of her most famous techniques (*Dagblade*t, 24 August 2003).

These examples show that being ordinary and human probably has a gender dimension. Traditionally, however, being ordinary has been a male discipline in Norwegian politics (Skjeie, 1993). For example, male politicians have showed their affinity with the people by revealing their interests for sport in general, and football in particular. Halvorsen and her female colleagues have demonstrated how it is possible to be ordinary and human in a more 'feminine' way, or rather that women may activate other fields in the national and cultural repertoires than men.

However, reference to personal experiences is by no means limited to female politicians. In a study of 41 televised election debates in connection with the parliamentary election of 2001, Krogstad (2004) found, both to her own and most politicians' astonishment, that more often than female politicians, male politicians referred to their own experiences. In interviews with party and deputy party leaders many of them maintained that "women use the empathy card", "women have a more personal touch", and "women more often use examples from their own personal experiences". However, the actual results from this study go against such stereotypical thinking.

What then about the sensuality which seems so prominent in French politics? Is there any sensuality in Norwegian politics? None of the earlier mentioned female candidates for the prime ministry in 1993, all good looking, behaved or dressed in ways which were perceived to be sensual. On the contrary, Kullman Five was considered to be cold and a prude. Lahnstein was considered to be warm, but not sensual. Brundtland was considered an excellent administrator, but apart from her first years in office she was not generally regarded as an exciting or sensual leader (Slagstad, 1998). First of all she was a respected national mother figure.

Even if the answer to the question of sensuality was "no" only a few years ago, the answer today seems to be "yes". First of all it is the female politicians who have introduced this element to the political scene. They have changed the look of Norwegian politics to a more glamorous one. The new glamour element has been tightly knit to sensuality and outer appearance, but not in a way based on a heterosexual alliance to men. Neither is this a sensuality where women are perceived as objects. On the contrary, we see examples of women who control the staging of their own sensuality and through the use of humour and irony, appear in a subject position. Even the female "heavy weight" Erna Solberg, the leader of the Conservative Party, has let herself be portrayed wrapped in a king blue gala dress, entering a pond as a water nymph (*Verdens Gang*, 22 October 2005).

The sensual appearance of Norwegian female politicians is quite different from that of male politicians in France. In Norway the aesthetic-sensual turn is less about seduction and more about appearing familiar to female voters, about being ordinary in a 'feminine' way. Kristin Halvorsen has explained her frequent appearances in women's magazines, in which she often poses in untraditional ways, with her wish to reach voters she does not normally reach. Even if the sensual factor does not seem to contribute to the charisma of female politicians, it may well have contributed to making some of them more well-known to the public.

Sensuality does not seem to contribute to the charisma of Norwegian male politicians either. Sensuality is not easily combined with the ascetic charisma of former male politicians, a charisma based on hard work, piety, community spirit and abstinence. The good looks and easy-going nature of Prime Minister Jens Stoltenberg is even used against him. Nicknames like "the ladies' Jens" has been used in an attempt to destroy some of his image as a serious politician, so much so that he says he deliberately tries to avoid flirting (*Tara*, 4 June 2005; *Kvinner og klær*, no. 34, 2005). In a Norwegian context a beautiful and elegant outer appearance is often interpreted as the opposite of the favoured inner character. Of course this does not mean that outward charm cannot have its attraction. The difference between France and Norway lies more in how this is interpreted and valued within the respective political culture.

CONCLUSIONS

The main point of this comparative study of charismatic political leadership is that French politics seems to gravitate toward a Weberian asymmetric type of charisma, whereas Norwegian politics would hardly meet this type of charisma. The Norwegian ideal of political leadership is not of the strong and heroic leader, but the anti-authoritarian, community-oriented leader. What Weber terms "ordinary men", not the extraordinary, will have the strongest legitimacy. Apparently, this political leadership ideal leaves little space for charisma. In this article, we have tried to demonstrate how an almost neglected dimension of Weber's writings on charisma nevertheless can assist in analyzing the Norwegian form of charisma, what we have called *the charisma of ordinary human beings*. This form of political leadership, which we regard as an expansion of Weber's form of charisma, has been analyzed on the basis of specific historical developments as well as more recent empirical examples in Norway.

Although other theoreticians, such as Little (1985, 1988) and Swidler (1979), have identified a more egalitarian type of charisma found among "personalities" or "eccentrics", their kind of charisma is not as egalitarian as the one we have described because it implies a type of intellectual superiority, which is not accepted in egalitarian Norwegian politics.

Charismatic leadership is a complex field in which many dimensions come into play. Different qualities make politicians charismatic in the two countries. In France charisma is closely knit to *heroism* and *seduction*. The concrete manifestation of a politician's charisma will also be dependent on other aspects such as class, physical appearance, prior merits and party representation. This has created variations such as the war hero (de Gaulle), the aristocrat (d'Estaing), the patriarch (Mitterand), the bully (Le Pen), the seducer (Chirac, Villepin, Sarkozy) and the lone rider (Sarkozy).

Our analysis has shown how different kinds of charisma are gendered. As can be seen from the above mentioned collection of politicians, charisma in France has mostly been a male quality. The charisma of the seductive hero appears to be especially difficult to live up to for female politicians. French women have had to experiment with other parts from the national and cultural repertoires in order to attain charisma. One example is Ségolène Royal. Whether her image as a mother and a loving wife can give her charisma remains to be seen. Another example is Simone Veil, who sometime has been described as charismatic. Veil's charisma, however, seems to be of a different sort than the above mentioned. It is based more on an ascetic rather than a heroic charisma.

Although an ascetic charisma is based on an asymmetrical relationship – i.e. a sort of moral superiority – the ascetic dimension is also found in Norwegian politics, albeit mainly in the past. Gerhardsen's and Tranmæl's ascetic lifestyles made them both extraordinary and ordinary in their time. Still today, Norwegian politicians try to avoid excessive consumption and prefer an ordinary way of life. Much of the ordinary charm we see in contemporary politics, however, is of another kind than the ascetic one. Because the Norwegian standard of living has become very high, an ascetic lifestyle would not make a politician ordinary. What nowadays seems to give Norwegian politicians their charm, is quite a different formula. The closest Weber came to deal with this kind of symmetrically based charisma we find in his anti-authoritative form of charisma. Consequently, we have termed the particular form of Norwegian politicians' charisma as an ordinary human charisma – a charisma created through being very human, made of flesh and blood. Psychic breakdowns, weight problems and other forms of human imperfections can make Norwegian politicians live up to this form of charisma. The Norwegian charisma of ordinary human beings seems to be just as suitable to female as to male politicians. However, the concrete way it is expressed may be somewhat different.

In our study the differences between France and Norway regarding charismatic leadership is explained by using the concept of national cultural repertoires, i.e. patterns of actions and interpretation developed through historical processes within particular national contexts. The heavy *emphasize* on charismatic leadership in France we attribute to the Versailles tradition of France, with its weight on emotions, personal appeal and outward appearance. Also the *form* of charismatic leadership, seductive heroism, still resonates the Versailles period, at least to a certain degree. Of course, the French revolution modified this aristocratic heritage. The French democracy thinkers emphasized reason and logic in political life. We believe that the *effortless superiority* which characterizes many male French politicians today represents a sort of mingling of these two historical traditions.

In Norway both the lesser emphasize on charisma and the type of charisma that actually does appear, is explained in a similar way. Norway had no aristocracy of its own to speak of, yet ideas from the French revolution had an impact. This meant that reason and logic did not have to compete with emotional persuasion in the same way as in France. The lesser stress on charismatic leadership in Norwegian politics we relate to this fact. The Norwegian puritan tradition, which led to a concentration on inner character, together with a strong accentuation on equality stemming from the old peasant society, laid the grounds for what we have called *the charisma of ordinary human beings*. Contrary to the French charisma, this Norwegian type does not imply an asymmetric relation between leaders and followers to the same degree. Consequently, this type of charisma does not threaten the impression of equality, which would otherwise be offended.

Renewal seems to be a central part of Norwegian politicians' charisma and charm. This is also an element in French politicians' repertoire. For example, some French politicians portray themselves as less pompous and more close to the people than their predecessors, something which breaks with tradition. The narrow recruitment to politics which characterizes the French political system as to class and gender however, demonstrates that renewal is less important than in Norway. Another difference is linked to formality and distance. In France, charisma is associated with a great, aloof, mystical and almost "supernatural" hero, while in Norway the more symmetrically based charm is associated with variations of ordinariness and being close to the people. The politicians in each country who challenge these national cultural repertoires can both gain and loose from this. However, they will certainly catch the voters' eye.

Put bluntly it seems mainly to be male politicians in France who radiate *eroticized heroic charisma* – with a positive evaluation. An eroticized image can also be seen in French women, but mostly with negative connotations. The Norwegian tradition of piety, moderation and inward orientation has not created very many seducers, neither male nor female. Interestingly, however, it is the Norwegian women who, from around 2000 and subsequently, are the main exponents of eroticism and glamour in Norwegian politics. Many of the female politicians have posed in quite astonishing outfits, thereby bringing humour and play into the solemn Norwegian politics. This does not seem to strengthen their position among the voters. However, it certainly raises interesting debates as to how far politicians can go in challenging national cultural repertoires of political leadership.

NOTES

1. Schein and Mueller (1992) illustrates that this has changed somewhat in the last decades. For example the leadership ideal in the Norwegian governmental sector has become more gender balanced (Storvik 2003).
2. It is possible that the evaluations given by journalists and biographers are not representative for the whole people as such. However, a main qualification of good writers seems to be their ability to express and reflect on thoughts common to large groups of people. Through their writings, journalists and biographers also influence how in fact politicians are perceived.
3. http://www.cnn.com/2005/WORLD/europe/05/31/france.candidates.reut/
4. Speech delivered by Trygve Bratteli at the unveiling of Tranmæl's memorial stone at *Vår Frelsers gravlund*, April 22, 1972.
5. What Swidler (1979) has in mind is more of an eccentric form of charisma. A Norwegian politician who would conform to Swidler's eccentric charisma is Anders Lange, who founded his own party, *Anders Langes Parti*. Lange described himself as one of the most prominent demagogues in Norwegian politics (*Aftenposten*, 30 November 2005).
6. A problem with this focus on heterosexual relations is that it seems to imply seduction and dominance, and consequently that men and women are positioned differently in the relationship. If this sexual relation is to be the prototype for leader-followership, is it likely that it creates special problems for women.
7. Sarkozy, probably the main rival of Royal in the 2007 presidential election, seems to acknowledge this dilemma. He has declared his admiration for Royal by stating that she is a beautiful woman and a mother of four (*Paris Match*, 15 March 2006)

ACKNOWLEDGEMENTS

We would like to thank Fredrik Engelstad, Trygve Gulbrandsen, Bernt Aardal, Bernard Enjolras and Nicole Hennum for valuable comments on drafts of this article. In addition we would like to thank Jannicke Hjelmervik, Rune Hoelseth, Jon Haakon Hustad and Sven Lindblad for their assistance with collecting data material.

REFERENCES

Aardal, B., Krogstad, A & Narud, H. M. (Eds). (2004). *I valgkampens hete*. Oslo: Universitetsforlaget.

Anderson, B. (1983). *Imagined communities, reflections on the origin and spread of nationalism.* London: Verso.

Apfelbaum, E. (1993). Norwegian and French women in high leadership positions. The importance of cultural contexts upon gendered relations. *Psychology of Women Quarterly, 17*, 409–429.

Bauhr, M., & Esaiasson, P. (2001). 'Trust me' – on the nature of ethos argumentation. In: K. Gomard & A. Krogstad (Eds), *Instead of the ideal debate. Doing politics and doing gender in Nordic political campaign discourse.* Århus: Aarhus University Press.

Bryman, A. (1992). *Charisma & leadership in organizations.* London: Sage Publications.

Chabal, P., & Daloz, J. P. (2006). The guises of political representation. In: P. Chabal & J. P. Daloz (Eds), *Culture troubles. Politics and the interpretation of meaning.* London: Hurst & Company.

Chalaby, J. K. (2002). *The de Gaulle presidency and the media: statism and public communications.* Basingstoke: Palgrave.

Connell, R. W. (1987). *Gender and power.* Oxford: Polity Press.

Daloz, J. P. (2003). Ostentation in comparative perspective: Culture and elite legitimation. *Comparative Social Research, 21*, 29–62.

Daloz, J. P. (2007). Political elites and conspicuous modesty: Norway, Sweden, Finland in comparative perspective. *Journal of Comparative Social Research* In: F. Engelstad (Ed.), *Comparative Studies of Social and Political Elites. Comparative Social Research* (pp. 173–212). Oxford: Elsevier Ltd.

Drake, H., & Gaffney, J. (1996). *The language of leadership in contemporary France.* Aldershot: Dartmouth.

Eckstein, H. (1966). *Division and cohesion in democracy. A study of Norway.* Princeton: Princeton University Press.

Ezekiel, J. (2002). Le women's lib: Made in France. *The European Journal of Women's Studies, 9*(3), 345–361.

Gaffney, J. (1988). *The French presidential elections of 1988.* Vermont: Gower Publishing Company.

Goffman, E. (1959). *The presentation of self in everyday life.* Harmondsworth: Penguin Books.

Goffman, E. (1961). *Encounters: Two studies in the sociology of interaction.* Indianapolis: Bobbs-Merril.

Gomard, K., & Krogstad, A. (2001). *Instead of the ideal debate. Doing politics and doing gender in Nordic political campaign discourse.* Århus: Aarhus University Press.

Gulbrandsen, T., Engelstad, F., Klausen, T., Skjeie, H., Teigen, M., & Østerud, Ø. (2002). *Norske makteliter.* Oslo: Gyldendal.

Gullestad, M. (2001). Likhetens grenser. In: M. Lien, H. Vike & H. Lidén (Eds), *Likhetens paradokser. Antropologiske undersøkelser i det moderne Norge.* Oslo: Universitetsforlaget.

Håkansson, N. (2001). Argumentative and symbolic discourse in Nordic electoral debate. In: K. Gomard & A. Krogstad (Eds), *Instead of the ideal debate. Doing politics and doing gender in Nordic political campaign discourse.* Århus: Aarhus University Press.

Halvorsen, K. (2004). *Rett fra hjertet.* Oslo: Gyldendal.

Hayward, J. (1991). Conclusion: Political science, the state and modernisation. In: P. Hall, J. Hayward & H. Machin (Eds), *Developments in French politics*. Basingstoke: Macmillan.

Heidar, K. (1997). Roles, structures and behaviour: Norwegian parliamentarians in the nineties. *Journal of Legislative Studies, 3*(1), 91–109.

Henningsen, E., & Vike, H. (1999). Folkelig elitisme? Om offentlighetens kultur i Norge. *Norsk antropologisk tidsskrift, 10,* 150–167.

Hernes, H. (1987). *Welfare state and women power: Essays in state feminism.* Oslo: Norwegian University press.

Hufton, O. (2000). *Europe: Privilege and protest 1730–1789.* Oxford: Blackwell.

Hunt, L. (1991). *Eroticisms and the body politic.* Baltimore: Johns Hopkins University Press.

Johansen, A., & Kjeldsen, J. E. (2005). *Virksomme ord: Politiske taler 1814–2005.* Oslo: Universitetsforlaget.

Jones, K. (1992). *Compassionate authority. Democracy and the representation of women.* New York: Routledge.

Kanter, R. M. (1977). *Men and women of the corporation.* New York: Basic Books.

Klausen, A. M. (1984). *Den norske væremåten.* Oslo: Cappelens forlag.

Krogstad, A. (1999). *Image i politikken. Visuelle og retoriske virkemidler.* Oslo: Pax forlag.

Krogstad, A. (2000). Antropologisk sammenlikning i 'tykt' og 'tynt'. Ti kjetterske teser. *Norsk antropologisk tidsskrift, 11*(2), 88–107.

Krogstad, A. (2004). Fjernsynsvalgkamp. Noen retoriske øvelser i skyld og ære. In: B. Aardal, A. Krogstad & H. M. Narud (Eds), *I valgkampens hete* S (pp. 85–111). Oslo: Universitetsforlaget.

Krogstad, A. (2006). En bok en blogg og en blondine. *Personsentrert politisk kommunikasjon.* Unpublished paper. (Sent to *Sosiologisk Tidsskrift* for publication).

Lamont, M., & Thévenot, L. (2000). *Rethinking comparative cultural sociology.* Cambridge: University Press.

Landes, J. (1988). *Women and the public sphere in the age of the French revolution.* London: Cornell University Press.

Larsen, T. (1984). Bønder i byen – på jakt etter den norske konfigurasjonen. In: A. M. Klausen (Ed.), *Den norske væremåten.* Oslo: Cappelens forlag.

Levy, D. R. (1989). Women of the French national front. *Parliamentary Affairs, 42*(1), 102–111.

Lien, M., Vike, H., & Lidén, H. (2001). *Likhetens paradokser. Antropologiske undersøkelser i det moderne Norge.* Oslo: Universitetsforlaget.

Little, G. (1985). *Political ensembles. A psychosocial approach to politics and leadership.* London: Oxford University Press.

Little, G. (1988). *Strong leadership.* Melbourne: Oxford University Press.

Melby, K., Pylkkänen, A., Rosenbeck, B., & Carlsson Wetterberg, C. (Eds). (2000). *The Nordic Model of Marriage and the Welfare State, Nord 27.* København: Nordisk Ministerråd.

Nylund, Mats. (2001). Projecting unity: Strategic uses of we in televised debates. In: K. Gomard & A. Krogstad (Eds), *Instead of the ideal debate. Doing politics and doing gender in Nordic political campaign discourse.* Århus: Aarhus University Press.

Perry, S. (2005). Gender difference in French political communication: From handicap to asset? *Modern and Contemporary France, 13*(3), 337–352.

Ramsay, R. (2003). *French women in politics, writing power, paternal legitimization and maternal legacies.* New York: Berghahn Books.

Røkenes, T., & Sirnes, T. (2005). In the name of love. *Nytt Norsk Tidsskrift, 22*(2), 127–140.

Safran, W. (1985). *The French polity.* New York: Longman.

Saguy, A. C. (2000). Sexual harassment in France and in the United States: Activist and public figures defend their definitions. In: M. Lamont & L. Thévenot (Eds), *Rethinking comparative cultural sociology*. Cambridge: University Press.

Schein, V., & Mueller, R. (1992). Sex-role stereotyping and requisite management characteristics among college students. *Journal of Organizational Behavior, 13*, 439–447.

Skjeie, H. (1993). Om autoritet, weberske idealtyper og norsk politikk. *Norsk statsvitenskapelig tidsskrift, 9*(3), 224–239.

Slagstad, R., Korsgaard, O., Løvlie, L. (Eds). (2003). *Dannelsens forvandlinger*. Oslo: Pax Forlag A/S.

Slagstad, R. (2003). Folkedannelsens forvandlinger. In: R. Slagstad, O. Korsgaard & L. Løvlie (Eds), *Dannelsens forvandlinger*. Oslo: Pax Forlag A/S.

Slagstad, R. (1998). *De nasjonale strateger*. Oslo: Pax.

Sørensen, Ø., & Stråth, B. (1997). *The cultural construction of Norden*. Oslo: Universitetsforlaget.

Steinsland, G. (2005). *Norrøn mytologi, myter, riter, samfunn*. Oslo: Pax forlag.

Storvik, Aa. (2003). Maskulinitet og makt i utakt. In: A. L. Ellingsæter & J. Solheim (Eds), *Den usynlige hånd? Kjønnsmakt i moderne arbeidsliv*. Oslo: Gyldendal Akademiske.

Swidler, A. (1979). *Organizations without authority. Dilemmas of social control in free schools*. Cambridge: Harward University Press.

Swidler, Ann. (1986). Culture in action: Symbols and strategies. *American Sociological review, 51*(2), 273–286.

Tjeder, D. (2003). *The power of character: Middle-class masculinities, 1800–1900*. Stockholm: Department of History, Stockholm University.

Walzer, M. (1967). On the role of symbolism in political thought. *Political Science Quarterly, 82*(2), 191–204.

Weber, M. (1947). *The theory of social and economic organization*. Translated by A.M. Henderson & Talcott Parsons. Edited with an introduction by Talcott Parsons. New York: Oxford University Press.

Weber, M. (1968). *Economy and society, an outline of interpretive sociology*. Edited by Guenther Roth & Claus Wittich. New York: The Bedminster Press.

Weber, M. (1994). Political writings. In: P. Lassman & R. Speirs (Eds), *Cambridge texts in the history of political thought*. Cambridge: Cambridge University Press.

Newspapers, Magazines and Websites

Aftenposten, 27 May 1989.
Aftenposten, 31 January 2000.
Aftenposten, 1 September 2005.
Aftenposten, 30 November 2005.
Dagbladet, 24 August 2003.
Dagbladet, 13 September 2003.
Dagbladet, 23 November 2005.
Dagbladet, 27 December 2005.
Femmeactuell,e 27 February 2006.
Globe, no. 27, 1988.
Kvinner og klær, no. 34, 2005.
L'Express, 19 January 2006.
Le Monde, 3 January 2006.

Le Monde, 31 January 2006.
Le Nouvel Imbécile, March 2006.
Le Nouvel Observateur, 30 June 2005.
Le Point, 5 January 2006.
Liberation, 13 March 2006.
Marianne, 14 January 2006.
Marianne, 17 March 2006.
Paris Match, 05 March 2006.
Paris Match, 15 March 2006.
Tara, 4 June 2005.
The Atlantic Monthly, September 2005.
Verdens Gang, 22 October 2005.
Verdens Gang, 29 December 2005.
http://www.cnn.com/2005/WORLD/europe/05/31/france.candidates.reut/ Accessed 3 October 2005.

PART III
REVIEW SECTION:
ELITES AND DEMOCRACY

DEMOCRACY AND ELITES

John Higley

Discussion of democracy and elites has long centered on the "theory of democratic elitism." As is well known, Joseph Schumpeter initiated the discussion by conceiving democracy as "an institutional arrangement for arriving at political decisions in which individuals [elites] acquire the power to decide by means of a competitive struggle for the people's vote" (Schumpeter, 1942, p. 269). Numerous works seeking to affirm, deny, or modify Schumpeter's formulation followed. Robert Dahl's concept of polyarchy – a regime "substantially popularized and liberalized, that is, highly inclusive and extensively open to public contestation" – was a key contribution (Dahl, 1971, p. 8). Giovanni Sartori combined the formulations of Schumpeter and Dahl to construct the most precise statement of democratic elitism that we have: "Large-scale democracy is a procedure and/or a *mechanism* that (a) generates an *open polyarchy* whose *competition* on the electoral market, (b) attributes *power to the people*, and (c) specifically enforces the *responsiveness* of the leaders to the led" (Sartori, 1987, p. 156, his emphases). As Sartori encapsulated it, democracy is an "elective polyarchy."

Democratic elitism holds that rule by the *demos* is not prevented by the existence and power of elites: in deciding elite competitions for government office, the people still rule. The theory has made interactions between mass publics and elites an abiding research focus, spawning countless studies that have investigated the degree of concordance between mass and elite opinions, the extent to which gender, ethnic, occupational, and other mass diversities are mirrored in elite make-ups, how mass publics are linked to elites

Comparative Studies of Social and Political Elites
Comparative Social Research, Volume 23, 249–263
Copyright © 2007 by Elsevier Ltd.
All rights of reproduction in any form reserved
ISSN: 0195-6310/doi:10.1016/S0195-6310(06)23010-2

through parties and career recruitment structures, how the approach of elections forces elite responsiveness to mass discontents, and how countervailing mass and elite groups create a stable democratic balance.

Democratic elitism pays surprisingly little attention to elites as such. The theory pertains only to party elites and says nothing about the wider elite stratum in which they are embedded. How business, trade union, state administrative, media, military, and sundry other elite groups influence party elite competitions goes unmentioned. Holding that party elites anticipate voters' reactions to policies and adjust policies and campaign promises accordingly, the theory does not consider that elites frequently deceive voters by distorting or withholding information or by colluding to keep some issues completely off the public agenda. The theory likewise discounts or ignores much of the nowadays brutal cut and thrust of party elite competitions, in which large financial and media resources and a variety of "dirty tricks" are employed to discredit and demonize opponents. Democratic elitism merely takes it for granted that party elites are restrained and mutually respectful in their competitions and that, as Schumpeter put it, this is an "institutionalized" condition. Finally, the theory has little to offer by way of causal analysis. How democratic elitism comes about, why and how it becomes institutionalized, and what causes it to wax or wane are questions to which the theory gives no answers.

One aim of my research on elites has been to remove, or at least lessen, these blind spots in democratic elitism. Influenced by elite theory as it evolved from the writings of Mosca, Pareto, and Michels (with more than incidental contributions by Weber), I have contended that *elites create and sustain democracies*, just as they create and sustain all other kinds of political regimes. Democracies are first and foremost creations of a distinctive type of political elite, which I term a *consensually united elite*. This elite formation is much wider and more complex than the party elites on which democratic elitism focuses. I have tried to uncover the origins and workings of consensually united elites, how they have fostered, usually over long periods, today's democracies, and what prospects there are for the spread of such elites and, thus, of democracies in the twenty-first century. I have hastened to add that democracies are not one-way, elite-to-mass streets. There is probably always a broad interdependence between elites and mass publics in the sense that mass interests and orientations constitute *parameters* within which elites can effectively and safely act. Elites who violate these parameters risk coming to grief. But the mass parameters are wide and they leave elites with a range of choices that are decisive for creating and sustaining democracies.

In a current book, Michael Burton and I show that no democracy has ever emerged without the prior or concomitant formation of a consensually united elite, and none has persisted when such an elite has broken down (Higley & Burton, 2006). Democracy's elite and mass dimensions are thus more separable and sequential than the theory of democratic elitism implies. An elite whose members and factions are disposed toward restrained and mutually respectful political behavior always forms *before* democratic precepts and practices are adopted by any large number of citizens and *before* democratic institutions become stable. There is, admittedly, a danger of tautology: if elites choose to practice democratic politics, then democratic politics will be practiced. Yet it is a matter of historical record that elites have seldom made this choice. Consensually united elites have been formed infrequently during the past several centuries and there is little reason to believe that their number will increase greatly in our new century. Disunited elites producing authoritarian regimes or illiberal and unstable quasi-democracies have been the rule historically, and they are likely to remain so. What interests me is how and why consensually united elites form, how they are propitious for democracy's emergence, why such elites strongly tend to persist over long periods, and whether current and foreseeable circumstances portend their continuation or breakdown. Answers to these questions provide the theory of democratic elitism with some of the dynamics that it lacks.

CONSENSUALLY UNITED ELITES

Elites are the principal decision-makers in the largest or otherwise most pivotally situated organizations and movements in a modern society. By commanding major business firms, large trade unions, state bureaucracies, the mass media, the military, important pressure groups, and mass movements, as well as political parties, elites are the persons and groups who have the *organized capacity* to affect political outcomes regularly and substantially. Researchers have estimated that elites in this sense number about 10,000 people in the United States (Dye, 2002, p. 139); roughly 5000 in middle-sized democracies like France, Australia, and Germany (Dogan, 2003; Higley, Deacon, & Smart, 1979; Hoffmann-Lange, 1993); and perhaps 2000 in smaller democracies like Denmark and Norway (Christiansen, Möller, & Togeby, 2001; Gulbrandsen et al., 2002). This is a narrow definition and identification of elites. It does not equate high occupational, educational, or cultural status with "elite," even though this "high status" definition is often employed. I understand elites in a much more restricted sense – as the few thousands of people who occupy a modern society's uppermost power positions.

Among modern historical and contemporary societies worldwide, the principal variations among elites are in the extent of their structural integration and value consensus. Structural integration involves the relative inclusiveness of formal and informal networks of communication and influence between elite persons and factions. Value consensus involves their relative agreement about norms of political behavior and the worth of existing governmental institutions. In these two respects, one can distinguish between *disunited* and *united* elites. The persons and factions forming disunited elites are divided and separated from each other, they disagree fundamentally about political norms and institutions, and they adhere to no single code of political behavior. Disunited elites view politics as a zero-sum game and a war-like struggle. Concrete examples range from chaotic extremes (Liberia, Sierra Leone, the Democratic Republic of the Congo, Somalia in recent years) to entrenched configurations of two or three well-articulated but deeply opposed camps (most European and virtually all Latin American elites from the time independent national states formed until well after World War II).

By contrast, united elites are characterized by dense and interlocking networks of communication and influence, together with basic value agreements and a common code of political behavior. However, there are two quite different types of united elites. In one type, the networks that signify structural integration are exceptionally tight and sharply centralized, running through a single party or movement and pivoting on a handful of its top leaders. As well, all elite members publicly profess consensus about the rightness of a distinct ideology, religious doctrine, or ethnic creed, even though other belief systems are known to exist. This is an *ideologically united elite*, principal examples of which are the Soviet Union's nomenklatura-based elite prior to the 1980s, the elite in the People's Republic of China down to the mid-1990s, the elite in the People's Republic of North Korea throughout its existence, and with some qualifications, the elite in Iran since the 1978–1979 revolution.

In the other type of united elite, the consensually united type, networks that signify structural integration are most dense and tight within functionally differentiated sectors – business, trade unions, state administration, the media, etc. But these networks overlap and interlock across sector boundaries to form "webworks" and "central circles" whose members enjoy access, whether direct or indirect, to key political decision-makers

(Higley et al., 1991). In addition, elite members and groups share a mostly tacit consensus about norms and rules of political behavior, best summarized as a "code of restrained partisanship" (Di Palma, 1973). They view politics as a bargaining process according to the principle of *do ut des* – give to get (Sartori, 1987, p. 229). Over time, bargaining enables disparate elite persons and factions to achieve or protect their main interests, and this inclines them to view the totality of political outcomes as positive-sum. I contend that these consensually united elites have been the creators and mainstays of today's democracies. Concretely, they have ranged from quite oligarchic formations (Mexico's omnibus National Revolutionary Party (renamed Institutional Revolutionary Party) elite cartel from 1929 until it became more open in the late 1990s; the elite condominiums in Colombia and Venezuela from the late 1950s until the early 1990s when the Venezuelan condominium broke apart and the Colombian teetered on disintegration; Malaysia's National Organization/National Front constellation throughout the country's fifty years of independence) to more broadly open and inclusive formations (elites in Britain progressively since the eighteenth century and in British settler countries from the times of their independence; elites in the Netherlands progressively from independence in 1813).

A consensually united elite approximates in politics what game theorists call a "stable equilibrium," in which no significant player has a strong incentive to alter its behavior (Przeworski, 1991, pp. 26–34; Weingast, 1997, p. 260). Elite factions find the existing political order rewarding because none stands any large risk of losing comprehensively in political competitions. This makes elite interactions "self-enforcing," which is to say that elites police themselves by penalizing members who violate norms of restrained partisanship. It is the core reason why consensually united elites strongly tend to persist, in some countries over several centuries and despite all manner of societal changes and upheavals. As Robert Putnam has observed of such elites, "[Their] commitment to 'the system' is doubtless...related to the gratifications the system gives them. Leaders are more likely to agree on the rules of the game, because it is fundamentally their game" (Putnam, 1976, p. 116). Over time the norms established and shared by consensually united elites become embedded in political institutions and the wider political culture. These norms acquire a life of their own so that what is and is not permissible in politics become widely recognized and this recognition proscribes much public behavior that could challenge a consensually united elite and the peaceful, broadly representative political practices that it fosters.

Gross differences between the three basic types of elites – disunited, ideologically united, or consensually united – are not hard to discern in modern historical perspective. By looking at countries' political patterns comparatively and longitudinally their basic elite configuration stands out. The origins of disunited or ideologically united elites are also quite readily discerned. Disunited elites have originated most often in the formation of independent national states, which has typically involved some elite factions forcibly suppressing and subjugating other factions. These suppressions and subjugations, and the unremitting resentments, fears, and hatreds they create, have routinely produced deeply disunited elites. This was the case in all European states when they first formed between 1500 and 1800, in all of the states that formed after the Spaniards and Portuguese were driven from Latin America early in the nineteenth century, and in the bulk of postcolonial states that became independent in Africa, the Middle East, and Asia during the decades after World War II. Disunited elites that originated in the formation of independent national states, the war-like politics these elites subsequently practice, and the authoritarian regimes they most frequently produce have been so widespread as to constitute the modal pattern of politics in the modern world.

Although a few ideologically united elites have formed in the process of fighting for and gaining national independence (the Vietminh elite throwing off French rule of North Vietnam; the Taliban elite's suppression of the several Mujaheddin groups that liberated Afghanistan from Russian military control), ideologically united elites have two principal origins. The first is the victory of a doctrinaire, secretive, and well-organized elite faction that capitalizes on state breakdown to seize power and liquidate other factions in a revolutionary struggle (the Bolsheviks between 1917 and 1921 in Russia; the quasi-revolutionary Fascist and Nazi accessions to power a few years later in Italy and Germany; the victory of the elite led by Tito in Yugoslavia's revolution 1943–1945; the similar victory of the elite led by Mao Zedong in China's revolution 1948–1949; the elite led by Khomeini that destroyed Iran's monarchical regime in 1978–1979). The victorious faction confines all political activity to its party or movement and establishes its doctrine as the only framework for political expression. The other principal origin of an ideologically united elite is its imposition by a conquering country that already has such an elite (Eastern Europe under Soviet control following World War II).

More interesting, but also more debatable, are the origins of consensually united elites and the emergence of democracies for which, I contend, such elites are the *sine qua non*. There are three ways and sets of circumstances in which consensually united elites have originated. All three origins have been uncommon and one is no longer a realistic possibility:

- *Settlements* of basic disputes among disunited elites that are deliberate and sudden, and depend upon highly contingent elite circumstances and choices;
- *Colonial opportunities* for local elites to practice cautious and limited representative politics during long periods of "home rule" while also leading politically complex movements for national independence;
- *Convergences* toward shared norms of political behavior among disunited elites competing for support amid economically prosperous electorates that are, on balance, averse to drastic alternations of the status quo.

Classic instances of settlements are the deliberate and sudden coming together of bitterly opposed Tory and Whig elites in England's Glorious Revolution of 1688–1689, and the comparable conciliation reached by opposing elite camps in Spain during the three years that followed Francisco Franco's death in 1975 (Burton & Higley, 1987; Higley & Burton, 1998). Classic instances of colonial opportunities are the long practice by American and Indian elites of cautious home rule politics under distant British control, augmented by risky struggles for national independence that further united these elites (Weiner, 1987, pp. 18–23). In our post-colonial world, however, this origin of consensually united elites is no longer likely. Classic instances of elite convergences are the gradual coming together of French elites under Gaullist electoral hegemony amid prospering economic conditions during the 1960s and 1970s, and the comparable coming together of Italian and Japanese elites under Christian Democratic and Liberal Democratic electoral hegemony, respectively, also amid prospering economic conditions, between 1963 and 1964 and the early 1980s (Higley & Burton, 2006).

Modern Scandinavian political history provides examples of all three origins of consensually united elites. To better see what they entail, I will summarize the Swedish, Norwegian, and Danish cases, although space limits and my amateur knowledge of Scandinavian political history undoubtedly do violence to the complexities actually involved.

SCANDINAVIA'S CONSENSUALLY UNITED ELITES

The only instance of an elite settlement in Scandinavia occurred in Sweden in 1809. Its background condition was the century-long and largely inconclusive struggle between "Hat" and "Cap" elite camps, both of them aristocratic in composition and mercantilist in orientation, although with opposing political programs and strategies. Their struggle opened the way to a peasant uprising and a march on Stockholm in 1743 and to the coup d'état in 1772 by Gustav III, who sought to restore royal absolutism after fifty years of eroding monarchical authority. At the famous masked ball in Stockholm twenty years later, an assassin mortally wounded Gustav, and his less politically astute son ascended to the throne as Gustav IV. A severe crisis capable of triggering an attempted elite settlement occurred in 1808: drastic economic decline, a series of military defeats by Russian forces, and Denmark's declaration of war against Sweden – all attributed to Gustav's incompetence.

Through a conspiracy of key Hat and Cap leaders, Gustav was deposed and exiled in March 1809. Fifteen of these leaders then secretly negotiated a new constitution that was drawn up and accepted by the *Riksdag* during five weeks, start to finish, in May and June 1809. It embodied basic agreement between the two elite camps to institute a constitutional monarchy (or "crowned republic") along English-British lines. The two camps then co-operated to foil a royalist counter-coup in 1810, and they duly recruited a new Crown Prince, Jean-Baptiste Bernadotte, the illustrious field marshal in Napoleon's armies who had fought the Swedes honorably before falling out with Napoleon. Bernadotte steered evenly between the Hat and Cap elites, and he prevented Sweden from being overrun by Russian forces. Moving with much circumspection, he waited until 1818 to ascend the throne as Carl XIV Johan. The collaboration between opposing elite camps that marked a new era in Swedish politics solidified under Carl Johan's restrained guidance, which continued until his death in 1844. From not later than 1818, the Swedish regime was a stable liberal oligarchy. After major democratizing reforms in 1907, it became the more or less fully representative democracy that has persisted to this day.

The way in which a consensually united elite formed in Norway was more ambiguous. It is plausible to view this Norwegian development as resulting from a long experience of limited and cautious elite politics under distant colonial rule augmented by a unifying struggle for independence, or, alternatively, as a gradual process of elite convergence during the decades after independence was won in 1905. Norway entered the modern historical period without an aristocratic and leisured class, the Viking ruling groups having been decimated in the Black Death of 1349–1350. After two centuries of political disorder and disintegration, Norway was annexed by Denmark in 1536. Officials and emissaries from Copenhagen ruled Norway for the next three centuries – the ruling structure of "officialdom" (*embetsverket*). When the Swedes took control of Norway late in 1814 as a consequence of Denmark being on the losing side in the Napoleonic Wars, it was a markedly egalitarian society without an indigenous bastion of conservatism and privilege. Before the Swedes fastened their grip on Norway, however, 112 leading citizens convened a constitutional convention at Eidsvoll, wrote a liberal constitution, and proclaimed Norway an independent constitutional monarchy. The dispatch with which this was done indicated a considerable amount of elite cooperation and consensus, derived from long resentment of Danish rule. The Swedish elite recognized the Eidsvoll constitution as the framework in which Norway would be governed, albeit as a distinct component of the Swedish kingdom.

Swedish rule of Norway during the nineteenth century was for the most part benign and distant; it afforded Norwegian elites considerable autonomy. After the elite settlement of 1809 in Stockholm, Sweden was itself a constitutional monarchy governed by a consensually united elite, and principles of liberal and at least somewhat representative politics had, therefore, to be followed in matters pertaining to Norway's governance, as well as to Sweden's. The parallel with Britain's governance of its colonies in accordance with political legacies of the English elite settlement of 1689 is striking. Thus, while their formal, occasionally very concrete, subordination to Stockholm's decisions and policies greatly irked Norwegian elites and nationalists, they acquired considerable experience in cautious home-rule politics.

Simmering Norwegian discontent with Swedish rule came to a boil during the 1870s in a struggle to make members of the cabinet in Oslo (then called Christiania), who were appointed by and responsible to the Swedish Crown, participate in meetings of the *Storting* and be otherwise responsible to that body. Faced with a considerable mobilization of Norwegian nationalists, the Swedes eventually acceded to this demand, and ministerial responsibility to the *Storting* was enacted in 1884. From that year, the political elite in Christiania/Oslo, though technically still subordinate to the Swedish Crown, controlled Norwegian domestic affairs in all practical ways. Independence in foreign affairs was obtained in 1905, although only after several risky confrontations with Sweden that involved considerable forethought, secret consultations, and cooperation within the Norwegian elite.

The Norwegian case has, thus, the earmarks of a consensually united elite that formed under colonial home rule and a unifying struggle for independence. But it is also plausible to regard Norwegian elites as disunited when independence was gained in 1905, so that the formation of a consensually united elite occurred through a process of gradual convergence during the next several decades. When they gained full autonomy in domestic matters in 1884, Norwegian elites were aligned in conservative and liberal camps, each of which exhibited considerable distrust of the other. Within a few years, moreover, elites leading disaffected manual industrial workers, whose numbers increased dramatically with Norway's rapid industrialization during the twenty-five years before World War I, emerged at the head of a powerful labor movement and allied Labor Party. These socialist elites were openly hostile to "bourgeois rule" and the putatively democratic regime that, in their view, embodied it.

After World War I, radically egalitarian goals and a revolutionary program were ascendant in the socialist elite camp. The Labor Party became the only western socialist or social democratic party to join the Bolshevik-controlled Comintern, although for just a brief period, 1919–1923. In the face of this professedly revolutionary movement, conservative and liberal elite factions mobilized enough voters to form governments that kept the Labor Party excluded from executive power. After repeated electoral defeats, the magnitude of which varied directly with the radicalism of socialist rhetoric and threats employed by Labor leaders during election campaigns, these leaders began to tone down their socialist program. Having had an 18-day taste of executive power when it emerged from the 1927 election as the largest party, Labor entered into coalition with the Agrarian Party to form a left-of-center government in 1935. Because it was beholden to powerful Agrarian interests and its Labor leaders recognized that a strict socialist program enjoyed nothing approaching majority support, this government pursued moderate reforms until Hitler's forces invaded Norway in April 1940. Further united by the experience of German occupation, which entailed the imprisonment of Norwegian political leaders of all stripes in the same concentration camps, the consensually united character of Norwegian elites, operating a fully liberal democracy, was almost immediately apparent once the country was liberated from German occupation in 1945.

The formation of a consensually united elite in Denmark involved neither an elite settlement nor colonial opportunities to gain experience in cautious home-rule politics. A civil war punctuated national state formation in the 1530s, and struggles among aristocratic and bourgeois elite camps culminated in royal absolutism after 1665. A century of rule by a few hundred landowners who were in league with the monarchy followed, but this arrangement was upset during the 1770s and 1780s by palace intrigues and power grabs, amounting to successive coups. Although Denmark was in principle a constitutional monarchy after 1849, its elites remained disunited over issues of parliamentary sovereignty and the monarch's power, as well as the extent of the suffrage. The cabinet was responsible to the monarch, not to the lower house of the *Folketing*, which was in any case elected on the basis of a sharply restricted male suffrage. But in 1901 the principle of cabinet responsibility to parliament was accepted by dominant conservative elites, and in 1914–1915 the suffrage was made universal, which further strengthened the *Folketing's* lower house. Coupled with Denmark's rapid industrialization during the century's first two decades, these changes increased the political power of socialist elites who, like their Norwegian brethren, were avowedly revolutionary in aim. To contain the socialists, conservative and liberal elites collaborated in numerous coalition governments during the 1920s, and their repeated electoral successes gradually forced leftist leaders to recognize that a socialist order had no chance of gaining majority electoral support. During the 1930s, leftist elites began to pose much less alarming alternatives to Danish voters, and once German occupying forces were driven out in 1945, this more moderate stance enabled the Social Democratic Party to dominate Danish governments during the next several decades, although it never won a majority of votes.

Changes among Norwegian and Danish elites during the interwar period could thus be said to approximate gradual elite convergences. In neither country did the main propellant of a convergence – the electoral hegemony of a party defending a relatively prosperous status quo, thereby forcing opposing elites to gradually abandon anti-system stances in order to compete credibly for executive power – actually materialize. One must look at elite patterns in other countries – West Germany under the Christian Democrats-Christian Socialists between 1949 and 1966; France under the Gaullists between 1960 and 1981; Italy under the Christian Democrats between 1963 and 1979; Japan under the Liberal Democrat juggernaut between 1964 and 1984 – to find more clear-cut examples of elite convergence. In Norway and Denmark anti-socialist elites merely cooperated to keep right-of-center governments in power so long as the socialist/anti-socialist divide remained deep. As well, the eventual uniting of all main elite factions received powerful support from the ways in which German occupation and resistance to it during World War II enhanced elite accommodation and cooperation. The analytical question of how disunited elites in Denmark and mutually suspicious elites in Norway became consensually united, finds a plausible answer in the thesis that gradual convergences within both elites took place prior to 1945.

THE ELITISM IN DEMOCRATIC ELITISM

When he wrote about democratic elitism two decades ago, Giovanni Sartori worried about an imbalance in the democracies he observed. Excessive emphasis on their horizontal or non-elite dimension – on electoral, participatory, and referendum democracy – was in his view stifling the vertical or elite dimension – subordination, superordination, and coordination – without which democracies become rudderless (Sartori, 1987, p. 131). Fareed Zakaria has recently echoed Sartori's worry: "The deregulation of democracy has gone too far. It has produced an unwieldy system, unable to govern or command the respect of people…Those who hold power [elites] devote themselves to placating popular demands while losing the independence that is a prerequisite for tackling issues whose complexities lie beyond the grasp of mass publics" (Zakaria, 2003, pp. 240–241, p. 256). Sartori and Zakaria call for more forceful and independent leadership by elites if democracies are to survive the challenges they confront. Democratic elitism has become too "democratic" and insufficiently "elitist".

There are signs, however, that the vertical or elite dimension is being reasserted. In several democracies elites are suddenly more conspicuous and forceful. In America, an exceptionally aggressive and cohesive elite clustered around George W. Bush has, for good or ill, been reshaping the country's democratic politics quite dramatically in a vertical direction (Higley, 2006). In Britain, Tony Blair and his entourage have given the core executive expanded resources and a streamlined capacity to impose policies, taking the grave step of participating in the US-led invasion of Iraq despite massive parliamentary, internal party, and public opposition (Burch & Holliday 2004–2005, pp. 1–21). The American and British patterns are duplicated by the elite centered on Australia's prime minister, John Howard, whose forceful actions – also participating in the Iraq invasion despite fierce opposition, launching risky military missions in East Timor and the Solomon Islands, threatening pre-emptive military strikes against terrorist redoubts in Southeast Asia, detaining and incarcerating large numbers of illegal refugees, and gaining three re-elections through bare-knuckled campaigns – have no clear precedent in Australia's hundred years of independence (Uhr, 2005). In Italy during the last four years, the governing elite led by Silvio Berlusconi played fast and loose with parliamentary, judicial, and electoral rules, exerted a near monopoly control of television, and, like the Blair and Howard elites, engaged militarily in Iraq in the teeth of public opposition (Ginsborg, 2004).

At the national level in all EU member states, a reassertion of elites is evident in expanded intelligence-security apparatuses, greater surveillance of mass publics, and numerous forceful actions against terrorist cells and migrant diasporas thought to harbor them. Acting jointly, these national elites have attempted to provide the EU – whose construction has always been an exclusively elite project (Middlemas, 1995) – with a power-centralizing constitution that was signed by the leaders of member states in 2004. The constitution's ratification was stalled in 2005 when Dutch and French voters voted "No" in referendums that governing elites in Amsterdam and Paris carelessly called. But it is likely that, by hook or by crook, EU elites will get their constitution, or a close approximation of it, adopted before the present decade ends. In any event, a symbiosis of European business and bureaucratic elites, headquartered in Brussels, is robust and little beholden to popular accountability (Siedentop, 2001, pp. 122–151; Judt, 2005, pp. 723–748).

There is, of course, cause for concern. Recent developments in the U.S. and some other democracies appear to involve a stronger articulation of competing elite factions and an increasing distance between them. Consensually united elites are tending to divide into more tightly organized and mutually antagonistic camps that deploy large financial and other resources, including heightened powers of office incumbency and the ability to manipulate mass media, in their contests for executive power. These camps increasingly portray competitions in winner-take-all terms. The mobilization of popular support is more plebiscitary, stressing patriotic and religious commitments that narrow the room for elite compromise and power sharing. Party elites organized tightly around leaders who evoke a sense of overwhelming crisis, the need for a closer integration of a purer community, and the superiority of their own instincts are advantaged in electoral competitions. Scurrilous accusations about the personal deficiencies of opposing leaders are drumbeats in campaigns and policy disputes. Although it is easy to mistake short-run developments for a longer trend, diminished mutual respect, trust, and restraint, among elites in some of the best-established democracies, is apparent and worrisome.

From the standpoint of democratic elitism, these changes and tendencies have an equivocal character. On the one hand, elites and a more vertical politics seem to be returning to democracy's center stage. On the other, the glue that binds elites together and keeps their competitions and disagreements from de-stabilizing democratic politics seems to be weakening. It is obvious that elites and the democracies they operate confront a bewildering kaleidoscope of ominous and inter-related threats: rapid environmental degradation; serious shortages and dramatically increased costs of natural resources; job out-sourcing and high levels of unemployment in ageing populations; prospective disease pandemics; deepening racial, ethnic, regional, and religious cleavages; confrontations with culturally traditionalist countries and sects that are frustrated in their development efforts but armed with weapons of mass destruction and fired by millenarian beliefs. The list of dire threats can easily be extended. What is their likely consequence?

Probably the elitism to which democratic elitism has always alluded but never emphasized will come more to the fore. Confronting lethal external threats, elites in democracies will become more aware of the historically usual need to defend the material and cultural achievements of their own people against the incursions of foreigners and alien cultures. They will discard some of the more idealistic aspirations to which they and their supporters have recently clung. They will realize, for example, that their power to transform countries that are not democratic is slight and that the costs of attempting such transformations are large. They will be more cognizant of the need to avoid circumstances in which there is no alternative but to pay blackmail or tribute to militant countries and sects that revile the democracies.

There is in my view no persuasive reason to forecast the breakdown of consensually united elites and democracies. But neither do I see a reason for thinking that this type of elite and the democratic politics, it fosters, will spread widely during the next decades. A main origin of consensually united elites – colonial home-rule opportunities – is no longer realistically available; the settlement origin is highly contingent and rare; and the convergence origin requires a condition of general prosperity that most countries in the world will not soon attain.

Instead of elite breakdown in today's democracies, I anticipate a recalibration of elite thinking and action. Elites sense that they must be bolder, although this will make their errors and misjudgments that much more costly. Based on its fearful – but some would say prudent – assessment of the Middle East's political deterioration, made well before the 9/11 attacks, the Bush elite's disastrous military plunge into Iraq is a striking example of such errors and misjudgments. But elites in all democracies now feel embattled by dangers and problems that have no clear solutions. My guess is that this feeling of embattlement will fuel a stronger awareness of the need for collective elite action and cooperation to avert horrible outcomes. As awareness of the grave challenges now at hand sinks in, elites in democracies may well become more, not less, consensually united, so that democracy will survive, albeit in a distinctly more vertical form. Elites are likely, in sum, to adopt a more self-consciously elitist frame of reference. For the many who hold grander egalitarian visions of democracy's prospects this is not a pretty picture, but I believe that it is a likely one.

REFERENCES

Burch, M., & Holliday, I. (2004–2005). The Blair government and the core executive. *Government and Opposition*, *39*(Winter), 1–21.

Burton, M., & Higley, J. (1987). Elite settlements. *American Sociological Review*, *52*(June), 295–307.

Christiansen, P. M., Møller, B., & Togeby, L. (2001). *Den danske elite*. Copenhagen: Hans Reitzels Forlag.

Dahl, R. A. (1971). *Polyarchy*. New Haven: Yale University Press.

Di Palma, G. (1973). *The study of conflict in western societies*. New York: General Learning Press.

Dogan, M. (2003). Is there a ruling class in France? In: M. Dogan (Ed.), *Elite configurations at the apex of power*. Amsterdam: Brill Publishers.

Dye, T. R. (2002). *Who's running America? The Bush restoration*. Englewood Cliffs, NJ: Prentice-Hall.

Ginsborg, P. (2004). *Silvio Berlusconi: Television, power and patrimony*. London: Verso Press.

Gulbrandsen, T., Engelstad, F., Klausen, T. B., Skjeie, H., Teigen, M., & Østerud, Ø. (2002). *Norske makeliter*. Oslo: Gyldendal Akademisk.

Higley, J. (2006). The Bush elite: Aberration or harbinger? In: B. O'Connor & M. Griffiths (Eds), *The rise of anti-Americanism* (pp. 155–168). London: Routledge.

Higley, J., & Burton, M. (1998). Elite settlements and the taming of politics. *Government and Opposition*, *33*(Winter), 98–115.

Higley, J., & Burton, M. (2006). *Elite foundations of liberal democracy*. Boulder, CO.: Rowman & Littlefield.

Higley, J., Deacon, D., & Smart, D. (1979). *Elites in Australia*. London: Routledge & Kegan Paul.

Higley, J., Hoffmann-Lange, U., Kadushin, C., & Moore, G. (1991). Elite integration in stable democracies: A reconsideration. *European Sociological Review*, *7*(May), 35–53.

Hoffmann-Lange, U. (1993). *Eliten, Macht und Konflikt in der Bundesrepublik*. Oppladen: Leske + Budrich.

Judt, T. (2005). *Postwar: A history of Europe since 1945*. New York: Penguin Press.

Middlemas, K. (1995). *Orchestrating Europe: The informal politics of the European Union, 1973–1995*. London: Fontana Press.

Przeworski, A. (1991). *Democracy and the market*. New York: Cambridge University Press.

Putnam, R. D. (1976). *The comparative study of political elites*. Englewood Cliffs, NJ: Prentice-Hall.

Sartori, G. (1987). *Democratic theory revisited, part one: The contemporary debate*. Chatham, N.J.: Chatham House Publishers.

Schumpeter, J. A. (1942). *Capitalism, socialism, and democracy*. New York: Harper & Row.

Siedentop, L. (2001). *Democracy in Europe*. New York: Columbia University Press.

Uhr, J. (2005). *Terms of trust: Arguments over ethnics in Australian government*. Sydney: University of New South Wales Press.

Weiner, M. F. (1987). *Competititve elections in developing countries*. Durham, NC: Duke University Press.

Weingast, B. (1997). The political foundations of democracy and the rule of law. *American Political Science Review*, *91*(June), 245–263.

Zakaria, F. (2003). *The future of freedom*. New York: W.W. Norton.

ELITES AND DEMOCRACY: ARE THEY COMPATIBLE?

Ilkka Ruostetsaari

According to John Higley, democracies are first and foremost creations of a distinctive type of political elite, what he calls a consensually united elite. His hypothesis is that no democracy has ever emerged without the prior or concomitant formation of a consensually united elite, and none has persisted when such an elite has broken down. In other words, such elites are the *sine qua non* for democracy. What interests Higley is "how and why consensually united elites form, how they are propitious for democracy's emergence, why such elites strongly tend to persist and whether current and foreseeable circumstances portend their continuation or breakdown".

Higley understands elites in a quite restricted sense, as the few thousands of people who occupy a modern society's uppermost power positions. In this he refers to the empirical elite research being conducted in the United States, Australia and Europe. His rigorous definition of an elite remains nonetheless an open question in this volume, even if he has formulated it specifically in other publications, following mainly the tradition of the positional approach (e.g. Dogan & Higley, 1998, p. 15, Burton & Higley, 2001, p. 182).

However, based on aspects such as the inclusiveness of networks of communication and influence and the degree of value consensus, he distinguishes disunited from united elites. Moreover, the latter group is divided into ideologically united elites (such as the Soviet Union's nomenklatura-based elite) and consensually united types. In these latter, again, the

Comparative Studies of Social and Political Elites
Comparative Social Research, Volume 23, 265–274
Copyright © 2007 by Elsevier Ltd.
ISSN: 0195-6310/doi:10.1016/S0195-6310(06)23011-4

networks that signify structural integration are the most dense and tight within functionally differentiated sectors such as business, trade unions, state administration and the media. These networks overlap and interlock across sector boundaries to form central circles whose members enjoy access to key political decision makers. According to Higley, these consensually united elites have been the creators and mainstays of modern democracies. In fact, a consensually united elite would appear to be largely similar to the concept of power elite.

The processes and circumstantial configurations resulting in the emergence of consensually united elites are threefold, namely settlement of basic disputes between elites, colonial opportunities for local elites and convergence towards shared norms of political behaviour among disunited elites. Testing Higley's hypothesis is a challenging task. However, he is thoroughly acquainted with Scandinavian history and argues that modern Scandinavian political patterns provide examples of all three modes of origin of consensually united elites. In a parallel way, David Arter has characterized the Scandinavian model of government as involving the concepts of consensus, compromise and cooperation (the three Cs) (Apter, 1999, p. 149).

My aim is, first, to consider whether Higley's hypothesis can be applied to the historical development of the fourth Nordic country, Finland, as well. Second, I analyse the connection between the consensually united elite and democracy. Higley's thinking has similarities with Etzioni-Halevy's theory of demo-elitism; affinities and differences between the two theories will be examined. Third, I raise a question whether cooperation between elites is necessarily based on consensus within them. More precisely, we ask whether Higley's analysis of the consensual development in Scandinavian elites focuses more on cooperation than on consensus within them. Finally, I try to outline under what kind of circumstances elites can exist simultaneously with democracy.

THE CASE OF FINLAND

As far as nation building is concerned, there are substantial differences between the Western and Eastern patterns. In the West nationalism generally developed only after the strong states had been formed, as a consequence of conscious efforts by the central power. In the Eastern European latecomer states in contrast, the process was reversed: ethnic similarities led to national consciousness prior to the formation or re-establishment of a state. Although Finland followed the latter pattern, it approximated the

Eastern pattern mainly in terms of the political dependence, but that of Western Europe, especially Scandinavia, as far as the class structure is concerned. This mixture explains the steady advance of national consolidation and nationalism in Finland (Alapuro, 1988, pp. 88–90).

Sweden lost Finland in 1809 and the country was annexed to Russia as an autonomous Grand Duchy. A Finnish polity was founded decades before the politicization of ethnic differentiation, i.e. before the rise of nationalism. As an autonomous unit with its own administrative apparatus, Finland's political dependence was comparatively limited. The necessity of fighting for a separate status, confronted by nationalist movements elsewhere, was not a primary problem in Finland (*ibid.*, p. 90).

The Finnish class structure was peculiar in two respects. Although ultimate control was exercised in St. Petersburg, domination within the country – political, economic and cultural – was not in the hands of the Russians but of the Swedish-speaking upper class. Thus, although linguistic, social and educational barriers coincided within Finland, the local elite was not an extension of the metropolitan elite. Such a situation was far from common in Eastern Europe, where the aristocratic upper classes often identified themselves both politically and culturally with metropolitan power (*ibid.*, p. 90).

Under Swedish rule, a non-feudal class structure with a large and strong indigenous peasantry had consolidated itself in Finland. Consequently, by international comparison the authority of the Finnish upper class rested on an exceptionally fragile foundation. Elsewhere, the power of the upper classes rested on a seemingly solid basis, by merit not only of the guarantees of metropolitan power but also of the prolongation of feudal class domination. But in Finland, the upper class had no solid basis in landownership; rather, its position was based almost exclusively on the central role played in administering the emerging state (*ibid.*, p. 91).

Nationalism in Finland did not play the role of a liberating force as it did in Eastern Europe; more or less from the outset it served strong elements of a "civic religion" for the territorially centralized state as well. The upper classes, with their Swedish culture, had exceptionally strong incentives to adopt or accept the language and culture of the large Finnish-speaking majority, both because of the country's political dependence on a great autocratic state, Russia, and of their own need, as civil servants, to establish a sense of obligation to the Finnish polity. As a consequence, a fairly unified national culture emerged. This implies that in Finland, in contrast to Eastern Europe, strong incentives for nationalist mobilization existed not only among the middle but also among the upper classes (*ibid.*, p. 92).

The Finnish nationalist movement, Fennomania, was a mixture of the "civic religion" of a state and a national liberation movement. It sought to strengthen the state upon which the position of the elite depended as well as to identify with the people and alongside them resist the foreign-speaking upper class. Both efforts were aimed at consolidating Finland's position separately from Russia. It was, thus, no surprise that upper-class representation among the nationalist activists was exceptionally large by international comparison. As a result of this, the Finnish-speaking or bilingual gentry adopted the Finnish language without coercion, or even contributed to this development (Alapuro & Stenius, 1987, p. 14). Although mainly Swedish speaking, the [L]iberals did not focus their main opposition on the cultural aspirations of the Fennoman movement; they opposed the creation of a unilingual Finnish national culture. Nonetheless, the preservation of existing political institutions and the continuity of the cultural heritage of the Swedish period were more important than language. In contrast, although the Finnicization movement was directed against the exclusively privileged Swedish-speaking upper class, this did not imply that the upper class needed to be eliminated to found a democratically organized society. Rather, the upper class, speaking Swedish and oriented to Swedish culture, should be replaced gradually by an upper-class speaking Finnish and oriented to Finnish culture (Alapuro, 1988, pp. 95, 97). All in all, in these circumstances the upper class culture – whether Finnish or Swedish – was united by many common elements. Many Fennomans had changed their language from Swedish to Finnish, and the whole of the gentry had studied together in a single place, the University of Helsinki. (Alapuro & Stenius, 1987, p. 17).

To conclude, prior to the parliamentary reform of 1906, which introduced democracy to Finland, the elite was cohesive in two different respects. On the one hand, it was internally cohesive inasmuch as top bureaucrats in the central administration were not exposed to competition from the academic sector, from the Church, or from business. There were no independent power centres separate from the bureaucratic elite. The gentry's position not as a landed upper class, but as bureaucrats of a dependent state made for a considerable tolerance of demands by the other segments of the population for organization and, finally, even for a popular say in national policies. The gentry were thus willing to seek the support and solidarity of the peasantry that materialized into Fennomania; a part of the Swedish-speaking gentry were allied with the Finnish-speaking peasantry and begot an ideology strengthening a state in which independent peasants played an important role. This tolerance and its linkage to state-making efforts of the dominant classes were demonstrated by the relation of popular organizations to the state. The Finnish mass organizations became markedly centralized, stable and state-centred and in only a few cases split into competing organizations as in Sweden (Alapuro, 1988, pp. 106–107; 1990, p. 242).

On the other hand, the front formed by the Finnish elite and the Russian government was also cohesive: the upper class in Finland had accepted the fact that they were dependent on the Russian Tsar. By international comparison, the Finnish peasantry during this period showed quite exceptional allegiance to authority (Alapuro, 1990, pp. 214–249). Although this authority structure collapsed in the early 20th century, when Russia began to enforce its policy of unification upon Finland, there can be little doubt that the centralized power structures of the 19th century left a deep imprint on the forms and styles of Finnish power structures once independence was gained in 1917 (Ruostetsaari, 1993, p. 309). All in all, Finland's historical development dovetails with Higley's analysis of the colonial origin of some consensually united elites.

THE LINK BETWEEN CONSENSUALLY UNITED ELITES AND DEMOCRACY

The connection between a consensually unified elite and democracy seems, however, to be an open question in Higley's theory. If the emergence of consensually unified elites precedes the entrenchment of democracy, why would the elite, despite their power, contribute to or even countenance the emergence of democracy, which might dig its grave? In other words, the entrenchment of democracy would very likely weaken the elite's power position. One explanation, for example, may be that several competing elites need support and allies among other groups in civil society in their mutual contestation.

In fact, Higley's theory has points of convergence with the theory of demo-elitism presented by Eva Etzioni-Halevy (1993). Both scholars specify the connection between certain characteristics of elites and the entrenchment of democracy, but their explanations are different, even contradictory. For Higley the precondition for democracy is a consensually unified elite, while for Etzioni-Halevy it is mutually autonomous elites.

Etzioni-Halevy's thesis is that the relative autonomy of elites and subelites constitutes an important condition for the subsequent development and stabilization of democracy. What counts for the preservation and further democratization of such a system is not a plurality of elites but their independence in terms of control of resources; i.e. they have significant resources, which cannot be controlled, or can only marginally be controlled from outside their own boundaries. It is their relative but not complete immunity in the control of resources such as coercive, material, administrative, symbolic and psycho-personal resources, which give elites their relative autonomy, and it is through the use of these resources that they can manifest such autonomy (Etzioni-Halevy, 1993, pp. 5–7, 99). This theory has been claimed by Burton and Higley (2001, p. 184) wherein the origin and basis of the relative autonomy of the elites is expressed too feebly.

Etzioni-Halevy sought support for her theory in actual historical development. Thus, states that developed into stable democracies should show evidence of the relative autonomy of their elites *before* the maturation of democracy. In contrast, in states where democratic development was followed by the breakdown of democracy there should be proof of a lack of elite autonomy *before* the collapse. She shows that in Britain, where elites have successfully struggled for and obtained relative autonomy, democracy has subsequently taken root. Conversely, in Germany the elites' struggles for autonomy were much less successful; democracy was not successfully stabilized even though in some respects it preceded the advent of democracy in Britain. It subsequently suffered a breakdown, which came even before the accession of Nazism to power. Furthermore, by 1991 Poland was far more advanced on the path to democracy than was the Soviet Union as an entity. Both under Communism and before, this difference may be explained in part by previous differences in the autonomy of the elites in them, this being clearly more highly developed and sturdier in Poland than it was in the Soviet Union (Etzioni-Halevy, 1993, pp. 7–8).

Higley argues that in the consensually united elite structure that is a precondition for democracy, networks between elites are dense and tight. In addition, elite members and groups share a mostly tacit consensus on the norms and rules of political behaviour. In other words, he argues that the coupling between elites should be tight, while Etzioni-Halevy's argument is the reverse, that is, there should be loose coupling.

Adopting Dahrendorf's distinction between social integration and social harmony, she argues that a similar distinction needs to be made between elite cooperation on the one hand, and elite solidarity and consensus on the other. Furthermore, she suggests that it is elite cooperation rather than elite consensus on rules or elite solidarity that is necessary for the proper functioning of democracy. Without such cooperation, the other elites would constantly obstruct the government and each other, the system would be in a perpetual stalemate and would eventually be self-destructive. In short, without elite cooperation there can be no democracy, but without elite autonomy there can be no democracy either (*ibid.*, pp. 109–110).

This raises the question of whether the cooperation of elites is necessarily based on consensus within them. Higley's view seems to be affirmative even if he does not define specifically the concept of consensus. Quite to the contrary, Etzioni-Halevy argues that if we define elite consensus procedurally, to mean actual adherence to democratic rules and procedures, then by definition the cooperation of elites in the maintenance of democracy requires such consensus. But if consensus is defined as signifying that elites share beliefs, values or norms with respect to the rules of democracy, the question of whether elite cooperation requires such consensus becomes an empirical one. According to Etzioni-Halevy, empirical research on various democratic countries shows that elite cooperation may well require some consensus about the desirability of democracy through free elections and civil liberties as such. However, elite cooperation may exist without consensus on the actual, concrete rules by which the electoral process and other democratic conflicts are to be waged, and by which civil liberties are to be implemented (*ibid.*, p. 110). It seems that the absence of conflict is not for Etzioni-Halevy a manifestation of consensus within elites.

COOPERATIVE RATHER THAN CONSENSUAL ELITES?

It may be that Higley's analysis of the consensual development in Scandinavian elites focuses more on the cooperation rather than consensus within elites. For instance, even today it is doubtful whether the Swedish elites are cooperative, let alone consensual in character. According to the Swedish power study (SOU 1990:44, 1990) the country is dominated by two blocs of rival elites; the business elite's economic power versus the labour movement elite's power of numbers. Although the study found no major differences between the views of elites and the people on political issues, the elites appeared to be fairly heterogeneous in several respects. The borders between these elites are largely impervious; networks of interaction and communication between elite members are confined to their "own camp" and cabinets are regularly composed *either* of the Social Democrats *or* the bourgeois parties.

In contrast to Sweden, Finland is clearly a more consensual society. There are no two dominating power blocs or competing elites representing economic power and political power based on business and the labour movement. In Finland the business and labour movement elites are part of a wider social network of interaction that is fairly closely interconnected. Wielding of power at the elite level is characterized by consensus rather than polarization. The pursuit of social consensus results, on the one hand, from historical experiences (the fight for independence during Russian rule and again during the Second World War) and, on the other hand, from the absence of any single dominant political party; in Finland no party could dominate the political arena as the Swedish Social Democrats do (Ruostetsaari, 2004, 2006). The same applies to the economic sphere, which in Finland has not been exclusively dominated by the bourgeoisie. Instead, the Centre Party, the former Agrarians, and the left-wing parties have also been involved in the exercise of economic power through state-owned companies and cooperatives. The "camp society" which emerged in the 1918 Civil War, where virtually all institutions and organizations were divided into Red and White, no longer exists (Ruostetsaari, 1993, p. 334). Since 1937 cabinet coalitions have regularly been composed of *both* bourgeois *and* left-wing parties.

In Sweden the debate between elites, and sometimes also within elites, is carried on publicly and the mass media play the primary role of mediator. In Finland, by contrast, discussion between the elites is carried on outside the public arena, mostly in informal groups. In Sweden debate has reflected different ideological views concerning the direction in which the Swedish society should move (e.g. the role of employee funds in the ownership of the business; European integration). The Finnish practice of informality contributes to the maintenance of an elite consensus in that the mass media and the public do not undermine the elites; indeed, the media elite is part of the wider elite structure, i.e. the power elite (Ruostetsaari, 2006). To put it concisely, Sweden is characterized by consensus within each of two elite blocs while in Finland consensus prevails between elite blocs.

THE COEXISTENCE OF DEMOCRACY AND ELITES

John Higley raises a core question in this context of democratic elitism inasmuch as popular control concerns only the elites of the political institutions, not those representing the administration, the business, the media, etc., which also wield significant power on the citizenry. Under what circumstances do elites coexist with democracy?

I have argued elsewhere (Ruostetsaari, 2006, pp. 27–28) that in an elite structure compatible with democracy (a fragmented elite structure) there is slight mutual interplay and consensus between the elites. However, there is consensus between elites regarding the societal rules of the game, not the goals of societal development. By contrast, mutual contacts between civic groups as well as between civic groups and the elites are close. Horizontal interaction, i.e. cross-connections between the elites and civic groups, is also intense. Moreover, such elites are open to the recruitment of new members from civil society. In other words, there are no impenetrable "glass ceilings" to block upward social mobility, and correspondingly, "the floor" is not so rigid that downward mobility from elites to civil society is impeded.

A fragmented elite structure, where elites are autonomous and fairly independent of each other in respect, for instance, of resources, and where civic groups are competitive and overlapping as far as their membership is concerned, is compatible with the pluralist principles of democracy. The conception of democracy outlined here differs from demo-elitism, according to which democracy calls for autonomy and weak interconnection not only between elites, but also between the elites and civic groups. It is intense interaction between elites and civic groups and control exercised by the citizenry that ensures the responsiveness of decision making, i.e. consideration of the interests of the citizens. In other words, the existence of elites is an inevitable fact of life in a post-modern society; however, as far as democracy is concerned, there is no problem provided the elites are open to various socio-economic groups, i.e. the circulation of elites is active and their entwining is slight, and yet the interplay and cooperation between them and the civic groups is close.

THE FUTURE OF DEMOCRACY?

John Higley's hypothesis regarding the role of elites in the future is twofold. On the one hand, elites seem to be returning to the centre stage of democracy. On the other, the glue that binds elites together seems to be weakening. According to my empirical findings in the context of only one country, Finland, such a developmental trend seems very likely. However, what will it mean for the future of democracy? The strengthening position of the elites together with the widening gap between them and the people – which also seems evident – is not beneficial for democracy, but increasingly challenges the legitimacy of political systems. Nevertheless, increasing competition and fragmentation between the elites may dissolve power structures and open up opportunities for citizens' participation and influence. This important hypothesis deserves to be analysed empirically.

REFERENCES

Alapuro, R. (1988). *State and revolution in Finland.* Berkeley: University of California Press.

Alapuro, R. (1990). Valta ja Valtio – miksi vallasta tuli ongelma 1900-luvun taitteessa? In: H. Pertti (Ed.), *Talous, valta ja valtio* (pp. 237–254). Tampere: Vastapaino.

Alapuro, R., & Stenius, H. (1987). Kansanliikkeet loivat kansakunnan. In: R. Alapuro, I. Liikanen, K. Smeds & H. Stenius (Eds), *Kansa liikkeessä.* Helsinki: Kirjayhtymä.

Apter, D. (1999). *Scandinavian politics today.* Manchester: Manchester University Press.

Burton, M., & Higley, J. (2001). The study of political elite transformations. *International Review of Sociology, 11*(2), 181–199.

Dogan, M., & Higley, J. (1998). Elites, crises, and regimes in comparative analysis. In: M. Dogan & J. Higley (Eds), *Elites, crises and the origins of regimes* (pp. 3–27). Oxford: Rowman & Littlefield.

Etzioni-Halevy, E. (1993). *The elite connection. Problems and potential of western democracy.* Cambridge: Polity Press.

Ruostetsaari, I. (1993). The anatomy of the Finnish power elite. *Scandinavian Political Studies, 16*(4), 305–337.

Ruostetsaari, I. (2004). L'évolution des élites Finlandaises après la crise des années 1990. *Nordiques, 4*(printemps), 83–101.

Ruostetsaari, I. (2006). Social upheaval and transformation of elite structures. The case of Finland. *Political Studies, 54*(1), 23–42.

SOU 1990:44. (1990). *Demokrati och makt i Sverige. Maktutredningens huvudrapport.* Stockholm: Allmänna förlaget.

SET UP A CONTINUATION ORDER TODAY!

Did you know that you can set up a continuation order on all Elsevier-JAI series and have each new volume sent directly to you upon publication? For details on how to set up a **continuation order**, contact your nearest regional sales office listed below.

To view related series in Sociology, please visit:

www.elsevier.com/sociology

The Americas
Customer Service Department
11830 Westline Industrial Drive
St. Louis, MO 63146
USA
US customers:
Tel: +1 800 545 2522 (Toll-free number)
Fax: +1 800 535 9935
For Customers outside US:
Tel: +1 800 460 3110 (Toll-free number).
Fax: +1 314 453 7095
usbkinfo@elsevier.com

Europe, Middle East & Africa
Customer Service Department
Linacre House
Jordan Hill
Oxford OX2 8DP
UK
Tel: +44 (0) 1865 474140
Fax: +44 (0) 1865 474141
eurobkinfo@elsevier.com

Japan
Customer Service Department
2F Higashi Azabu, 1 Chome Bldg
1-9-15 Higashi Azabu, Minato-ku
Tokyo 106-0044
Japan
Tel: +81 3 3589 6370
Fax: +81 3 3589 6371
books@elsevierjapan.com

APAC
Customer Service Department
3 Killiney Road #08-01
Winsland House I
Singapore 239519
Tel: +65 6349 0222
Fax: +65 6733 1510
asiainfo@elsevier.com

Australia & New Zealand
Customer Service Department
30-52 Smidmore Street
Marrickville, New South Wales 2204
Australia
Tel: +61 (02) 9517 8999
Fax: +61 (02) 9517 2249
service@elsevier.com.au

30% Discount for Authors on All Books!

A 30% discount is available to Elsevier book and journal contributors on all books *(except multi-volume reference works)*.

To claim your discount, full payment is required with your order, which must be sent directly to the publisher at the nearest regional sales office above.